INTELLIGENCE

AND THE

STATE

INTELLIGENCE
AND THE
STATE

ANALYSTS AND DECISION MAKERS

JONATHAN M. HOUSE

Naval Institute Press
Annapolis, Maryland

Naval Institute Press
291 Wood Road
Annapolis, MD 21402

Library of Congress Cataloging-in-Publication Data
Names: House, Jonathan M. (Jonathan Mallory), 1950- author.
Title: Intelligence and the state : analysts and decision makers / Jonathan M. House.
Description: Annapolis, Maryland : Naval Institute Press, [2022] | Includes bibliographical references and index.
Identifiers: LCCN 2021045965 (print) | LCCN 2021045966 (ebook) | ISBN 9781682477724 (hardcover) | ISBN 9781682477748 (ebook) | ISBN 9781682477748 (epub)
Subjects: LCSH: Military intelligence—United States. | Intelligence service—United States. | Civil-military relations—United States. | National security—United States. | United States—Military policy.
Classification: LCC UB251.U5 H68 2022 (print) | LCC UB251.U5 (ebook) | DDC 355.3/4320973—dc23
LC record available at https://lccn.loc.gov/2021045965
LC ebook record available at https://lccn.loc.gov/2021045966

♾ Print editions meet the requirements of ANSI/NISO z39.48-1992 (Permanence of Paper).
Printed in the United States of America.

30 29 28 27 26 25 24 23 22 9 8 7 6 5 4 3 2 1
First printing

Dedicated to the memory of my parents,
two wartime intelligence officers:
Lt. Col. Albert V. House, U.S. Army Air Forces, and
Lt. Laura M. (Griffin) House, U.S. Naval Reserve

And to the memory of
Col. Russell P. Vaughn, U.S. Army (Ret.)
and GG-15, Defense Intelligence Agency

Contents

Preface

In 1957, Samuel Huntington published *The Soldier and the State: The Theory and Politics of Civil-Military Relations.* In this landmark study, he attempted to define the interrelationships between military professionals and the civilians who controlled military force in a democracy. Huntington was concerned by the manner in which the sustained partial mobilization of the Cold War seemed to endanger the traditional concept of civilian supremacy over the armed forces. Military proconsuls such as Douglas MacArthur had acquired both experience in and control over large portions of national security policy and strategy, subjects traditionally left to the civilian government. Senior military leaders understandably believed that they had both technical expertise and practical experience unmatched by most politicians. Indeed, the growing possibility of nuclear war seemed to give American generals and admirals overwhelming control over national policy.

Huntington's solutions were somewhat simplified and even unrealistic, attempting to apply hard and fast rules to a variety of nuanced relationships. Nonetheless, his prescriptions offered a useful framework for exploring those relationships. Fifty years later, Gen. David Petraeus, who had studied Huntington's book while in graduate school, used the Harvard theorist's principles as a starting point for discussions with Secretary of Defense Robert Gates about Petraeus' new appointment to command forces in Iraq.

The Cold War and the subsequent era of insurgency and terrorism placed stress not only on civil-military relations, but also on civil-intelligence relations. To a large extent, the U.S. intelligence community is a product of the post-1945 era, when policy makers had to rely constantly on the expertise of intelligence officers, whose education, motivation, and experience differed markedly from those of politicians. Successive administrations have attempted to co-opt and politicize the senior leaders of both defense and the intelligence community, in each case to the detriment of national security.

While I cannot pretend to the brilliance of Huntington, this study attempts to address a civil-intelligence interface that has become just as fraught with misunderstanding and error as civil-military relations have ever been. Civilian leaders often assume a political bias on the part of analysts, whereas most analysts attempt to exclude such factors from their considerations. The analysts in turn suspect that the decision makers are unable to overcome their own biases and partisan politics in order to understand foreign cultures and interests. Intelligence leaders are just as prone as others to make errors, but on balance those leaders are correct more often than they usually receive credit for, if only because their successes are classified while their failures, real or alleged, are trumpeted to the world. The most recent example of this was the alleged "intelligence failure" to warn of the January 6, 2021, attack on the U.S. Capitol, when the threat of such an attack was apparent weeks ahead of the event.

In writing this book, I am indebted to a number of research facilities, most especially the Dwight D. Eisenhower Presidential Library in Abilene, Kansas; the Ike Skelton Combined Arms Research Library at Fort Leavenworth, Kansas; and the Deryck Maughan Library of King's College, London. I must also acknowledge the contributions of my colleague and retired intelligence officer John Kuehn, whose comments significantly improved this study.

Like my father before me, I was liberally educated as an historian before becoming a working-level intelligence analyst in a wartime Pentagon. Other observers have greater experience with the intelligence community than do I, but I hope that my combination of education and practical service has equipped me to offer useful evaluations of a complex problem set.

The views expressed in this study are those of the author and do not reflect the official policy or position of the United States, the U.S. intelligence community, the Department of Defense, or any other U.S. government agency. Any assertions or errors are solely my responsibility.

Leavenworth, Kansas
June 2021

Acronyms and Abbreviations

AEC	Atomic Energy Commission
BCRA	Gaullist Bureau central de renseignements et d'action (Central Bureau of Information and Action, 1940–44)
CI	counterintelligence
CIA	Central Intelligence Agency
CIG	Central Intelligence Group (1946–47)
COMINT	Communications Intelligence
COMINTERN	Third or Communist International
CORDS	Civil Operations and Revolutionary Development Support
CRITIC	address list of agencies to receive urgent indications and warning messages
DCI	Director of Central Intelligence (1946–2004)
DD/P	CIA Deputy Director for Plans (later Deputy Director for Operations)
DGER	French Direction générale des études et recherches (General Directorate for Studies and Research, 1944–46)
DGSE	French Direction générale de la sécurité extérieure (General Directorate for Foreign Security, post-1982)
DIA	Defense Intelligence Agency
DIRNSA	Director, National Security Agency
DNI	Director of National Intelligence
DST	French Direction de la surveillance du territoire (Directorate of Territorial Surveillance, 1944–2005)

ELINT	Noncommunications electronic intelligence
FBI	Federal Bureau of Investigation
FHO	Fremde Heere Ost (German Foreign Armies East)
FISA	Foreign Intelligence Surveillance Act of 1978
FSB	Federal'naya sluzhba bezopasnosti Rossiyskoy Federatsii (Federal Security Service of the Russian Federation, since 1995)
GCCS	UK Government Code and Cypher School (to 1946)
GCHQ	UK Government Communications Headquarters (since 1946)
GRU	Glavnoye razvedyvatel'noye upravleniye (Soviet/ Russian General Staff [Military] Intelligence Directorate)
HUMINT	human intelligence
I&W	indications and warning
IAC	U.S. Intelligence Advisory Committee
IAEA	International Atomic Energy Agency
IC	intelligence community
IIC	U.S. Interdepartmental Intelligence Conference
IMINT	Imagery Intelligence
INR	Department of State Bureau of Intelligence and Research
JCS	Joint Chiefs of Staff
JIC	UK Joint Intelligence Committee
KGB	Komitet Gosudarstvennoy Bezopasnosti (Soviet Committee for State Security)
MI5	informal designation for UK Security Service
MID	U.S. Army Military Intelligence Division
MVD	Russian/Soviet Ministry of Internal Affairs
NSA	National Security Agency *or* National Security Assistant/Advisor
NSA 47	National Security Act of 1947
NSC	National Security Council
NSCID	National Security Council Intelligence Directive
ODNI	Office of the Director of National Intelligence

Okhrana	literally, Guard (Russian Department for Protecting the Public Security and Order, 1881–1917)
ONI	U.S. Office of Naval Intelligence
OPC	CIA Office of Policy Coordination
OSO	CIA Office of Special Operations
OSS	Office of Strategic Services (1942–45)
PBCFIA	President's Board of Consultants on Foreign Intelligence Activities (1956–61)
PFIAB	President's Foreign Intelligence Advisory Board
SD	Nazi Sicherheitsdienst (Security Service)
SDECE	French Service de documentation extérieure et de contre-espionnage (Service for Foreign Documentation and Counter-Espionage, 1946–82)
SERE	survival, evasion, resistance, and escape training
SIGINT	signals intelligence, including COMINT and ELINT
SIS	UK Secret Intelligence Service
SVR	Sluzhba vneshney razvedki Rossiyskoy Federatsii (Foreign Intelligence Service of the Russian Federation, since 1991)
USCIB	U.S. Communications Intelligence Board
USIB	U.S. Intelligence Board
WMD	weapons of mass destruction

Chapter One

Professions and Professionalism

And Joshua the son of Nun sent two men secretly from Shittim as spies, saying, "Go view the land, especially Jericho." And they went, and came into the house of a harlot whose name was Rahab, and lodged there. . . . [T]he woman had taken the two men and hidden them; and she said, "True, men came to me but I did not know where they came from; and when the gate was to be closed, at dark, the men went out. . . . [P]ursue them quickly, for you will overtake them."

—Joshua 2:1 and 2:4–5, RSV

According to a sexist cliché, prostitution is the oldest profession. Regardless of the accuracy of that statement, one can fairly argue that intelligence is at least the second oldest profession. When Joshua sent two anonymous men to reconnoiter Jericho, those men hid with a harlot, both because she was Jewish and because she could give them information she had learned from her customers, the rulers of the town.

The two professions share certain characteristics. Each requires a profound knowledge of human nature and a healthy skepticism, bordering on cynicism, about human behavior. To avoid surprise, intelligence officers tend to expect the worst of an opposing state and suspect the motives of anyone who provides information about that state. An aura of immoral or at least sordid activity surrounds both careers, in part because traitors and other suppliers of information are often flawed human beings. Most significantly, neither profession's customers respect the service provided and often display contempt for its practitioners, whose skills and motivations remain largely unknown to the consumers. In fact, amateurs commonly believe that they can perform the necessary services more effectively than professionals, whether providing sexual favors or analyzing raw intelligence reports. In an era where only a small minority of Americans ever serve in the armed forces, most educated people have at least heard of Carl von Clausewitz and Sun Tzu. Yet for many of those same educated people, intelligence collection is associated only with fiction writers such as Ian Fleming and Tom Clancy, while intelligence analysis is a complete unknown. When Sen. Daniel Inouye, himself a distinguished combat veteran, first encountered the intelligence community while chairing a Select Committee on Intelligence in 1976, he acknowledged that "my views changed. I had no idea of what I was getting into. I thought of [novelist] Robert Ludlum and what you read in magazines and newspapers. In reality, it is such a complex, all-encompassing organization with fancy devices. After about a month I felt that this [Robert Ludlum, James Bond] was a grossly distorted view of reality."[1]

Government officials have the right and even the duty to evaluate the information provided by intelligence professionals, but it stands to reason that such officials, with many different responsibilities, cannot hope to match the time and effort that analysts invest in understanding a particular culture or situation. As we shall see in this study, intelligence analysts are by no means infallible, but the vast majority labor honestly to help their governments understand the foreign threats they face. Yet long before Donald Trump gave the Russian intelligence services more credibility than he accorded their American counterparts, many decision makers were convinced that they "knew better" than the analysts. When told something that clashed with their expectations, well-intentioned political appointees often rejected the information and blamed the analyst, alleging bias and negligence simply because the analyst's interpretation of current affairs was unfamiliar to the policy makers. To cite one obvious example, many politicians understand and empathize with the Israeli view of the Jewish state's national security issues but have little knowledge of how those same issues appear to Palestinians. The intelligence analyst often finds himself or herself acting as devil's advocate without even getting a fair hearing for Satan.

If anything, a decision maker should actively encourage his or her intelligence services to provide a different viewpoint, one that does *not* reflect that decision maker's own beliefs. A politicized intelligence community is worse than useless, reinforcing the policy maker's own preconceptions rather than providing independent analysis to challenge those beliefs. For the intelligence services of Nazi Germany frequently failed to understand and predict Hitler's opponents precisely because those services had internalized the racist and conspiratorial beliefs of their own regime.[2]

Is Intelligence a Profession?

As a first step in exploring this field, one must define terms, particularly "intelligence," "intelligence officer," and "profession" or "professional." "Intelligence" as used by governments and military organizations may have many definitions, but most of them are variations on the following: "'Intelligence' is the product resulting from the collection, evaluation, and interpretation of information which concerns one or more aspects of foreign nations or of functional or geographic areas, and which is immediately or potentially significant to the development and execution of plans, policies, and operations."[3] In other words, intelligence is *collated and analyzed information* related to the development and execution of policy, not just random factoids or salacious anecdotes. By contrast, "information" is just that, a report—whether true, partially true, or false—that is not yet confirmed by other sources. A news story about civil disorders in a foreign city is a form of information that may cause intelligence personnel to direct other means of collection on that city, but that report, even when the journalist (presumably) attempted to confirm the event, is not intelligence.

The Central Intelligence Agency (CIA) has often used the term "intelligence officer" very narrowly, in an effort to distinguish between its own human intelligence collectors and the agents or sources those collectors deal with in the field. In fact, "intelligence officer" of course describes a large number and variety of career personnel, both civilian and military, found in most governments and even some nonstate actors of the world. These experts fall into three categories, although in some instances the same person may perform more than one role. First are the collectors, the skilled people who plan and conduct efforts to acquire information not just from human sources (foreign officials, spies, travelers, and prisoners of war), but also through the use of electronic emissions, imagery, or other means of obtaining data. Second come the counterintelligence and security personnel who protect both the organization and its intelligence operations from the opposition's collectors. As subsequent chapters will describe, these security personnel have historically been the nucleus of what are today considered intelligence agencies.

The third category of intelligence officers are the analysts, the people who evaluate and interpret the resulting information in an effort to provide decision makers with reliable intelligence about the opposition's capabilities and intentions.

Each of these categories of intelligence officers requires considerable education, training, and experience to contribute to the overall process. Collectors and security officers often perform their roles at considerable personal risk, in contrast to the analysts who sit in government buildings or field headquarters and whose most common health risk is acid reflux induced by mental stress and excess caffeine. Yet the focus of this discussion is on the analysts, who are most likely to provide finished intelligence and interact with the decision makers.

"Professional" is one of the most overworked and abused words in American English, to the point where the word often denotes little more than an individual who is paid to perform a particular function on a full-time basis. Such a definition of a professional requires greater specificity before we can apply it confidently to intelligence and other grave matters of national security. We need to describe the nature of a profession to determine whether intelligence collectors and analysts really deserve to be designated as members of such a group.

In his 1957 study *The Soldier and the State*, Samuel Huntington offered three criteria to define a profession.[4] To paraphrase his argument,

1. Society delegates an important function to be performed exclusively by these professionals;
2. Practicing the profession requires a combination of both formal education and extensive experience; and
3. The profession is a self-regulating corporate body that disciplines its own members to enforce standards.

A host of careers—physicians, soldiers, attorneys, teachers, nurses, and others—easily meets these three standards. Yet of these criteria, only the second unquestionably applies to intelligence, and even then the education requirement is of necessity vaguely defined. In order to understand foreign developments, intelligence agencies need an array of expertise ranging from language and area studies through history, economics, and political science to rocketry, electronics, epidemiology, and agricultural management.

Many of these fields of study, especially in the humanities and social sciences, are so esoteric that outsiders sometimes find it difficult to understand not only their value to analysis but also the intellectual processes involved and the motivations of those who specialize in such fields. Civilian decision makers, military commanders, and staff planners may concede the expertise of these specialists in principle while unconsciously relegating such academics to a status that has limited effect on "real" operations.

During the two world wars, some of the most successful British intelligence practitioners were eccentric academics such as T. E. Lawrence (archaeologist) in Arabia, Arnold Toynbee (historian) in the Foreign Office, or F. Harry Hinsley (historian) and Alan Turing (mathematician) at Bletchley Park.[5] Wartime American intelligence activities depended upon similar if less famous academics who served as "amateur" officers only for the duration of the conflict. To some extent this was inevitable, because career officers who specialized in intelligence often did so at the cost of their own chances for promotion.

Only the processes of intelligence, not its content, are at all standardized. The tendency to use academic learning in intelligence analysis is in sharp contrast to the professional knowledge and experience of line officers in the armed forces, who have mastered not only the technical dimensions of weapons systems but also the elaborate procedures necessary to plan and synchronize the employment of such systems. Military intelligence officers, in turn, straddle the line between these two groups, expected to be proficient at military, naval, or air operations as well as their intelligence skills and in some cases foreign area studies.

With the advent of the Cold War, the intelligence communities of major powers not only expanded but acquired a permanence not seen during the world wars. Throughout the Cold War era, the American armed services were the major source of intelligence analysts and collectors, both as uniformed operators and as veterans in civilian garb. While serving in the armed forces, these analysts and collectors not only procured their initial security background investigations but also learned the rudiments of order of battle, imagery interpretation, and communications traffic analysis. Civilian intelligence agencies regularly borrowed or recruited military experts in special operations, counterintelligence, psychological operations, and analysis.

With the end of the Cold War, the shrinking size of the armed forces has reduced the pool of such intelligence recruits at the same time that earlier generations of skilled recruits reached retirement age. Moreover, the intelligence agencies reached a certain maturation that led to more structured career patterns.

The new century has seen an increase in civilian institutions, both governmental and private, aimed at developing intelligence professionals in a systematic manner.[6] Perhaps the most obvious example of this trend has been the expansion of the Joint Military Intelligence College, a small part of the Defense Intelligence Agency, into a National Intelligence University, although the new entity is still growing into its potential. Yet the very concept of intelligence education and careers is a recent development in the West.

For much of history, rulers and commanders were their own intelligence analysts. As will be discussed in chapter 4, rulers in the early modern period used diplomats and spymasters, but they focused as much on domestic threats as they did on foreign adversaries. If people thought of intelligence at all, they often assumed that it was a purely military, wartime activity, just as it was when Joshua planned to take Jericho. Gen. George Washington had to operate his own spy network, supplemented to some extent by a Connecticut dragoon regiment that provided scouts and messengers.[7] In the Spanish peninsular campaigns of 1808–13, Arthur Wellesley had the services of not only a gifted cryptographer, quartermaster George Scovell, but also an infantryman turned intelligence officer, Major W. Colquhoun Grant. In an age before reliable maps, the function of Grant and other "exploring officers" was as much topographic engineering as it was tactical reconnaissance of their French opponents. Such exploration was also crucial to opening the American West. Beginning with the Lewis and Clark Expedition and continuing with topographic engineers such as John C. Frémont and Stephen W. Kearny, the U.S. Army collected basic intelligence throughout the Louisiana Purchase.[8] Robert E. Lee performed a similar role, with greater emphasis on enemy dispositions, for Gen. Winfield Scott during the advance on Mexico City in 1847.

Napoleon's apparent ability to be his own spymaster and planner led to an unrealistic expectation that future commanders would perform the same functions without assistance, an expectation reflected in the dominant military theories of Antoine-Henri de Jomini.[9] The American Civil War was strewn with examples of generals who were unable to match the Napoleonic model of either intelligence or maneuver.

In practice, this habit of allowing the statesman or general to be his own intelligence officer retarded the development of intelligence agencies and professions to support national or strategic-level decision-making. Intelligence collection was easily understood, but intelligence evaluation or analysis was rare for both generals and rulers. In turn, this delayed development meant that many decision makers were ill prepared to deal with the increasing complexity of intelligence sources and methods during the twentieth and twenty-first centuries. Joining the traditional skills of espionage, encrypting messages, and reconnaissance came new fields such as aerial imagery, signals intercept, and the arcane technical details of radar, sonar, and unattended ground sensors. These and others offered vast new sources of information about the enemy, but only if the recipient of that information could interpret and integrate all these indicators. It is no reflection on their capability to say that many decision makers displayed a limited understanding of intelligence sources, methods, and analysis—a limitation that produced disastrous mistakes. Analysts are by no means infallible either, but the decision makers' belief that they could be their own analysts, when those decision makers had so many other tasks to perform, was and remains perilous.

In May 1916, Vice Admiral Reinhard Scheer commanded the German High Seas Fleet as it prepared to leave its ports in northern Germany, seeking to lure Scheer's British counterparts into a submarine ambush. "Room 40," the British Admiralty's cryptanalysis center, had identified that Scheer's radio call sign was "DK." The analysts also correctly detected that, in an attempt to conceal his preparations for sailing, Scheer had moved that call sign from his flagship to his headquarters ashore. However, Rear Admiral Thomas Jackson, the Admiralty's director of operations, was contemptuous of the amateur naval officers who manned Room 40, a not uncommon issue even in more recent situations. On May 31, Jackson asked the analysts on duty in Room 40 *not* to explain a particular message but simply to tell him the meaning of the call sign DK; when told it was Scheer's call sign, he misinterpreted that to mean that DK represented Scheer's flagship rather than his headquarters. Jackson therefore misunderstood a message stating that DK remained on the Jade River, adjacent to the German naval base at Wilhelmshaven; it could hardly have done otherwise, since the headquarters building was stationary. Jackson incorrectly informed the British fleet commander, Admiral John Jellicoe, that signals intercepts showed the German fleet was still in port. This miscommunication, compounded by delays in translating other German messages, allowed Scheer to surprise Jellicoe at the battle of Jutland, a chance encounter of the two fleets at a time when Jellicoe believed his opponent was still in port. The result of this confusion was to make Jellicoe mistrust Room 40's analysis, when the fault lay at least as much with an operator asking a half-informed question.[10]

Such misunderstandings reflect one of the fundamental arguments for developing and respecting intelligence as a separate profession. Decision makers are perfectly capable of mastering the technical procedures and cultural nuances of intelligence, but as a practical matter those decision makers lack the time and inclination to do so and must rely on specialists to collect and analyze intelligence information, just as they rely on other experts to coordinate military operations, fly aircraft, or organize secure communications.

This brings the discussion back to the first of Huntington's criteria for a profession. For more than eighty years in the United States and longer in Europe, societies have indeed delegated the function of intelligence collection and analysis to intelligence professionals, just as those societies have delegated the legal use of force to the military. While both professions must be subordinate to civilian leaders, it is counterproductive if not dangerous for those leaders to consistently bypass and ignore the designated professionals when they make decisions.

One implication of recognizing intelligence as a profession is the importance of imposing stability on its senior leadership. Not counting interim appointments, at least seventeen men served as Director of

Central Intelligence (DCI) between 1946 and 2005; only one survived for eight years and two more for six each. With a few exceptions, such as Robert Gates (acting director 1986–87 and director 1991–93), these men were politicians or clandestine operators rather than experienced analysts. Once the Director of National Intelligence (DNI) succeeded the DCI as head of the intelligence community in 2005, only one DNI—James R. Clapper, who had already headed two intelligence agencies after a career in Air Force intelligence—managed to serve for six and a half years. Even he was criticized for not knowing every new intelligence fact while attempting to manage the entire intelligence community. In other words, Clapper was judged by his performance as a current intelligence briefer rather than his overall ability to manage the intelligence community (IC) and identify broad trends.

Many of the men who occupied the positions of DCI and DNI were knowledgeable about intelligence, and a few were even experienced practitioners of the craft. Still, the political atmosphere in Washington produced such a frequent turnover that few presidents had the benefit of fully prepared intelligence subordinates who, like Clapper or J. Michael McConnell, had devoted their professional military careers to intelligence.

By comparison, admirals and generals spend up to thirty years studying and practicing their professions before they reach the four-star level, where they typically serve for four years in a particular command before moving to a related position elsewhere. Perhaps because of the (perceived) technical nature of the role, the uniformed director of the National Security Agency (NSA), who is simultaneously chief of the Central Security Service and (since 2009) commander of U.S. Cyber Command, has had greater longevity in position. Between them, two men (Lt. Gen. Michael Hayden and Gen. Keith Alexander) occupied this post during a fifteen-year period (1999–2014). The other senior managers of the intelligence community need the same kind of longevity and experience.

Or course, even if civilian leaders were willing to accept the concept of the intelligence community as being functionally equivalent to the armed forces, they are often intolerant of and even mystified by the idea that intelligence agencies should be headed by apolitical experts. In theory, one could cite the Federal Bureau of Investigation (FBI) directorship as an institutional example of how to develop senior expertise while limiting abuse of the position. In 1976, Congress belatedly acknowledged the obvious truth that allowing one man—J. Edgar Hoover—to occupy such a key position for forty-eight years was highly undesirable and posed a threat to civil liberties. The congressional solution was to limit the directorship to a term of at least ten years. In practice, however, only one subsequent director (Robert Mueller, 2001–13) was able to serve a complete term. President Trump's abrupt firing of director James Comey in 2017 reflected the continuing politicization of the post. Again, agency heads need much greater stability in order to provide the government with effective intelligence and counterintelligence.

Responsibilities of the Profession to the State

In addition to his definition of a profession, Huntington also postulated the responsibilities that senior military leaders owed to their governments:

> The responsibilities of the military man to the state are three-fold. He has, first, a representative function, to represent the claims of military security within the state machinery. . . . Secondly, the military officer has an advisory function, to analyse and to report on the [military] implications of alternative courses of action. . . . Finally, the military officer has an executive function, to implement state decisions with respect to military security even if it is a decision which runs violently counter to his military judgement.[11]

One obvious problem with this formulation is that Huntington seemed to expect the civilian decision makers to submit various courses of action to the military commanders for review and approval. In practice, those decision makers tend to follow the opposite procedure, in which the general or admiral offers a variety of military courses of action, accompanying each option with an estimate of the positive and negative outcomes of that option. Moreover, because of their domestic political experience, civilian decision makers are in the habit of seeking partial solutions or compromises to problems and as a result may tell the commander to seek the same outcome with half the resources the professional considers necessary. The result may well be a program that, like American policy in Vietnam, lacks both combat power and domestic political support. This half-step approach to military decisions was precisely what Secretary of

Defense Caspar Weinberger warned against in the famous Weinberger/ Powell Doctrine of 1984.[12]

Huntington himself recognized another problem, although he attempted to define it out of existence. He raised the possibility that an officer might be tempted to disobey his civilian master because the civilian orders violated military competence, the officer's understanding of the law, or the officer's sense of morality. In each case, however, Huntington insisted that the soldier owed obedience and a presumption of legality to any orders, without even the option of resignation in protest. Huntington assumed that the judicial system would resolve any questions of legality without action on the soldier's part. Consequently, he condemned not only Douglas MacArthur's confrontation with President Truman about Korean policy, but also the German officers who opposed Hitler. He argued that "only rarely will the military man be justified in following the dictates of private conscience against the dual demands of military obedience and state welfare."[13] In effect, therefore, Huntington advised senior officers to follow the discredited Nuremberg defense, claiming they bore no personal responsibility when they executed illegal or immoral orders. In practice, military and intelligence officials, being both responsible and ethical, need some alternative to the kind of blind obedience that Huntington demanded.

All these and other difficulties arise when military leaders must advise their civilian masters, even though in many if not most instances the disagreements are about the optimal means to achieve an agreed-upon policy outcome. In the case of intelligence, however, the analyst may well be trying to convince the decision maker that the reality of the situation differs from what the politician believes it to be, which implies that the desired policy outcome is inappropriate or impractical. Thus intelligence leaders not only begin the discussion with less credibility than their military counterparts, but also must seek to persuade the decision maker to change his or her perceptions of reality.

If we then attempt to translate Huntington's three responsibilities for military leaders into the equivalent functions of senior intelligence leaders, we arrive at a formulation such as the following:

1. Representative: Represent the profession to decision makers, advising generally on what the intelligence community believes

are the risks to the state and society, as well as what that community needs to help mitigate those risks, but recognizing that some of these needs may be politically unacceptable. Above all, help decision makers understand the strategic viewpoints of likely adversaries.
2. Advisory: When asked about a particular course of action, provide the most reasoned interpretation of opponent and third-party responses and risks for that course of action. This includes identifying both the most likely and most dangerous enemy courses of action; the latter is important so that neither the intelligence officer nor the policy maker assumes that they have identified opponent intentions accurately.
3. Executive: If the decision maker disputes or rejects the intelligence officer's best estimate of the opponent's capabilities and intentions, that officer should reconsider the estimate but still ensure that his subordinates follow and predict enemy actions in an unbiased manner.

As for questions of conscience, the intelligence professional, like his military counterpart, may well conclude that some form of disobedience is required under rare circumstances of illegality or immorality. Here the intelligence officer has the added burden of maintaining information security about such matters. Adm. Bobby Ray Inman, who resigned as deputy DCI in 1982 because he believed that DCI William Casey was misrepresenting assistance to the Nicaraguan Contras, is a rare example of ethical resistance to intelligence impropriety.[14] In Inman's case, however, he was curtailing a thirty-one-year naval career that included director of the NSA, giving him an unassailable position for dissent that few others possessed. Moreover, because he did not breach security regulations nor (apparently) dissuade the Reagan administration, his action had little influence on the Contra issue.

A brief consideration of congressional involvement in decisions may illustrate related difficulties an intelligence professional faces with regard to maintaining information security.

In 1974, the Hughes-Ryan Amendment mandated that the executive branch notify as many as 57 senators and 143 representatives of sensitive information collection or covert actions. This large number was clearly incompatible with the security of an operation. The Intelligence Oversight Act of 1980 finally limited such notification to the "Gang of Eight," which included congressional leaders of both parties, intelligence committee chairs, and ranking members of the minority party on those committees.[15] Even then, however, the definition and timing of such notification remained vague, and in practice it is extremely difficult for Congress to force presidential compliance. Presidents naturally argue that certain information is too sensitive to be shared even with the Gang of Eight, leaving the door open to executive actions without prior consultation.[16]

The justification for an intelligence officer to bypass the hierarchy and inform an agency inspector general or Congress of apparent illegality is even less clear. In 2019, the Trump administration strongly objected to invocation of the Intelligence Community Whistleblower Protection Act of 1998 when career intelligence officers reported questionable actions in Ukraine. As a practical matter, any government employee, and still more one with access to classified information, endangers his or her career even when reporting actions within classified channels. Regardless of the outcome in court, a disapproving supervisor can withdraw the employee's access to classified information, blocking his or her future employment.

During the early Cold War, some former intelligence professionals were able to publish their memoirs because the government was reluctant to air classified issues in open court. In 1981, however, President Reagan introduced a requirement that all individuals with access to sensitive compartmented information must sign a pledge not to publish information that was classified or "classifiable," with penalties for such publication. A subsequent requirement extended similar restrictions to those with access to lower levels of classified information. These restrictions made it easier for the government to punish publication of sensitive information, even when the intelligence officer was identifying improprieties.[17] Conscientious intelligence officers thus remain at a severe disadvantage in dealing with their consumers if the latter engage in illegal or unethical behavior.

Chapter Two

The Intelligence Process

Before considering the history and issues of relationships between government and intelligence institutions, a brief review of the basics of the intelligence process is in order. What follows may be obvious to practitioners and students of intelligence, but both the general public and decision makers sometimes have misconceptions or blind spots concerning the fundamentals.

The Intelligence Cycle

Different publications use different terms to present the process of intelligence, but there is little dispute over what must occur. The traditional explanation describes a four-step procedure, including direction, collection, processing, and dissemination.[1] Within an intelligence unit or agency, most or all of these steps occur simultaneously, although rarely is a single individual involved in all phases. One must also recognize that the process does not always follow the four steps in order; both intelligence officers and decision makers may short-circuit the cycle, retasking the system on the fly to confirm or elaborate upon a development.[2]

Direction, also described as collection management, is the process of establishing requirements and priorities for collection. Contrary to what conspiracy theorists say, no intelligence community in the world is capable of learning every possible item of useful information in a timely manner, and some events are simply unknowable in advance. Ideally, the intelligence consumers/decision makers assign detailed and realistic tasks, but many intelligence consumers have little knowledge of what can and cannot be collected and lack the time to monitor a myriad of tasks on a regular basis. Clearly, any subject on which the consumer asks for information must be a priority for the intelligence cycle: what is sometimes termed "mission-based planning."[3] Yet those consumer requests will rarely cover all possible collection requirements. Indeed, almost by definition, if the consumer only hears about topics of which he or she is already aware, that consumer runs a serious risk of being blindsided by new developments.

Instead, collection managers must decide which developments—whether diplomatic, information/propaganda, military, or economic—are most important to the decision maker and what specific indicators of those developments can actually be identified with available resources. Such decisions require collection managers to learn about their principal consumers in terms of both responsibilities and personalities. Wherever possible, managers choose to search for multiple indicators of the same anticipated event, seeking to collect two or more independent confirmations that such an event has occurred or is imminent. While every society seeks to anticipate threats to its welfare, an adversary will naturally attempt to conceal indications of those threats, making it difficult if not impossible to anticipate the adversary's actions.

Collection systems have limited capabilities, so establishing or changing collection priorities always comes with a cost. Particularly when assigning tasks to the technical collection systems involved in signals intelligence (SIGINT) or imagery intelligence (IMINT), a focus on one development may reduce that system's capacity to monitor other possible indicators or events on different frequencies or at different locations. In the case of human intelligence (HUMINT), asking a particular source to obtain a different set of information may expose that source to increased risk of detection by the adversary. Reassigning a collection system in response to current concerns may also cause the intelligence community as a whole to lose focus on equally significant but longer-term problems. Some of the most important potential threats, such as nuclear attack, have a high priority for warning but a low probability of occurring. Thus a collection manager must balance the real risks from such threats against the tendency to reprogram a system ad hoc to collect information about a current event that in reality poses a lesser threat to national security.[4]

In the American intelligence community, maintaining this balance between current and long-term interests is further complicated by a multiplicity of specialized agencies, each of which has its own needs and preferences for collection. Furthermore, no collection management system can anticipate every possible development that may be of interest to decision makers; there is a low but real possibility that a "black swan" event will appear unheralded despite the best efforts of all concerned.

Collection management also requires moral or ethical decisions. HUMINT may in some instances involve violence in other countries, while ethics are especially important when the collection involves counterintelligence or domestic surveillance of perceived terrorist threats. Free societies are understandably opposed to such surveillance, especially when it involves violation of privacy and other rights. Governments may be tempted to abuse this capability by conducting surveillance against legitimate domestic opponents. Still, every government needs a procedure for validating and conducting collection against genuine internal threats. In those instances, security agencies may need to intrude on civil rights to ensure the survival of the society. In an article for the journal *Intelligence and National Security*, Ross Bellaby suggested that such limited intrusions must be justified by a careful assessment of the trade-offs between ethical considerations and severity of the risk. He therefore proposed that the equivalent of "just cause" morality in warfare would be "sufficient threat" to balance the harm involved in intelligence collection.[5] Unfortunately, such threats are in the eye of the beholder, and people in power may believe they are justified in unnecessary intrusions.

The practical application of such ethics sometimes involves very fine distinctions. For decades, the British Security Service (aka MI5) regularly used listening devices and phone taps to monitor the Communist Party of Great Britain and similar organizations that followed the Moscow line and in some instances acted at the behest of the Soviet Committee for State Security (KGB). On several occasions, however, senior leaders of the Security Service demurred when conservative politicians wanted to go beyond monitoring of subversive activities to "bug" union or party leaders engaged in legitimate opposition actions.[6] Moreover, even after collecting appropriate information on domestic subversion, additional safeguards are still necessary to restrict disclosure of the resulting personal information to those with an absolute need to know.

Once managers assign tasks for collection, the next and most complex step in the intelligence process is to collect the raw information. For a major intelligence community such as that of the United States, this collection is continuous and relentless. Inevitably, however, the collectors may overlook or miss a small number of individual events because of equipment malfunctions, personnel shortages and fatigue, miscommunications, and various other forms of friction. Adverse weather or maintenance problems may delay the launch of a SIGINT aircraft so that it misses the opportunity to collect indications of a specific technical or military activity. This risk is yet another reason for seeking multiple confirmations of the same possible event.

Moreover, on occasion a picture is *not* worth a thousand words, at least not when that picture or other piece of raw data is taken out of context. For this reason, individual collectors often provide qualitative evaluations of the inputs they are forwarding. A HUMINT officer may comment that the source is not known to have access to the type of information he or she claims to have learned and may be inventing that information in hopes of reward. A SIGINT site might note that the technical parameters of a certain radar do not match those of the emitter operating in the same area on the previous day. An economic attaché in an embassy may observe that the host government's announced figures for unemployment do not seem to match the visible indications of joblessness. Without such contextual comments, it would be easy to misinterpret the bare contents of a report.

In the same vein, one must recognize that not all HUMINT comes from espionage. Career foreign service officers, especially those who serve repetitive assignments in the same region of the world, are often the most sophisticated observers of a foreign government's intentions and worldview. Joseph C. Grew, the U.S. ambassador to Tokyo from 1932 to 1941, recognized that Japan was *not* closely tied to the Tripartite Pact with Germany and might instead be amenable to a pragmatic compromise with the United States. By contrast, Secretary of State Cordell Hull insisted that Japan was part of a global network of aggressors who needed to be halted by firm policies. Although Japan undoubtedly began the Pacific War, American policies and perceptions contributed to Tokyo's decision in this regard.[7]

Every potential intelligence indication is subject to misinterpretation. Imagery interpreters may misidentify one piece of equipment as being another, similarly shaped item that the interpreters expect to see; a mine-laying plow and a towed mortar look remarkably similar from overhead.[8] A well-placed HUMINT source that reflects the beliefs of the adversary does not necessarily describe the reality of the situation—only the flawed perceptions or unconscious self-deceptions of that adversary. Just as trial lawyers regard "eyewitnesses" as unreliable sources, so a HUMINT officer must be alert for agents who report what they themselves believe, or what they think that officer expects to hear, rather than what is really happening. Similarly, signals intercepts that appear to indicate preparations for an offensive may actually be part of a deception plan or some irrelevant event. In short, analysts at every level must exhibit a healthy skepticism about the reality and meaning of any indication that comes their way.

Analysis

The results of such collection, provided in their context, are then subject to analysis, which is sometimes subdivided into collation, evaluation, analysis, integration, and interpretation.[9]

Many external characteristics of analysis have changed during the past four decades. The predictable, conventional structure of the Cold War and containment has given way to a more unpredictable world in which nonstate actors are often a major threat. The information revolution produced not only innovative collection devices but also open-source intelligence, digital searching and manipulation of classified collection reports, and rapid exchange of draft analyses and comments between analysts. People have developed an expectation of instantaneous access to information, often without realizing that typical internet search results are composed of equal parts fact, opinion, and outright misinformation.[10] Search algorithms frequently identify the most often cited sources, but "most often cited" is not the same as "most accurate." The subconscious belief that a "Google search" can correctly answer any question constitutes yet another barrier to communication between decision makers and analysts.

Despite such massive changes, the objective of analysis remains the same: using carefully developed knowledge of other cultures and environments, assemble and analyze the available, often incomplete data to discern what is happening and how an adversary may react to those developments. Intelligence organizations have to create and refine structures and procedures to accomplish that objective in the Information Age.

For a major power with extensive intelligence collection capabilities, the volume of raw reports often exceeds the time and attention span of any one person to absorb. There are a number of solutions to this volume. For example, the same analytical section may have multiple Boolean logic programs to search incoming electronic reports. One of these programs would be common to the entire office, based on the same search terms, which every analyst uses as a basis of situational awareness with other programs, customized by and for the different analysts to reduce the possibility that they overlook a particular event.

Another approach is to stratify analysis into different time frames. Many government organizations and a few large businesses maintain a twenty-four-hour monitoring office sometimes called a situation, alert, or watch center where analysts with broad areas of responsibility seek to identify and publicize time-critical developments. These watch officers issue reports in brief, short-fuse messages that contain only minimal explanatory analysis. Such reports are the essence of current intelligence but are rarely decisive in their own right. Beyond that monitoring center, one or more levels of analysis may produce more complete reports of increasing sophistication and decreasing time constraints, ranging from daily and weekly current intelligence summaries out to longer-term estimates for a particular state or region. Most of the experienced intelligence officers who perform such in-depth analysis are organized by expertise concerning a particular region, such as the Levant or Southeast Asia. In other instances, the organization is topical rather than regional, with analysts who specialize in, for example, rocketry, weapons of mass destruction (WMD), or transnational terrorism.

In connection with such specialization, many observers lament what they regard as inefficiency and duplication of effort between the different agencies that comprise the U.S. intelligence community. The competitive existence of these organizations—especially the Central Intelligence Agency (CIA), Defense Intelligence Agency (DIA), and State Department Bureau of Intelligence and Research (INR)—poses the possibility of lowest-common-denominator joint reports with watered-down community assessments.[11] Although all three agencies have access to the same information, there is a natural tendency, sometimes termed an "analytical stovepipe," to put greater trust in reports from the field representatives (station chiefs, defense attachés, foreign service officers) of one's own organization.[12] The result may be a disagreement concerning the likelihood and rapidity with which a particular future event, such as the 1992 division of Czechoslovakia into two different states, might occur.

The existence of multiple agencies, each with a different institutional charter and incentives, has the potential to ensure multiple perspectives that will reduce the probability that a threat or opportunity goes unnoticed. That said, there is no guarantee that this pluralism within the intelligence community will always ensure independent intellectual perspectives on an issue.[13]

On occasion, one intelligence agency (or one major decision maker, as chapter 3 addresses) may become so convinced of a particular interpretation that it insists on that interpretation despite all IC efforts to reach a consensus. Unlike those who spread propaganda, the advocate of an outlying intelligence viewpoint is not deliberately lying, but the effect may be equally misleading. The nature of intelligence analysis is that one can rarely if ever *disprove* an interpretation that has at least some factual basis, which results in muddled or inaccurate community assessment.

The president or other decision maker may be tempted to regard such disagreements within the IC as reasons to either ignore analysis completely or choose the interpretation that best supports a preferred policy. On the other hand, the very existence of multiple agencies, many of which have specific areas of focus (such as terrorism, weapons proliferation, or financial trends), reduces the probability that an outlying event or indication is ignored or misinterpreted.

In theory, the 2005 creation of the director of national intelligence (DNI) position reduced the undesirable effects of having multiple intelligence agencies. Even before that event, however, experts from different organizations often worked together on ad hoc or standing committees/task forces to provide an integrated assessment of a high-priority threat. Given existing issues with classified information, it may be decades before historians can evaluate the institutional effects of the DNI on the coherence of IC assessment.

The mental processes involved in intelligence analysis may vary considerably depending upon the nature of the subject, the skills of the analyst, and the needs of the intended consumer. Analysis is not simply "establishing the facts" or "connecting the dots," since in many instances some of those facts or dots are unknown or unknowable.[14]

Perhaps the closest, albeit imperfect, analogy to intelligence analysis is the experience of writing a history or social science research paper the night before that paper is due. The parallel is particularly apt when late-breaking information or an ongoing crisis limits the time available for analysis while fatigue hampers the mental processes. The writer does not have and cannot obtain all the facts about the situation, but instead must interpolate the available data, applying his or her understanding of an adversary's capabilities or likely intentions to discern the most likely eventuality. Within these restrictions of time and information, the analyst attempts to achieve three things in the intelligence product: provide context and insight to the known facts, warn of possible adverse events in a timely manner, and where applicable identify opportunities for the decision makers to intervene in the developing situation. This last is not always possible, and in any event the analyst must resist the tendency to describe the situation selectively so as to (consciously or unconsciously) "sell" the decision maker on a particular course of action. In short, as veteran analyst Thomas Fingar observed, "spies collect data, analysts provide insight."[15]

Unless the analyst is a very senior intelligence official, the first draft of intelligence production is just that: a draft. Good staff work requires that the analyst coordinate with other experts, both within and sometimes outside his or her agency, after which the supervisor will at least proofread the result if not make substantive suggestions and modifications.

The final step in intelligence production is the dissemination of the finished analysis to decision makers, using some combination of written products and deskside briefings. The term "dissemination" suggests that this is a simple distribution procedure, analogous to delivering a daily publication on a paper route. In fact, however, this final act is often the most difficult step in the process.

Critical Nodes in the Intelligence Cycle

Even before an analysis reaches the decision maker's desk or computer screen, the intelligence cycle may fail in several different ways. To avoid classification issues, the following discussion is based primarily on a familiar example, the Allied ability (ULTRA intelligence) to read German messages that had been encrypted using the supposedly unbreakable ENIGMA machine.[16]

The first issue for any successful intelligence effort is that it must be possible to detect the opponent's preparations in advance. If the opponent does not exhibit any indications of what is about to occur, by definition no advance proof is possible except in the rare instance when a HUMINT source has access to the opponent's decision makers. In the ULTRA example, German army communications often went via courier or landlines, severely reducing the opportunity of interception except where Resistance workers copied and forwarded those messages. German navy and Luftwaffe messages, as well as signals transmitted across the Mediterranean to commanders in North Africa, were far more likely to be intercepted simply because they were transmitted over the air.

When detection or interception of indications is impossible, the most that intelligence analysts can do is suggest that a particular action accords with the opponent's known policy objectives and previous actions. Political, diplomatic, or economic policy changes may well fall into this category, because they require few if any visible preparations prior to the event. By contrast, the classic examples of surprise ground invasion, such as the German invasion of the Soviet Union in 1941, involved thousands of troop movements and logistical preparations, all of which were identified but not interpreted correctly at the time (see chapter 7).[17] Naval offensives often begin with fewer but more massive preparations, primarily the movement of naval task forces that can minimize their electronic emissions to reduce the chances of detection. Thus, for a naval attack such as that on Pearl Harbor, there will be fewer intelligence indications than for an equivalent land attack, thereby reducing the probability of timely leads and warning.

The second issue is ensuring that the intelligence collector in question actually collects the indication(s) of impending action by the opponent. Even if management has prioritized such collection, there are numerous reasons why it might fail to happen. In the case of ENIGMA-encrypted messages, for example, radio propagation varied from hour to hour and place to place, preventing some signals intercepts.

Third, once the intelligence community collects the raw message or other data, it must be able to decrypt and interpret that data correctly. On May 1, 1940, Germany changed virtually all of its ENIGMA encryption keys. That change alone was an indication of impending major action, but the details of that action were not available until the British rebroke the code some three weeks later. In the interim, the German advance through the Ardennes had doomed France. On February 1, 1942, the German navy adopted a new code known as "Triton" for its Atlantic submarine operations. The British ULTRA effort was again unable to break this code, this time until December of the same year. Some analysis of training operations in the Baltic and of the external characteristics (traffic analysis) of Triton messages still occurred during this ten-month period, but the Royal Navy was not privy to the details of German operations.[18] Deciphering older messages whose code is better understood may still have some intelligence value, but it is unlikely to provide the time-sensitive information that the analyst or decision maker needs from current communications.

Fourth, the collectors need to receive not just one critical message but rather a group of such indications, if at all possible coming from different sources and by different means. Not only does decryption require multiple messages to break a code, but no one report, however critical, provides reliable proof of what an opponent intends to do. Consider, for example, the German defeat of American forces at Sidi Bou Zid and Kasserine Pass in February 1943. The Allies relied too much upon ULTRA decrypts indicating that German higher headquarters had disapproved a counterattack in Tunisia. The analysts could not know that Field Marshal Erwin Rommel had returned to the region from sick leave. He met his subordinate commanders face-to-face on February 9 and developed a plan that was not reflected in any signals intercepts, resulting in a disastrous surprise for the Allies.[19] In modern terms, all-source analysis is the best safeguard against such surprises.

Finally, this entire intelligence process must result in a coherent estimate or prediction that reaches the decision maker in a format to convince that leader to take action in time to influence the situation. The purpose of all intelligence is to give the leader a more complete understanding of the situation with fewer ambiguities, permitting that leader to either counter or if possible deter the undesirable actions of the opponent. If the decision maker does not read, understand, agree with, and act upon the considered analysis of his or her intelligence officers, the entire process of intelligence production is a waste of resources for the government and an exercise in frustration for both leader and intelligence personnel.

There are in fact two aspects of time with regard to influencing the policy maker. An intelligence estimate must arrive both before the decision maker has made up his or her mind and while there is still time for the government to influence the outcome—a narrow window.[20] Chapter 3 focuses on this critical interface between leader and analyst.

Qualitative Grading of the Assessment/ Prediction: The "Weasel Words"

Regardless of how convincing an assessment may be, almost by definition a prediction of future behavior cannot be certain. Telling a decision maker that such a prediction is ironclad would therefore be at best misleading and at worst an unprofessional lie. One of the most infamous (if dubious) examples of false confidence of this type occurred in 2002, when DCI George Tenet allegedly assured President George W. Bush that the case for WMD in Iraq amounted to a "slam dunk," a statement with which many analysts might have disagreed (see chapter 3), and which the Bush administration later used to blame Tenet for the invasion of Iraq.[21] In practice, responsible intelligence officers seek to qualify their statements with indications of the probability or likelihood that the statements are completely accurate. Unfortunately, some decision makers regard qualifying adverbs—including "apparently," "probably," and "presumably"—as being an effort not to report accurately but rather to avoid responsibility for being wrong. In the military, such terms are sometimes referred to, scornfully, as "weasel words."

In recent years, the U.S. intelligence community attempted to explain and quantify the terminology used in estimates. A 2007 report from the Office of the Director of National Intelligence (ODNI) noted,

> We do not intend the term "unlikely" to imply an event will not happen. We use "probably" and "likely" to indicate there is a greater than even chance. We use words such as "we cannot dismiss," "we cannot rule out," and "we cannot discount" to reflect an unlikely—or even remote—event whose consequences are such it warrants mentioning. Words such as "may be" and "suggest" are used to reflect situations in which we are unable to assess the likelihood generally because relevant information is non-existent, sketchy, or fragmented. In addition to using words within a judgment to

convey degrees of likelihood, we also ascribe "high," "moderate," or "low" confidence levels based on the scope and quality of information supporting our judgments.

- "High confidence" generally indicates our judgments are based on high-quality information and/or the nature of the issue makes it possible to render a solid judgment.

- "Moderate confidence" generally means the information is interpreted in various ways, we have alternative views, or the information is credible and plausible but not corroborated sufficiently to warrant a higher level of confidence.

- "Low confidence" generally means the information is scant, questionable, or very fragmented and it is difficult to make solid analytic inferences, or we have significant concerns or problems with the sources.[22]

This approach to intelligence analysis was codified in Intelligence Community Directive 203, June 21, 2007.[23] It remains to be seen whether this commendable effort has in fact clarified understanding in the minds of decision makers.

Security Classification

Such definitions also highlight the often misunderstood meaning of security classifications on sensitive information. While the markings and meaning vary between national governments, the U.S. definition for designating information as "Top Secret" is "whether its unauthorized disclosure could reasonably be expected to cause exceptionally grave damage to the national security."[24] In the case of operational information, such as the dispositions and plans of certain military forces, this definition is literally true, since divulging such plans might allow an adversary to destroy those forces.

When applied to intelligence reports, however, the security classification often refers not to the information itself but rather to the sources and methods used to acquire and confirm that information. The actual data may be relatively unimportant, but if an adversary knew how and when the United States collected that data, that adversary might take measures that blocked access to an entire class of similar raw information. The classified information may or may not be essential to the all-source analysis contained in a particular document, but the future ability to collect such data could be critical.

One of the most famous cases of compromising intelligence sources and methods occurred in the United Kingdom in 1927. For years, British signals intercept and analysis had provided the government with a steady stream of information showing that the Soviet Union's trade representatives in Britain were directing and financing labor strikes and other disruptions there, all while denying any involvement. A raid on Soviet offices failed to provide conclusive evidence of these efforts. In frustration, the British government quoted decrypted messages in public as a justification for expelling the Soviet agents. Moscow eventually responded with radical changes in communications security, including the introduction of almost unbreakable one-time code pads. For more than a decade thereafter, Britain had no access to Soviet encrypted communications.[25]

A related matter is that the most highly classified/sensitive data point in a particular document determines the classification of the overall document, of the page on which that data point appears, and of the classification marking on the paragraph containing that information. In theory, the entire assessment, PowerPoint briefing slide, or classified article might be based on otherwise unclassified information, but it will still be classified in accordance with the one item that reflects the intelligence capabilities, sources, and methods. In practice, however, good all-source analysis weaves together elements from multiple sources—a factor that makes subsequent declassification review complex and time-consuming.

Consider a hypothetical example of a multiparagraph classified article concerning a major training exercise for an armored division in a foreign country. Unclassified newspaper or confidential defense attaché reports provided the cue for collection management to focus efforts on the upcoming exercise. SIGINT, imagery, and even cyberpenetration of the division's network may have offered pieces of information concerning this exercise, perhaps noting that the division is conducting an expensive, full-blown maneuver with all of the division's troops and equipment in the field, as opposed to a command post exercise in which staff officers simulate such maneuvers without moving the units. Just as a student should not submit a term paper based on only one reference, so the intelligence officer attempted to include all these data points in the final product. The real value of the final report, however, lay not in the high-technology, sensitive collection capabilities, but rather in the analysis that indicates a higher tempo of training—a tempo intended either to send a diplomatic warning to a potential adversary or to prepare the division for actual deployment. The analyst must justify which of these two explanations is more probable.

Now, imagine that years later someone submits a Freedom of Information Act (FOIA) request for a group of classified reports that includes the analysis of this division exercise. The highest security classification or sensitive information compartment attached to this article may suggest which of the "INTs" (HUMINT, SIGINT, IMINT, etc.) was involved and therefore which intelligence agency collected that particular form of information. Only an experienced analyst may be able to identify all the possible inputs, retrieve the corresponding messages from a database of messages from that time period, and then consult with each of the contributing agencies to determine how much of the resulting article can be declassified and released to the public. Small wonder, then, that FOIA requests often take years for security review.

Covert Action

One activity often associated with foreign intelligence is missing from the preceding discussion: covert action. Illegal or violent action may sometimes be necessary in the ordinary course of intelligence gathering. A century ago, a number of intelligence agencies burgled the diplomatic facilities of their adversaries as a means of obtaining encryption codes. Even within the United States, the FBI under J. Edgar Hoover ordered illegal invasions of the offices of organizations or people the agency was investigating. Regardless of the moral issues involved, such crimes in support of intelligence collection differ in both scope and intent from "covert action" as it is usually defined: a deniable military or political action undertaken abroad to achieve a specific political effect. This may range from funding a foreign political organization to manipulating foreign social media to conducting an armed uprising. Any such action puts the individuals at risk of detection and apprehension. These efforts are thus antithetical to the basic role of field officers as invisible information gatherers. In fact, many covert operations are conducted by organized military units rather than by intelligence officers. As we shall see in chapters 4 through 6, however, intelligence agencies often become involved in covert operations at the expense of their primary mission.

There are many reasons for such diversions from the primary purpose of intelligence. Yet one of these factors is a very human one. When a senior intelligence officer presents a decision maker with the often difficult, nuanced challenges posed overseas, those challenges put pressure on both participants to find a response or solution. This relationship between operator and intelligence analyst is the critical nexus of intelligence and may often lead to distorted results. No one is satisfied when a subordinate reports a problem but has no solution. The intelligence officer, seeking to build credibility with his or her chief, may be tempted to offer a seemingly simple covert response. Conversely, decision makers regard intelligence agencies and especially espionage officers as having the ability to go beyond information gathering to influence the situations they report. Once an "intelligence" agency diverges from collection to covert action, however, that agency becomes invested in a particular policy and thereby reduces the likelihood of dispassionate, rational analysis of events. A short-term win by covert action may contribute to a long-term blindness on the part of analysts and leaders.

Chapter Three

The Operator-Analyst Interface

[F]or it is a habit of mankind to entrust to careless hope what they long for, and to use sovereign reason to thrust aside what they do not desire.

—Thucydides[1]

I said I don't want either intelligence organization [Iraqi Intelligence Service or General Military Intelligence Directorate] to give me analysis—that is my specialty . . . which is what I used with the Iranians, some of it out of deduction and some of it through invention and connecting the dots, all without having hard evidence.

—Saddam Hussein, 1990[2]

At the heart of most intelligence successes and failures is the relationship between the operator or decision maker on the one hand and the intelligence analysts or managers on the other. In the majority of cases, this relationship is quite effective, although subject to the usual risks of misunderstanding found in any human communication. On occasion, however, the operator-analyst interface becomes so dysfunctional that it leads to organizational and intelligence failure.

It is natural and appropriate that the decision maker will compare intelligence analysis to other sources of information before arriving at a decision. Some of these "customers" are sophisticated and well-informed.[3] Yet, particularly when the intelligence product differs from those other sources, the customers may reject the intelligence estimate as an unsupported or deliberately biased "opinion."

The issue is not whether the analysts will support the operators, but rather whether the analysts understand what the operators need, and the operators comprehend and respect the support they receive. In examining this relationship, one must first consider the common errors of perception that may afflict both intelligence consumers and producers, and then examine other impediments to mutual communication and understanding.

Operators and Analysts

A recurring motif of the American government's response to the COVID-19 pandemic in 2020 was the image of political leaders making public assertions that were at odds with what their scientific advisors, from the Centers for Disease Control down to local public health officers, believed. Unlike the classified arena of intelligence, these issues of public health played out in the full glare of the media, but the disagreements involved in epidemiology and intelligence were remarkably similar. In each instance, the advisors had extensive expertise but could not predict the future with absolute certainty, which somehow gave the decision makers the false impression that their own preferences were by definition more likely to occur than the experts' projections.

Mark Lowenthal, a distinguished practitioner and author on intelligence matters, has observed that "policy makers tend to be optimists" while "intelligence officers are skeptics."[4] This generalization is undoubtedly correct; most politicians believe that the policies they advocate can make government more effective, just as most flag officers want to implement organizational improvements and military offensives. By contrast, many intelligence officers are motivated in part by the desire to protect their state from harm. Intelligence analysts often unite this defensive, cautious mindset with a desire to teach others the nuances they have learned concerning foreign adversaries, even though their decision-making "students" may be unwilling to learn. On the surface of it, combining optimistic operators with pessimistic analysts would seem to be a sensible precaution to ensure a balanced approach to any situation. In practice, however, the interaction of policy makers with intelligence producers is far from balanced.

In many if not all large organizations, military or civilian, there is an ill-defined but very real divide among the participants. On the one hand are the operators—owners, business partners, team leaders, managers, staff chiefs, elected officials, and operations officers—who are determined to accomplish what they perceive to be the objective of their organization. The objective or mission may be profit from a business, completion of a project, passage of a law, implementation of a policy, or defeat of an enemy force. This determination to succeed, this drive to completion, is essential to the success of most endeavors. Yet it can spin out of control when the operator subconsciously assumes away any difficulties that might impede mission accomplishment and demands that everyone "get on board" with his plan.

On the other hand are the specialists, whom operators often describe as "support staff." These specialists are essential to the organization, yet the specialists' contribution to the group often takes the form of objections or modifications to a plan, giving the appearance of being obstructionist and negative. The financial officer may argue that the organization cannot afford a particular course of action, the attorney may advise that such a course of action borders on illegality, and the logistician may argue that the distances involved will require additional time and resources to refuel vehicles. Experienced operators will take measures to address constructive criticisms, but over time they may come to regard the support staff as naysayers.

In most instances the specialists generate visible products and detailed calculations to bolster their contentions about a course of action. Logistical plans, for example, may be far more detailed than the overall concept of the operation. By contrast, the products and sources used by an intelligence analyst are either highly classified or based on unfamiliar cultural norms, or both. Under such circumstances, it is human nature for the "operator" in a particular situation to disregard or downplay the intelligence officers' concerns about the operator's preferred course of action.

The marvels of instantaneous communication have encouraged the military decision maker, at least, to believe that he or she knows as much about the situation as the intelligence manager. Two pieces of technology should suffice to illustrate the pitfalls of such situational awareness.

The first of these is Blue Force Tracker, one of a number of GPS-enabled devices that depict the current position of a particular friendly military element. "Blue" in this instance is a generic term for friendly forces, as opposed to hostile or "Red" troops. In 2003, one vehicle in each company-sized American military unit had such a device installed, allowing observers to view, almost instantaneously, the location on a monitor as the soldiers entered Baghdad. In special operations applications, each individual soldier might carry a tracker. This was a priceless command-and-control advantage, permitting American commanders to know the current location of the fighting force.

Unfortunately for organizational effectiveness, the same level of accuracy was impossible when plotting the suspected positions of "Red" (adversary) troop units. Intelligence analysts strove to position Red units as accurately as possible in the tracking system. Still, the habit of thinking that the monitor depicts "ground truth" could easily lead operators to reach a distorted understanding of the situation when looking at tracking monitors that show only projected enemy locations, let alone actual enemy activities. This was especially difficult when attempting to track irregular formations such as the Fedayeen Saddam. Even today, a commander still needs input from his or her intelligence officer as to the actual locations, capabilities, and intentions of the opposing force, and he or she can never expect to have absolute omniscience concerning those opponents.

Unmanned aerial vehicles (UAVs) require similar cautions. Israel originally designed such systems to collect intelligence, although later the United States pioneered arming the larger ones with missiles. Even without such armament, a UAV can loiter over an area for hours, collecting information without endangering a friendly pilot. There are indeed times when a commander needs to watch the UAV "feed" personally to identify targets and anticipate an enemy attack. The UAV, however, only shows one portion of a potential battlefield. If a commander becomes focused on the images coming from one or even multiple UAVs, that commander may easily believe that he or she has total knowledge of the situation even though he or she unintentionally ignores much of the battle area. It is also easy to misinterpret innocent activity as enemy military preparations—a misinterpretation that can lead to an ill-considered attack. Only time and experience can develop the knowledge to differentiate such activities, and few commanders have the time to devote exclusively to one system. Most of the time, therefore, the commander should let his or her staff, both intelligence and operational, monitor such technology and produce a summary of the result. To do otherwise may mislead the commander or decision maker about the situation with which he or she must deal.

Problems of Perception

All of us see what we expect to see. Most Westerners, however sophisticated, are susceptible to cognitive dissonance and its counterpart, confirmation bias. We often ignore or reject information that contradicts preconceived notions while clinging to those familiar viewpoints even in the teeth of the evidence. If a human receives indications that reality is at odds with those notions, he or she tends to ignore or explain away the dissonant factors while overemphasizing other indications that appear to support the preconceived notion.

In arguing that national security decision makers do not necessarily follow the rational actor theory, political scientist Matthew Wahlert postulated what he called "motivated bias." Confident in past successes and present policy, the operator ignores or misinterprets data that might constitute warning of an impending failure. He cited the Bay of Pigs invasion and the Iranian hostage rescue effort as examples of plans that a president persisted in implementing despite low probability of success.[5]

Keren Yarhi-Milo, a Princeton professor of politics and international affairs, described this phenomenon as the "selective attention thesis," arguing that policy makers give disproportionate weight to two factors: their own theories and their personal experiences in dealing with an adversarial leader.[6] This combination of cognitive dissonance and confirmation bias is exacerbated by a number of related issues.

The first such problem is the sheer volume of individual reports and factoids generated on a daily basis by the multiple collection efforts of a major government. In such circumstances, genuine indications of an opponent's future actions can easily be lost in a background of irrelevant or even contradictory information. Influential military intelligence historian Roberta Wohlstetter used an engineering concept, the signal-to-noise ratio, to describe this phenomenon. Just as an electronic device needs to differentiate between the voice or signal it is amplifying and the background noise of static and other sounds, so the analyst needs to pick out the fleeting indications of opponent action against the "noise" of other reports as well as opponent deception measures. Analyzing the American failure to anticipate the Japanese attack on Pearl Harbor, Wohlstetter concluded that "we failed to anticipate Pearl Harbor not for want of the relevant materials but because of a plethora of irrelevant ones."[7] Even if an analyst or intelligence agency identifies the correct "signal," the analyst or agency still has to convince the policy maker to focus on that event rather than on the irrelevant background noise. If, as sometimes happens, that policy maker wishes to see the raw information reports, he or she may seize upon a piece of chaff that supports preconceived notions while ignoring the wheat the analysts seek to highlight.

Mirror-imaging also discourages correct signal identification. It is tempting to assume that your opponent assesses the situation in the same manner and with the same priorities as do you. In practice, however, two potential adversaries often have radically different priorities and assessments. Governments vary in both vital interests and national cultures, so that experience learned in one political or business system may be completely inappropriate when dealing with a foreign actor. Yet decision makers naturally rely on their own experience and may unconsciously adjust their understanding of the facts to conform to that experience.[8] Prior to the start of World War I, the French army commander-designate, Joseph Joffre, and many of his colleagues felt that they could not rely on units composed of French reservists to perform well under fire. Joffre therefore applied mirror-imaging to his German adversaries, believing that they, too, would hesitate to employ their reserve formations despite numerous intelligence indications to the contrary. The French concluded that without such reserve troops, Germany could not execute the rumored Schlieffen Plan by invading through Belgium. In reality, the German planners could and did use reserve units in their offensive.[9]

Intelligence officers are vulnerable to these mistakes as well, tending to apply "common knowledge" or "institutional wisdom" even if the adversary may have changed. There is no such thing as a completely "objective" analyst, but career analysts, whatever their other faults, are less likely to be biased in favor of a particular policy than are the leaders who designed that policy. Unfortunately, this *lack* of bias may appear to a decision maker as disloyalty or nitpicking.

Analysts and decision makers both tend to focus on the opponent's supposed *intentions* but also need to consider *capabilities*. When an adversary is capable of conducting some action in the international arena, policy makers as well as intelligence analysts should not dismiss that possibility simply because they believe the adversary has no such intention. In the months prior to the 1973 Yom Kippur or Ramadan War, Israeli leaders were well aware that Egypt had the capability to cross the Suez Canal, even if they grossly underestimated the speed of such crossing. The Egyptian armed forces included forty battalions of engineers that frequently rehearsed erection of Soviet ribbon bridges under cover of an elaborate air defense system. The Israelis assumed, however, that the Egyptians intended to recapture the entire Sinai Peninsula, which would require first-line fighter-bombers and other new weapons to neutralize Israeli airpower. Thus, Israeli and most Western intelligence analysts assumed that the Egyptians would not attack until they acquired and mastered these advanced weapons.[10] Instead, of course, the Egyptians deliberately planned a limited offensive to seize shallow bridgeheads on the east bank of the canal and then stand on the defensive, covered by Soviet-supplied air defense systems, so their war plan had less need for fighter-bombers with skilled pilots. Instead of seeking air superiority, Egyptian commanders relied upon their air defense to negate Israeli air superiority.[11]

Yarhi-Milo has emphasized, correctly, that military intelligence organizations in particular, charged with tracking trends in foreign military armaments and doctrine, are more likely to emphasize capabilities than are politicians, who often focus on the personalities and current behavior of their opposite numbers.[12] Moreover, the national intelligence agencies have attempted to educate their analysts and structure their processes against the dangers of cognitive biases.[13] If nothing else, professional intelligence agencies have at least some opportunity of escaping the "motivated bias" of those who are closely associated with a particular course of action.

Decision makers may be more vulnerable to deliberate or self-deception, both because those leaders/managers cannot devote all their time to looking at all indications and because they subconsciously expect the data to conform to their desired policy outcomes. Rare, indeed, is the executive who, like President George H. W. Bush or Secretary of Defense Robert Gates, has significant previous experience (in each case including time as DCI) with the strengths and limitations of intelligence assessment.

Organizational Constraints

Consequently, mixing policy and intelligence may lead to dangerous misunderstandings. Any organization that permits an "operator" to decide what intelligence reports are presented to the next higher level of decision-making is encouraging such wishful thinking, yet this is a recurring institutional problem for different organizations. The operator's responsibility is always apparent, whereas the analyst appears to produce nothing but a few vague yet highly classified documents and briefings. Therefore, the unconscious assumption is that the intelligence staff is less important and less involved than the operations staff.

As Japan expanded during the later 1930s and early 1940s, its operations officers frequently criticized their more junior intelligence counterparts for failing to produce targets. Before occupying French Indochina, the General Staff operators did not bother to consult intelligence experts on the region, and they co-opted intelligence collection for their own purposes.[14] In the German armed forces and especially the Luftwaffe, intelligence officers were consistently junior in rank and subordinate to the operations officers in the same headquarters. Those operations officers routinely wrote their own "intelligence" estimates and dismissed any views provided by the intelligence staff.[15] Throughout the Cold War, U.S. Army and Air Force tactical staffs gave nominal independence to the intelligence officer, but again the operations officer at any given level was usually of a higher rank and often had authority to issue orders on behalf of the commander. On the staff of the Department of the Army, the assistant chief of staff for intelligence did not have the same organizational rank as the deputy chief of staff for operations until 1987. Although such organizational minutiae may appear petty, they reflect a continuing habit of giving the operator precedence and preference over his intelligence counterpart, thereby invalidating any independence in discussions between the two.

A related problem is that decision makers often expect that the manager of their intelligence programs will personally brief them on a daily basis. While many military commanders have recognized the inherent contradiction in these two roles, political leaders often confuse the two. It is easy to say that the intelligence manager should undertake this role to establish a personal relationship and trust with his or her boss, but the organizational consequences can be negative.

This briefing relationship may increase the decision maker's trust of his or her intelligence staff chief, but it also insulates the decision makers from the actual analysts. This insulation, in turn, means that the leader does not benefit from the expertise of specialists while the specialists may not have a clear sense of what the leader needs from them.

From the time of the first DCIs under Harry Truman, presidents expected that their chiefs of intelligence would personally brief the executive on a daily basis. This meant that the DCI had to invest up to six hours a day in preparing, practicing, waiting outside offices, and then presenting such briefings to the president, leaving the intelligence manager with far less time than any other manager or departmental secretary to oversee his organization and process. Subsequent presidents varied in their approach to the daily intelligence briefing. A group of well-qualified national intelligence officers (NIOs), established during the 1970s when Henry Kissinger was the National Security Assistant, became the primary presidential briefers. Yet presidents continue to expect that their DCIs and later DNIs be omniscient about current events. When George W. Bush became president, DCI George Tenet chose to accompany his NIO to every daily intelligence briefing, which meant that he had to review the briefing ahead of time. Tenet gained influence and credibility but lost much of the time needed to manage the CIA. Some critics have alleged that his closeness to the administration made it difficult for Tenet to assert analytical differences with that administration concerning Iraq.[16] As the Silberman-Robb Commission on the Intelligence Capabilities of the U.S. Regarding Weapons of Mass Destruction urged Bush, "while the DNI must be ultimately responsible for the content of your daily briefing, we do not believe that the DNI ought to prepare, deliver, or even attend every briefing. For if the DNI is consumed by current intelligence, the long-term needs of the Intelligence Community will suffer."[17]

Once the CIA created the NIOs, the DIA followed suit with its own set of defense intelligence officers—senior analysts who regularly briefed Congress and other senior officials. Still, the defense secretary and chairman of the Joint Chiefs of Staff continued to expect that their principal intelligence staff officer would provide deskside briefings. For example, in 2003 the Joint Staff J2 (a rear admiral or major general) had to devote at least half of his time—often starting at 3:15 a.m.—to editing, practicing, mastering, and personally presenting the current intelligence brief to the defense secretary, the chairman of the Joint Chiefs, and sometimes other senior officials. Again, this reduced the senior manager to a glorified briefer while insulating the intelligence consumer from the expertise of actual analysts. In many instances, the operator and heads of other staff divisions sat back while their subordinates gave the daily updates.

There are solutions to this inefficient relationship, of course. In 1991, while working as a lowly analyst who assembled the Joint Staff's daily intelligence assessment, I briefed the personal staff of the secretary of defense early each morning before the secretary reached his office, and then the J2 himself briefed the secretary an hour later. My opposite number on the night shift also used a secure telephone to brief the regional defense intelligence officer before that officer, in turn, explained the situation on Capitol Hill. This allowed an alternative line of communications between decision makers and analysts, although I'm not sure that either side was conscious of the opportunity. It was at best an imperfect methodology, since the secretary continued to receive his background information second- or thirdhand and the J2 still lost half his day being a current intelligence briefer.

Consequences

Subsequent chapters will trace the evolution of intelligence organs in both Europe and the United States. For the purposes of this discussion, two examples should suffice to illustrate the psychological and institutional differences between decision makers and intelligence analysts. At best, these relationships are inefficient. In extreme cases, as Richard Samuels observed of Imperial Japan's leaders in *Special Duty: A History of the Japanese Intelligence Community*, operators may choose to follow "essentialist stereotyping and wishful thinking."[18]

Secretary of Defense Robert S. McNamara was a brilliant and decisive executive who had to balance many conflicting considerations in his support of President Lyndon Johnson's conduct of the Vietnam conflict. Unfortunately for later events, this combination of brains and loyalty to his boss made McNamara impatient with anyone, including intelligence analysts, who disagreed with him about the war. McNamara recognized that Vietnam represented a difficult problem that did not lend itself to conventional or special warfare solutions. This lack of clarity prompted the secretary to view intelligence reports about the war as attempts to justify increased resources for it or as criticism of national policy, leading him to disregard such intelligence if it clashed with his personal interpretation.[19] On September 22, 1965, the CIA published a special national intelligence estimate (SNIE). This assessment argued, quite correctly, that Washington's repeated interruptions of the Rolling Thunder bombing campaign offering to negotiate while avoiding the industrialized northeastern region of North Vietnam tended to stiffen Hanoi's resistance by giving the impression that the United States lacked determination to prosecute the war. Instead, the SNIE suggested that the United States escalate the bombing campaign. Secretary McNamara apparently resented such critique. He persuaded the president to appoint a panel of "experts," who naturally predicted that escalation would not influence Hanoi's conduct of the war; the panel instead urged leveling off the rate of attacks.[20] The self-defeating cycle of bombings and hesitations continued for another three years.

The tangled tale of WMD in Iraq involved a collective exercise of similar preconceived notions on the part of executives. The supposed presence of WMD became the major justification for the 2003 invasion of Iraq and is often depicted as a significant failure of "American intelligence." The reality was more complex.

The origin of beliefs concerning Iraqi WMD dates back at least to the 1991 Desert Storm operation when, contrary to Western expectations, Saddam Hussein remained in control of Iraq despite his defeat in Kuwait. United Nations Security Council Resolution 687, dated April 3, 1991, demanded that Iraq destroy all chemical and biological weapons as well as all missiles with a range of more than 150 kilometers (93 miles).[21] The United Nations Special Commission (UNSCOM) on Iraq took up the task of enforcing these rules, while the International Atomic Energy Agency (IAEA) sought to bring Iraq back into compliance with its treaty obligations against military uses of nuclear materials.

Between 1991 and 1994, Iraq destroyed, under UNSCOM supervision, more than 38,000 filled and unfilled bombs and shells, 690 tons of chemical agents, and a host of other materials.[22] Saddam's ability to conceal the extent of these programs prior to 1991 encouraged many observers to believe that he would continue to develop and produce WMD. As time passed, the Iraqi government increasingly resisted the required inspections, which it found insulting to its sovereignty. In the mid-1990s Saddam made major efforts to conceal programs and evade inspections. Baghdad issued a series of certifications that claimed it had destroyed all of its prohibited missiles and WMD. When inspectors noted discrepancies in these certificates, the Iraqis corrected and then repeated their claims to be WMD-free.[23] The Iraqi government blocked both ground and air movements of international inspectors and threatened to fire on reconnaissance overflights used to verify compliance. In December 1998, UNSCOM came to a halt in the face of continued Iraqi intransigence. Many observers believed that Saddam still had WMD stockpiles.[24]

This long, frustrating process of resistance to UN inspections gave rise, among analysts, reporters, and politicians alike, to a conviction that the Iraqi dictator would never tell the truth about his weapons programs. The "conventional wisdom" in Washington and other Western capitals was that Iraq's stiff-necked evasion must be in order to conceal additional WMD.[25] Given Iraq's repeated use of chemical weapons in the past, there seemed to be little question that Saddam Hussein still possessed such munitions. Indeed, right up until the 2003 invasion the Iraqi government fostered this belief. Although Baghdad publicly denied the presence of such weapons, it still sought to deter its enemies, both foreign and domestic, by encouraging rumors that it had poison gas.[26] Even some of its generals apparently believed those rumors; ironically, the U.S. government's insistence that WMD still existed may have reinforced these beliefs inside Iraq. It was impossible for Iraqi leaders to have accurate knowledge of weapons development and inventories when virtually no one reported the truth for fear of punishment.[27]

American intelligence analysts were divided, however, concerning the status of Iraqi nuclear and biological weapons programs. Some observers believed that these programs remained active, while others suspected that the Iraqi government was waiting for an end to sanctions before resuming development.[28] In retrospect, this latter suspicion was probably the correct one; UNSCOM found no evidence of production as opposed to research of WMD after 1991,[29] and the IAEA certified that Iraq had no *ongoing* nuclear weapons program. Investigations after the 2003 conflict strongly suggested that Saddam had done away with his existing WMD to satisfy inspectors while keeping his weapons development programs ready to restart as soon as the UN Security Council lifted sanctions.[30]

The Iraqi resistance to inspection also fostered a prolonged period of undeclared hostilities with the United States and some of its allies. In August 1992, after the Iraqi regime ignored UN warnings not to repress uprisings in the southeastern part of the country, the United States established Operation Southern Watch, a series of air patrols to prevent Iraqi fixed-wing aircraft from operating south of the 32nd parallel (extended north to the 33rd parallel in 1996). After Saddam similarly persecuted Kurdish rebels in northern Iraq, the United States, Britain, and Turkey established an equivalent Operation Northern Watch in January 1997, patrolling a no-fly zone north of the 36th parallel.[31] The United States launched periodic air attacks in an attempt to pressure Iraq into compliance; the most significant of these was Operation Desert Fox (December 16–19, 1998), during which the United States and Britain struck a number of targets with precision-guided missiles. Following this strike, Iraq announced that it would no longer respect the no-fly zones, and confrontations in those areas increased. When Iraqi air defense fired at Southern Watch aircraft, it provided a pretext for those aircraft to strike various targets within the no-fly zones, further degrading Iraqi defense capabilities.

These coercive measures depended upon periodic reauthorization by both the UN Security Council and (for Northern Watch) the Turkish legislature. Turkey in particular had suffered serious economic damage by limiting trade with its neighbor and had little motivation to continue. International support for sanctions enforcement waned steadily, to the point that without the advent of the U.S. "War on Terror," these measures would eventually have expired, leaving Saddam free to resume his weapons development. Similarly, the UN's Oil for Food program, designed to permit Iraq to care for its people by selling oil to purchase nonmilitary goods, was a subject of frequent abuse. The Iraqi regime received at least $1.8 billion in kickbacks from both oil purchasers and goods suppliers, allowing it to finance various military programs.[32] It also used Oil for Food money to purchase dual-use equipment, such as trucks suitable for moving armored vehicles rather than construction equipment over long distances. Again, the knowledge of these abuses contributed to a general perception among policy makers, intelligence analysts, and journalists that the Baghdad regime was concealing numerous illegal activities, including acquisition of additional materials for WMD.

Misperceptions of Iraqi WMD

Such was the atmosphere even before the terrorist attacks of September 11, 2001. In addition to the assumption about Iraqi WMD, however, the Bush administration came to believe that the Iraqi government was in league with Islamist terrorist groups.

Although he went through the motions of being a Sunni Muslim, Saddam Hussein was a secular dictator, and his Iraqi Ba'ath Party was a national socialist organization not associated with any religious extremism. On the contrary, Saddam tried to impose the Ba'athist belief that Islam was an essential if subordinate aspect of Arab nationalism.[33] Saddam was particularly unlikely to cooperate with Tehran after fighting a ten-year war against Iran. Nor were the Shi'a fundamentalist leaders of Iran likely to work with Osama bin Laden's Sunni followers. Nonetheless, many Americans in and out of office drew the emotional conclusion that our Middle Eastern adversaries must be cooperating with each other in some unspecified manner. In his State of the Union address on January 29, 2002, President George W. Bush described the three dissimilar states of Iraq, Iran, and North Korea as an "axis of evil" and warned that these states might provide WMD to terrorists.[34] On April 3, 2002, Secretary of Defense Donald Rumsfeld branded Saddam as supporting terrorism because Iraq paid compensation to the families of Palestinian suicide bombers.[35] Although this statement was technically correct, the secretary seemed unwilling to acknowledge that Saddam, like other Middle Eastern leaders, had little interest in the Palestinian cause; he made such gestures primarily to woo Arab public opinion.

After the 9/11 attacks, the U.S. intelligence community was engaged in a massive effort to track down all aspects of international terrorism. Of necessity, this attempt to understand nonstate conspiracies depended heavily on HUMINT reports obtained by espionage, interrogation, and similar means. The best intelligence analysts in the world find it difficult to conclusively confirm or deny such reports, which are based on eyewitnesses with unique access to the inner workings of small conspiracies. Therefore various individuals, perhaps seeking personal gain or promoting an invasion of Iraq, were tempted to tell the U.S. government what it wanted to hear. The U.S. intelligence agencies received a series of allegations concerning contacts between the Iraqi government, al Qaeda, and other enemies of America. Other sources claimed to have witnessed WMD inside Iraq. Most experienced Middle East analysts were skeptical of such allegations, but unfortunately not everyone read these reports with critical eyes. In fact, when the intelligence agencies did not provide the expected confirmation of some political appointees' beliefs, the appointees concluded that those agencies—rather than the politicians themselves—were politicizing the process, so they decided to bypass those agencies and create their own "intelligence." This was another form of cognitive dissonance, with the decision maker attributing bias to the analysts without recognizing his own preconceived notions.

Even before 9/11, John R. Bolton, the undersecretary of state for arms control and international security, excluded his liaison officer, assigned by the State Bureau of Intelligence and Research, from daily meetings. Instead, Bolton insisted that he and his staff must have access to the raw intelligence reports normally filtered by analysts with experience in the subject matter.[36] A similar process occurred in the Pentagon immediately after 9/11, when Deputy Secretary of Defense Paul D. Wolfowitz created an Office of Special Plans that combined existing intelligence reports with the claims of Iraqi exiles such as Ahmed Chalabi; many of these exile assertions were later discredited. One member of the Office of Special Plans insisted that "I did a job when the intelligence community wasn't doing theirs. We recognized the fact that they hadn't done the analysis. We were providing information to [Secretary] Wolfowitz that he hadn't seen before."[37] This was an inherent conflict of interest, in which policy organizations were creating "intelligence" to justify their desired policy outcomes. In practice, career intelligence analysts had rejected the reports by exiles and others because those reports were inconsistent with what they knew about the situation—a body of knowledge with which few policy makers were familiar.

Douglas Feith, the undersecretary of defense for policy, organized the Policy Counter Terrorism Evaluation Group within the Office of Special Plans. This group claimed, contrary to the opinion of intelligence agencies, that there was a cooperative relationship between Iraq and al Qaeda. Secretary Feith not only circularized these allegations to the White House as if they were finished intelligence products, but also told senior officials within the White House staff that there were "fundamental problems with how the intelligence community is assessing information."[38] By contrast, DCI George Tenet stopped a briefing by two of Feith's subordinates in which they described their "intelligence" on the supposed relationship between al Qaeda and Iraq. Tenet dismissed the briefing as "the policy-planning shop's ideologically driven fantasies."[39] As DCI, Tenet could have challenged the creation of these pseudo-intelligence entities, but he was apparently too enmeshed in the administration's policies to do so.[40] Indeed, by one account Feith's "intelligence" operation, encouraged by Israeli intelligence officials, aimed to pressure the CIA into supporting the policy focus on Iraq rather than al Qaeda.[41]

In his memoirs, Feith cited reports, especially by the CIA, that appeared to agree with his analysis.[42] Without conclusive evidence to disprove the more extreme allegations concerning Iraq, however, there was no way for intelligence agencies to completely reject such claims, especially when policy makers were so determined to believe those allegations. Consequently, intelligence community reports tended to accept disputed "evidence" of WMD as at least plausible if not proven.

In the spring of 2002, the intelligence analysts working on Iraq within J2, the intelligence section of the Joint Staff, concluded that it was highly *un*likely that Iraq intended to use UAVs to deliver biological weapons. Some elements of the IC had embraced this idea, but dispersing biological agents in this manner would be ineffective at best. When the head of the Iraqi intelligence working group briefed Feith that this alleged biological weapon was improbable, however, the secretary's response was "You're wrong; go try again."[43]

By July 2002, the Bush administration, influenced by these misleading "intelligence" reports as well as an IC that could not disprove them, had decided that it must overthrow Saddam Hussein "to end a range of threats."[44] The United States persuaded the UN Security Council to pass Resolution 1441, declaring Iraq to be in breach of its obligations and offering it a "final opportunity to comply."[45] This resolution put the onus on Iraq, not the inspectors, to prove that it had complied with these obligations, and indeed the regime excavated various sites to demonstrate to the UN the destruction of certain chemical and biological materials. Now Iraq was in the same position as the American IC, trying to disprove an assumption that was wrongly presented as fact. The inspectors even found, and Iraq neutralized, sixteen chemical warheads for 122-mm rockets.[46] Meanwhile, however, dozens of intelligence reports from different sources indicated that Iraq was concealing something from the inspectors. It was rarely apparent precisely *what* was being concealed, but in context many analysts assumed that there were additional, unreported components of chemical weapons. At the very least, there was no means to completely disprove that assumption.

After the fact, however, the investigating commission concluded that "the Intelligence Community was dead wrong in almost all of its pre-war judgements. . . . This was a major intelligence failure."[47] That same commission appeared to be unaware of the pseudo-intelligence reports created by operators.

One final factor should be noted: in order to pressure Iraq into accepting renewed inspections, the United States began to build up its forces in the region, especially in Kuwait, beginning almost a year before the war began. Once large numbers of troops had deployed in this manner, the clock to war was in effect ticking. As a practical matter, the United States could not maintain such a high concentration of troops, aircraft, and ships indefinitely because of the expense of the deployment and the perishable nature of training and readiness among those forces. Moreover, the heavy concentration of such units within the small area of Kuwait appeared to be an invitation for Iraq to use its suspected WMD. Therefore, the U.S. government had to choose between withdrawing its forces, which would have given the impression of backing down to Saddam, or using them to attack, preferably before the extreme heat of the summer of 2003.

As in so many other instances, both the analysts and the policy makers were wrong. The intelligence community made many errors in this situation, but so did the administration, and the latter's errors created an atmosphere that discouraged and disregarded any analysis that contradicted the narrative of Iraqi violations. By early 2003 the Bush administration had backed itself, as well as Iraq, into a corner concerning alleged WMD. Other factors such as Iraqi petroleum and a desire to promote democracy may have had some bearing on the matter, but the false sense of urgency in 2002–3 was based to a considerable extent upon the decision of multiple officials to manipulate the raw information available to them so that this material appeared to support their own beliefs. The result was a prolonged and bloody occupation that distracted attention and forces from the genuine terrorist base in Afghanistan and helped recruit supporters for al Qaeda.

The urgency of going to war gave the WMD issue of 2002–03 a particular intensity. Yet it was not a unique instance of politicians pressuring analysts to change their conclusions.[48] Intelligence exists to serve policy decisions, but that does not mean the analytical products should bend to the preferences of policy. Paul Wolfowitz, who appeared in the aforementioned narrative on WMD, was a distinguished public servant who held multiple senior positions in both the Defense and State Departments. In the mid-1990s, he had asserted that intelligence personnel had to be closely integrated with policy makers, and that intelligence had to understand and conform to the decision-making process of the policy makers.[49] This approach reinforces the superior-subordinate dynamic, between analysts and operators, with its tendency to disregard what the intelligence person(s) brings to the policy discussion. Perhaps because Wolfowitz had more intelligence experience than his counterparts, he apparently overlooked the corollary that decision makers need to understand how intelligence is generated along with what it can and cannot do and should and should not say.

As analyst Moni Chorev observed in a study of Israel's 1973 strategic surprise, "If the intelligence service is dominated by a group of powerful decision makers, it will become the prisoner of these decision makers' images, dogmas, and preconceptions."[50]

Chapter Four

The European Precedents

[Ministers and their senior officials had] a natural tendency . . . to equate subversion with [any] activity which threatens a Government's policies or may threaten its very existence.

— Deputy Director General John Jones, MI5[1]

In comparison to the United States, the European great powers have a much longer experience with intelligence and security organizations. Not only do such precedents provide context for the development of the U.S. intelligence community, but those structures also had considerable influence on the Americans who came into contact with the British, French, and other intelligence communities during the world wars.

What follows is an historical overview that illustrates three generalizations. First, most European intelligence organizations arose in response to ideologically motivated movements that, like Islamic extremist terrorism in the present day, threatened the security of the state.[2] In the sixteenth and seventeenth centuries, such movements were often a combination of religious fanaticism manipulated by the raison d'etat of hostile powers. In the nineteenth and twentieth centuries, the threat took a variety of forms including radical republicanism, Marxist socialism, anarchism, and nationalistic separatism. The current focus on counterterrorism is thus, in effect, a return to the original roots of government intelligence operations five centuries ago.

Second, these ideological movements were internal threats that had foreign sanctuaries or backers. The governmental structures that opposed these threats began as internal security organs that developed a foreign intelligence component, rather than the reverse. Several governments formed some kind of secret police that, in order to protect internal security, branched out to collect information and act against opponents in foreign countries. The exact form of this new organization depended on the politics and culture of the individual state.

Finally, because early modern states lacked the budgets and bureaucratic traditions to institutionalize these security services, such services often withered when the threat declined. The intelligence and security structure had to be reinvented in its modern incarnation during the later 1800s and early 1900s, when new security threats appeared.

Early Modern England

Beginning with Henry VIII, the Tudor state became a battleground of the Protestant Reformation. Henry's chancellor, Thomas Cromwell, was a staunch supporter of the king's claim to control the church, and he thus employed informants to curb both defenders of Catholicism and the machinations of the Habsburg state. The personification of Tudor security and intelligence was, of course, Sir Francis Walsingham. He began his career as a diplomat, but by 1569 Queen Elizabeth's principal minister, William Cecil, had given Walsingham control over the crown's secret agents both at home and abroad.[3] The budding spymaster's personal religion was Evangelical, making him a more radical Protestant than his queen, but he loyally served her interests throughout his career. Over two decades, Walsingham planted spies among his enemies, including one among the exiled English Catholics in Rome and another in the household of the French ambassador to England. He also searched for Catholic priests and Habsburg agents at home, supervised interception and decryption of secret messages, and famously trapped Mary, Queen of Scots in the conspiracy that led to her execution.[4] He even paid fishing boats to track the movements of the Spanish Armada.[5] In addition to juggling intelligence abroad and countersubversion at home, Walsingham continued as a political advisor and diplomat for Elizabeth.

Domestic opponents, motivated in part by dynastic loyalty and in part by religion, continued to threaten the state during the 1600s, especially during and after the English Civil War. The mathematician John Wallis decrypted opponents' correspondence for both Charles I and II; Oliver Cromwell's secretary John Thurloe not only managed counterintelligence and intelligence against the royalists, but also, in his capacity as postmaster general, supervised the interception and reading of that correspondence.[6]

With the exception of periodic Stuart pretenders to the throne, the Glorious Revolution of 1688–89 temporarily sidelined issues of political security. Thereafter, funds derived from an annual secret service vote in Parliament were as likely to support royal mistresses as to finance bribes for diplomatic information. Nonetheless, Great Britain employed at least three agents, all posing as pro-American, to spy on Benjamin Franklin's diplomatic mission to France during the American Revolution.[7] During the French Revolution and Napoleonic period, London expanded its activities to include supporting a French royalist terrorist bomb aimed at Bonaparte, but such covert activity declined sharply again after 1815. Still, occasional security threats meant that the British government required help deciphering encoded letters; from 1716 through 1844 one family of intellectual clergymen, led by Bishop Edward Wiles, provided this service on a part-time basis. A scandal about reading private correspondence ended this service just as the advent of the telegraph raised the possibility of rapid communications with more time-sensitive decryption.[8]

Growth of British Intelligence

Meanwhile, for more than a century and a half, the focus of English/British intelligence shifted from countersubversion and counterintelligence at home to support for military operations overseas. The limited staffs and communications available to naval commanders meant that, like Napoleon, they often acted as their own collectors and analysts,[9] but land campaigns required much more in the way of intelligence. As noted in chapter 1, field commanders—including John Churchill (later Duke of Marlborough) and Arthur Wellesley (later Duke of Wellington)—used conventional reconnaissance, topographic engineers, and code breaking to develop an understanding of the situation. Some of the adventures of Wellington's exploring officers surpassed those of any espionage novel. In April 1812, Major Colquhoun Grant became a French prisoner but still found ways to send messages to Wellington from captivity. The

French took him to Bayonne, where he escaped; posing as an American, he traveled to Paris and continued to collect intelligence for Britain.[10]

Such brilliant efforts concealed the fact that Wellington's intelligence officers often had stunted military careers because they were not commanding or otherwise performing conventional duties. Deputy Assistant Quartermaster General George Scovell eventually succeeded in decoding most of the Grand Cipher used by senior Napoleonic commanders, thereby giving Wellington priceless insight into his opponent's intentions. In addition to this intensive effort, Wellington put Scovell in command of two improvised field organizations: the Mounted Guides, recruited originally from Portuguese troops to reconnoiter and carry messages, and later the Staff Cavalry, composed of troopers detached from various regiments to serve as military police and rear-area security. Despite these services, Wellington ignored Scovell in peacetime and never acknowledged either him or the Grand Cipher as contributing to British success.[11] The elaborate intelligence structure of the peninsula withered rapidly after 1814, along with the careers of those who led it.

The British Army improvised various intelligence collection operations during conflicts such as the Boer War (1899–1902) and the long-running "Great Game" rivalry with Russia in Central Asia. At home, national-level intelligence operations were revived primarily due to threats of subversion and terror, beginning with renewed efforts for Irish independence. From 1867 onward, the Fenians undertook a series of bombings, assassination plots, and military attacks. Regarding this as a police matter, in March 1883 the British government created the Special Irish Branch within the London Metropolitan Police; the "Irish" qualifier disappeared several years later. From the beginning, this office regarded Irish immigrants to the United States as a source of finances and activists for the Fenian cause. Thomas Beach, an outspoken Fenian advocate in the United States, was actually a Special Branch agent. Within two years, however, the poor bomb-making skills of the Fenians had defeated that wave of Irish unrest, and the small number of police detectives in the Special Branch found themselves looking at other threats such as anarchists. Neither the public nor the police force itself was comfortable with any form of political police, and the Special Branch instead switched to providing protective services for the royal family.

In the early 1900s, fear of foreign agents again prompted the British to form intelligence and counterintelligence agencies that finally became permanent. The difficulties of the Boer War shocked Great Britain and prompted the War Office to reorganize its staff into a Directorate of Operations and Intelligence. As the title suggests, this section was dominated by operators and, once the Boer War ended, did not reorient its collection and planning toward European threats. The growing rivalry with Germany gave rise to a rash of improbable novels in which German agents reconnoitered England in advance of an invasion. This type of fiction appeared quite plausible because the British Army and Royal Navy had already attempted their own espionage in Germany. In 1909, a subcommittee of the Committee of Imperial Defence recommended the creation of a secret service bureau with both offensive and defensive responsibilities.[12]

The first steps of this bureau bore many of the hallmarks of amateurism that sometimes plagued Victorian and Edwardian governments. The funding for the new bureau came from the Foreign Office, while the Admiralty and the War Office struggled for control. Because all three departments wanted deniability, they insisted that the two heads of the bureau, Commander Mansfield Smith-Cumming of the navy and Captain Vernon Kell of the army, must not be on active duty. Once both were retired for medical reasons, however, the War Office refused to give any information, or even access to its building, to the "unofficial" Cumming. Although Cumming was supposed to direct espionage while Kell headed counterespionage, the War Office tried to insist that its man, Kell, must be involved in all interviews and meetings with foreign agents. Worse still, in 1910 Kell contradicted Cumming's instructions to two junior officers turned amateur spies, contributing to their apprehension and imprisonment in Germany.[13]

After such a rocky start, Britain's intelligence services proved remarkably successful during World War I. Working through the Special Branch, Kell arrested twenty-two German agents at the outbreak of the conflict, blinding their opponents to the deployment of the British Expeditionary Force to northern France. After a series of staff reorganizations, Kell's counterespionage effort received the designation of MI5, which survived as an informal term for the Security Service for the remainder of the century. The service was so successful that, following a further roundup in June 1915, Germany abandoned the effort to place resident agents in Britain, relying instead on commercial travelers to pick up information. Yet this very success brought Kell into conflict with the Special Branch and other elements of the police. Police forces not only got public credit for arresting spies but also tried to exclude MI5 from any form of countersubversion or countersabotage outside of the armed forces. Basil Thomson, Kell's rival as head of Special Branch, briefly won this bureaucratic argument when, in 1919, he became head of a Directorate of Intelligence under the Home Office.[14]

Foreign intelligence was almost equally productive during the war. Working out of the neutral Netherlands, Cumming's subordinates in the Secret Intelligence Service (SIS) built networks in occupied Belgium and France that tracked German railroad troop movements. These reports provided advance warning of events such as the Ludendorff offensives of 1918. Despite such success, both the director of naval intelligence, Captain William Hall, and his army counterpart, General George MacDonogh, expressed a vague dissatisfaction with the SIS, imposing various staff reorganizations. Their criticism probably reflected the pressure placed on Hall and MacDonogh by their superiors, who were concerned by unrestricted U-boat warfare and an inability to break the stalemate on the Western Front. At one point in late 1917, Cumming offered to resign, but the friction gradually subsided.[15]

At the end of the war, both the Secret Intelligence and Security Services were severely reduced in staffing and funding. Cumming's successors and Kell therefore had to call upon unpaid amateurs and alumni of their wartime operations in order to operate. Officially subordinate to the Foreign Office, the SIS was responsible for foreign clandestine collection for a variety of departments, both civil and military. In practice, both agencies focused largely on the Irish and Soviet issues. Several specialized committees also analyzed available data on foreign industrial capacity and economic warfare.[16]

In addition to landing British troops in northern Russia, the United Kingdom engaged in a covert struggle with the new regime in Petrograd. In August 1918, the Bolsheviks (wrongly) suspected the Allies of inspiring the murder of the head of the Petrograd secret police and attempted murder of Vladimir Lenin. They responded by seizing the British embassy, killing the naval attaché in the process. The following summer,

SIS agent and Royal Navy lieutenant Augustus Agar used torpedo boats to penetrate the Kronstadt naval base on several occasions; on his own initiative he sank the heavy cruiser *Oleg* and two other warships to ensure British control of the Baltic, a feat for which he received the Victoria Cross. For years thereafter, SIS agents, including the gifted but erratic Sidney Reilly, tried in vain to overthrow the Bolsheviks.[17]

Once again, an internal ideological threat in this case Marxism seemed to pose a danger to the British state. As noted in chapter 2, the leadership of the Communist Party of Great Britain followed the Moscow party line, actively helping the young Soviet Union against Britain. Moreover, the "Cambridge Five," a group of believing Marxists recruited while at university who then rose through the ranks as penetration agents within the security services, breached British national security for decades.[18] When this betrayal gradually emerged during the 1950s and 1960s, many officers of both the British and American intelligence communities developed near-paranoid fears of double agents. Oddly enough, during the great purges of the 1930s, Soviet intelligence had been equally paranoid, suspecting their star British recruits of being elaborate plants.[19]

Focusing on the Soviets amid restricted budgets meant that the SIS and Security Service were forced to neglect the German threat until the later 1930s, when they belatedly scrambled to prepare for another war. After the 1935 Italian invasion of Ethiopia, the chief of SIS finally convinced the government to increase his budget.[20] The series of diplomatic crises from 1935 to 1939 created a classic conflict between policy makers on the one hand and career officials—both diplomatic and intelligence—on the other.[21] Critics such as Winston Churchill argued that Neville Chamberlain and other British leaders willfully ignored reality in dealing with Adolf Hitler, but that conclusion was by no means clear at the time. World War I had left both the leaders and the populations of the Western democracies unprepared and unwilling to risk another conflict, making it politically difficult for Chamberlain to stand firm against German expansionism. Giving concessions to an adversary in order to gain time or conserve resources is a time-honored approach to diplomacy.[22] Delay and compromise seemed especially appropriate when German propaganda gave the appearance of military superiority in comparison to the British and French; the error was in not understanding Adolf Hitler's character and goals.

Still, in private the British government was divided about appeasement. Sir Robert Vansittart, the senior permanent official in the Foreign Office, was so anti-German that he found himself shunted aside in 1938. Both Vansittart and the SIS made contacts with German civilian and military officials who insisted that only firm British resistance would cause Hitler to pause. Some of the information that was funneled through Vansittart may have been German disinformation that led the British to believe that attacks on Czechoslovakia and Poland were scheduled earlier than was in fact the case. Additionally, credulous politicians had accepted the exaggerated claims of Luftwaffe strength, while RAF officers wrongly thought the Luftwaffe was designed for strategic bombardment. Still, the SIS and Foreign Office staff developed a fairly accurate view of German ground capabilities and political intentions.[23]

Two significant organizational developments occurred during the interwar period, beginning with the blossoming of British signals intelligence. After the success of Room 40 during World War I, Whitehall centralized the SIGINT elements of the armed forces in the Government Code and Cypher School (GCCS, redesignated in 1946 as the Government Communications Headquarters, or GCHQ). Churchill was a strong advocate for this operation; he insisted on seeing raw decryptions on a daily basis, but his long experience with SIGINT made him a more sophisticated intelligence consumer than most of his contemporaries.[24] GCCS's most famous achievement, the cracking of the German ENIGMA codes, was possible only because of German spies as well as Polish and French mathematicians. This ULTRA success laid the groundwork for Britain's long-standing intelligence cooperation with the United States, whose government contributed both MAGIC decryptions of Japanese codes and some early computing devices to assist in ENIGMA decryption in the later years of World War II.

The Joint Intelligence Committee (JIC) provided the mechanism to coordinate the British intelligence community. The JIC had an intermittent existence until the eve of the Second World War, when the Foreign Office assumed the leading role and meetings became more frequent. In 1941, the JIC acquired a permanent joint staff for all-source analysis.[25]

For centuries, Parliament voted intelligence funding on an annual basis but avoided discussion or oversight of the agencies who collected and analyzed information. After the Cold War, a series of laws such as the Intelligence Services Act (1994) and the Regulation of Investigatory Powers Act (2000) belatedly defined the status and limits of intelligence organizations in the United Kingdom.

At the conclusion of a 1996 study, Mark Urban deliberately oversimplified by remarking that "More than anything else, British intelligence is a system for repackaging information gathered by the USA."[26] He meant that after 1945 the United Kingdom, like other Western states, was dependent on the United States to provide the complex and expensive machinery of SIGINT and IMINT collection. Moreover, GCHQ had difficulty finding personnel with languages and other skills after the end of national service conscription in 1960.[27] Beyond signals and imagery, however, the United Kingdom still retained considerable skills at HUMINT collection and analysis. The renewed importance of counterterrorism in the twenty-first century has brought those human skills back to their central position in intelligence. Britain's counterterrorism efforts, currently headed by an assistant commissioner of the Metropolitan Police, were built upon the tradition of cooperation between Special Branch and Security Service officers. The latter expanded markedly, establishing regional centers for identification and monitoring of the newest radical threat to British security.

France

In history as in fiction, Cardinal Armand Jean du Plessis, Duke of Richelieu, and his successor as first minister, Cardinal Jules Mazarin, appear omnipresent in seventeenth-century France. This applies equally to their roles in espionage and internal security. Even before these two statesmen, King Henry IV had initiated the interception and opening of letters, which by 1789 had developed into an elaborate "black chamber." The French government was especially concerned with counterintelligence against the Jesuit Order's attempts to achieve undue political influence in the country.[28]

Internal political policing occurred at more than one level. The unusual importance of Paris prompted establishment of a police force in the later Middle Ages, centuries before the equivalent developed in London. Furthermore, the term "police" in France had a much wider meaning than the Anglo-Saxon definition of the term. In addition to maintaining order, the police of Paris supervised public health, trade practices, vagabond control, public decorum, and other administrative matters. Among these manifold responsibilities, the police under various names used informants to monitor public opinion and forestall disorders, including those that might threaten the stability of the state.[29] In two decrees of 1666 and 1667, Jean-Baptiste Colbert, Louis XIV's minister of finance, regularized this police responsibility under the twin chiefs of lieutenant-civil and lieutenant of police of Paris. By the later 1700s, this hierarchy, mutating into the Lieutenant General of Police, was a major office of the French government.

This vigilance enabled the government to control numerous disorders motivated by economic and political dissatisfaction. Only the unusual confluence of high food prices, government bankruptcy, agitation for political reform, and disaffection among the French Guards allowed the assault on the Bastille to begin the French Revolution on July 14, 1789.[30] During the tumultuous decade that ensued, French governments often collected information about rebellious provinces as well as efforts at regime change in the capital. On May 10, 1796, police spies enabled the Thermidorian regime known as the Directory to pre-emptively arrest the leaders of Gracchus Babeauf's Society of Equals, a fate that befell a number of subsequent conspiracies that attempted regime change.[31]

In 1799, the Directory appointed the former radical politician Joseph Fouché as minister of police, but later that year the new minister betrayed his trust by failing to report the conspiracy that permitted General Napoleon Bonaparte to seize power.[32] Fouché's opposition to some of Bonaparte's policies led to the abolition of his position in 1802, although the First Consul consoled him with money and a legislative position. Continued royalist conspiracies to kidnap or assassinate Bonaparte brought Fouché back into office, and when Napoleon declared himself emperor in 1804 he revived the Ministry of Police. The focus of this office remained stopping internal conspiracies and subversion, but Fouché's efforts in this regard involved covert operations abroad. In one instance, the minister bribed the cook of the exiled King Louis XVIII in England. Fouché was also notorious for his role in the kidnapping, trial, and execution of the Duke of Enghien, a royal prince whom the emperor suspected of conspiring against him.[33] In 1810, Fouché's own dealings with both royalists and the British prompted Napoleon to replace him with René Savary, who emphasized defensive measures such as increased press censorship and sealing ports to prevent information leaks before a new campaign.[34]

Following Napoleon's final defeat and exile, succeeding governments in France still needed counterintelligence and countersubversion. Although the Bourbon government abolished a separate police ministry in 1818, the Prefecture of Police devoted considerable resources to spying on political opponents in Paris.[35]

For three decades after Waterloo, not only France but much of Western Europe was plagued by secret society conspiracies organized by radical republicans such as Louis-Auguste Blanqui. There was even a loose transnational group of such revolutionaries, often referred to as the Carbonari ("charcoal burners") because groups first appeared under that name in Italy. These conspiracies had a simple plan, beginning with the secret recruitment and arming of a few hundred would-be revolutionaries. At a given signal, this band would seize control of government buildings in the capital and then hold off the forces of repression until the urban population rose up in revolt. In most instances, however, the conspirators' security was so lax that police spies could infiltrate a society, identify its leaders, and warn the government to call out the armed forces and arrest the conspirators on the eve of the planned uprising. The one exception to this pattern was Blanqui's Society of the Seasons, which outwitted the undercover police and surprised the government on May 12, 1839. Unfortunately for Blanqui, he was so successful at security on this that potential supporters were as surprised as the police; the regular army and National Guard repressed the revolt in a single day.[36] Just as in 1789, the successful revolutions in Paris involved numerous causes, including large, peaceful crowds rather than small groups of violent extremists. Moreover, the decline of revolutionary radicalism in France after 1871 permitted a similar relaxation in undercover political police.[37]

Despite Jomini's portrayal of Napoleon as his own intelligence officer, in practice the emperor had used an elaborate intelligence collection system to support him. The Foreign Ministry and various agents, including smugglers, collected information to be forwarded to the emperor's headquarters. Within that headquarters, chief of staff Louis-Alexandre Berthier had an extensive intelligence section that included topographic scouting and tactical espionage.[38]

All this withered away with the end of the Empire. Of necessity, French commanders in North Africa and other colonies developed tactical intelligence against their local opponents. Overall, however, the French Army neglected military intelligence from 1815 until the disaster of 1870. While the Germans besieged Paris at the end of that year, the vaguely titled Statistical Section began to collect information and search for spies. After France surrendered, this section, which became the core of the army's Deuxième (Second) Bureau, worked to make up for previous neglect using agents, attachés, and open-source reporting to develop detailed information about France's adversaries. In a forerunner of Cold War espionage, French and German military intelligence officers situated in border towns used agents, travelers, and newspapers to collect information on each other. The French police also assigned special commissioners to monitor the German governance of Alsace-Lorraine.[39]

Unfortunately for its own credibility, however, the army's Deuxième Bureau became tainted politically by the affair of Alfred Dreyfus, a Jewish officer falsely accused of spying for Germany. Even France's excellent cryptologic capacity was compromised by decrypts falsified to implicate Dreyfus. During the early 1900s, French politicians proved more concerned about partisan politics than the value of decryption; one even asked the German ambassador for copies of messages so that he could compare them to the French decryptions! Such selfish concerns led to a rivalry between the police and foreign office decryption efforts and compromised the ability to read German diplomatic cables.[40]

Whatever France's rivalries with other governments, the political police within the national Sûreté (civil police force) cooperated closely with their foreign counterparts in tracking anarchists, communists, nihilists, and other radicals that posed a terrorist threat in the later nineteenth century. The Sûreté maintained agents in various foreign capitals and supported or at least tolerated Imperial Russian activity against extremist exiles within France.[41]

Like the other powers, France made strides in developing new means of intelligence collection during World War I. British and French aircraft helped track German troop movements during the initial battles, and soon thereafter individual airmen experimented with aerial photography. On October 7, 1914, Lieutenant Maurice Grout photographed German batteries near Verdun and aided French artillery in subsequent fire missions. Conservatism hampered development of the new technique. When shown aerial photos in December 1914, General Henri M. Berthelot, head of both the Second (Intelligence) and Third (Operations) Bureaux, replied that he already had a map and that "I don't care about your pictures."[42]

Within a year, however, both the quality of photography and the speed of interpretation had improved markedly. The static nature of the Western Front permitted almost daily photographic coverage, enabling interpreters to detect enemy movements despite efforts at camouflage. When the American Expeditionary Force (AEF) arrived in 1917, General Philippe Pétain assigned Captain Eugene Pépin, a pioneer in photo interpretation, to advise Gen. John Pershing; French procedures predominated in the AEF.[43]

The French army became equally effective in other forms of intelligence collection, such as prisoner of war interrogation. Sloppy procedures hampered the war effort, however, and intelligence officers often found themselves diverted to other duties. Poor communications procedures, especially mixing code and clear language in the same message, gave the Germans considerable information, while French counterintelligence was often ineffectual.[44]

After the high point of World War I, the next two decades of French intelligence were a period of neglect.[45] Efforts to counter the influence of Bolshevik covert operations became enmeshed in the bitter partisan politics of the Third Republic. Intelligence agencies collected information but had no system for analysis and distribution.

Even before the invasion of France, the greatest Allied intelligence success of the era backfired. On January 10, 1940, a German aircraft became lost in the fog and landed by mistake at Mechelen in neutral Belgium. The Luftwaffe staff officer on board was carrying large portions of Case Yellow, the overall plan for invading France and the Low Countries, and this plan fell into Belgian and eventually Allied hands.[46] Unfortunately for the French, the plan confirmed their expectations that Germany would attempt to repeat the Schlieffen Plan of 1914 by moving through the Low Countries. Instead, the lost order at Mechelen prompted the Germans to develop a new plan that included the movement of mechanized forces through the Ardennes Forest. Even if intelligence analysts had identified that thrust as the main German effort, they were unlikely to dissuade the French commander in chief, Maurice Gamelin, from dispatching his main counterattack force deep into Belgium, where the Ardennes penetration eventually encircled it.

In the ensuing campaign, France was unable to employ the usual methods of military intelligence. No amount of pilot courage could make French reconnaissance aircraft survivable over German lines. Fighting on the defensive, the French had few opportunities to interrogate prisoners or capture enemy documents. General Gamelin had split his headquarters staff, including intelligence analysts, among multiple locations that lacked secure communications between them. Finally, as noted in chapter 2, a German change in ENIGMA codes on May 1, 1940, left the Allies blind with regard to SIGINT.[47]

The ensuing 1940–44 occupation by Germany not only produced great suffering but exacerbated the politicization and division of the French government, including the intelligence services. Charles de Gaulle's Free French government in exile improvised a Central Bureau of Information and Action (Bureau central de renseignements et d'action, BCRA); when career intelligence officers joined later in the war, they were understandably contemptuous of the BCRA's amateurism and lax security. In November 1944, after most of the country was liberated, the amateurs and professionals were unified nominally as the General Directorate for Studies and Research (Direction générale des études et recherches, DGER). The DGER eventually merged into the External Documentation and Counter-Espionage Service (Service de documentation extérieure et de contre-espionnage, SDECE), but antagonisms continued. Meanwhile, numerous officials took advantage of wartime improvisations to line their own pockets, including selling intelligence to allies.[48]

French communists and moderates alike sought to control the postwar intelligence effort, but their sympathies to Moscow made the communists highly suspect, and thus anticommunists predominated in the SDECE. Over time, the proportion of career military officers also grew, increasing the conservative tendencies of the agency.

The postwar Interior Ministry had three counterintelligence agencies, of which the most effective was the Territorial Surveillance Directorate (Direction de la surveillance du territoire, DST). Not content with defensive counterintelligence, the DST sent its own agents abroad, which produced turf battles with the SDECE.[49]

Both during and after the war, various political groups within France tried to claim leadership of the Resistance. For reasons of national pride, both Frenchmen and their allies emphasized and perhaps exaggerated the wartime role of the Resistance. This carried over into a peacetime belief in the efficacy of insurgency and covert action.[50] Between 1949 and 1954, France trained and parachuted some one hundred exiles into Eastern Europe under Operation Minos; few of them survived to provide any useful intelligence. Anticipating a possible Soviet occupation of France, the government and some right-wing individuals tried to set up stay-behind networks. In 1946, one such effort recruited French veterans of the British Special Air Service and American Jedburghs; the group evolved into the 11th Shock Battalion (11e Choc), the special operations element of the SDECE. Following their belief in insurgency, the French Army in Indochina recruited and equipped local insurgents to fight against the Viet Minh. During the Algerian Conflict (1954–62), the 11e Choc engaged in terror attacks intended to sow suspicion between various ethnic groups. When the battalion became notorious, it was disbanded temporarily in 1963, but some of its members transferred into its successor, the 13th Parachute Dragoon Regiment (13ᵉ Régiment de dragons parachutistes, 13e RDP).[51] Thus, during the bitter period of French colonial wars the intelligence services continued their tendency to engage in partisan politicization and direct action rather than intelligence collection.

Particularly under Charles de Gaulle, France attempted to maintain its influence in Africa through various covert operations. Yet de Gaulle, like his successor Georges Pompidou, had little use for intelligence assessments that conflicted with his diplomatic initiatives. Both French presidents suspected that their intelligence services and the supposedly nefarious CIA were seeking to thwart those initiatives. After repeated cutbacks and efforts at reform, in 1982 François Mitterrand reorganized the SDECE into the Directorate-General for External Security (Direction générale de la sécurité extérieure, DGSE), which was forbidden to operate inside the national territory. Instead, Mitterrand followed his predecessors, bypassing these formal agencies and instead conducting sensitive political intelligence out of his own office.[52]

Whatever useful intelligence France gathered during the Cold War remained largely unknown. Like their British and American counterparts, the French security services periodically discovered Soviet penetrations of the national security structure. Such penetrations encouraged many to view every event through the prism of the Cold War. One example of this was the belief that the environmental activist group Greenpeace was a dupe of the Soviet KGB. In 1987, French operatives placed a bomb on the Greenpeace vessel *Rainbow Warrior*, blowing it up and killing one person in the port of Auckland, New Zealand.[53] In response, the French government dismissed the head of DGSE and paid damages to obtain the freedom of its agents, but it drew no larger lessons about the ineffective nature of covert operations.

In short, modern French intelligence has been handicapped by excessive politicization and reliance on covert operations. Meanwhile, it fell behind in the expensive fields of signals and imagery intelligence as well as the prosaic techniques of order-of-battle analysis. This came to light during the 1991 Desert Storm operation, when French leaders from the president on down were embarrassed to depend on American military intelligence about Iraq. Immediately after the conflict, Paris established a Military Intelligence Exploitation Center (Centre d'exploitation du renseignement militaire, CERM), but its staff was too small to provide effective defense intelligence at the national level.[54]

The Habsburgs

While by no means the only multinational empire in Europe, that of the Habsburgs was the most vulnerable to the nineteenth-century flowering of nationalist ambitions.[55] Beginning in 1852, the Interior Ministry actively tracked nationalists and socialists; labor organizers and Bolsheviks followed later. After the Compromise of 1867 established the dual monarchy, the growing political police of both Austria and Hungary worked to track and control radicals.

Austrian intelligence efforts actually began much earlier. In 1711, the Habsburgs had established a black chamber to decipher intercepted letters; three decades later, the Empress Maria Theresa's Chancellor Wenzel Anton von Kaunitz began to use counterespionage agents. As part of his efforts to maintain European stability and quash revolution after 1815, Chancellor Klemens von Metternich organized an information bureau at Mainz, which sent reports of radical activity to other European powers. In 1850, well ahead of its European peers, the Habsburg Empire formed a separate Evidenzbureau as a centralized intelligence agency for the entire empire, developing espionage networks and code-breaking capabilities despite limited budgets. Unfortunately for the empire, one of the bureau's senior officials, Colonel Alfred Redl, was a Russian agent from 1907 until his suicide in 1913 and betrayed many Habsburg sources within the Russian Army.[56] The Evidenzbureau recovered from this blow to function effectively during World War I, but neither it nor the political police forces could preserve the weakened empire from collapse under the stress of prolonged nationalist agitation and warfare.

Rise of German Intelligence

Translating between German and English is an inexact process. "Nachrichten," a term often used as an equivalent to tactical intelligence, is literally "news" or "tidings"—in other words, "information"—rather than "intelligence" (see chapter 1). Carl von Clausewitz was probably speaking of uncorroborated "information" rather than intelligence when he described wartime reports as contradictory, false, or uncertain.[57] Similarly, Abwehr, the organizational name for German military intelligence during World War II, literally means "defense," reflecting the same primacy of counterintelligence and countersubversion exhibited in Britain and France.

Although various German states opened correspondence and collected political intelligence in dealing with each other for centuries, the prevalence of revolutionary radicalism during the nineteenth century demanded a modern counterintelligence operation in Prussia. Following the overthrow of France's King Louis-Philippe in February 1848, a mixture of democratic, socialist, and nationalistic movements produced uprisings in many major cities of continental Europe. In Berlin, the conservative King Friedrich Wilhelm IV at first tried to repress these disorders, but soon decided to identify himself with the popular movement, apparently hoping to become monarch of a unified Germany.

Amidst this revolutionary agitation, a young police inspector named Wilhelm Stieber distinguished himself as a supporter of the crown. According to his own immodest memoirs, Stieber dissuaded a crowd from attacking a man who appeared to be the king but was actually an actor posing as Friedrich Wilhelm. Whatever the facts behind this story, the king soon promoted Stieber within the Berlin police and assigned him to perform a series of investigations that affected the political security—and sometimes the personal reputation—of the ruling Hohenzollern family. Although Stieber was engaged primarily in domestic countersubversion, he traveled to various German states as well as Paris and London on the trail of radical movements. In the latter capital, he claims to have met Karl Marx and fraudulently obtained the membership records of an early communist group. Stieber and his subordinates also discovered that an officer in the Prussian royal palace was copying royal documents and selling them to both France and Russia.[58]

With the death of Friedrich Wilhelm in 1861, Stieber lost his patron and eventually his official position. A few months later, however, Chancellor Otto von Bismarck rehired him, this time to collect information against Prussia's main rival, the Habsburg Empire. Stieber established a false news bureau as a cover to flood the Habsburg lands with agents; when these agents found no indications of Austrian aggression, Bismarck had him incite their opponents with false information. Just prior to the Austro-Prussian War of 1866, Bismarck terminated this operation to conceal it, and Stieber returned to his more normal role of security officer for the king. When war loomed with France in 1869–70, Stieber again sent out a large number of agents who bribed disaffected Frenchmen to spy on their own country. During the resulting conflict, Stieber was simultaneously responsible for the king's security in the field—including heading the field security police—and coordinating agent reports on French troop movements. In the latter capacity, Stieber claims to have told the Prussian/German chief of the general staff, Helmuth von Moltke (the elder), the direction taken by the French army of Marshal Patrice de MacMahon. This warning facilitated the capture of that army and the French emperor at Sedan in September 1870.[59]

Allowing for the exaggeration and self-promotion in Stieber's memoirs, his account generally conforms to known events. He had an unprecedented career countering subversion and foreign intelligence efforts while conducting information and collection operations against Prussia's foes. To some extent, one may argue that Stieber's success was only possible in an era when Prussia's enemies had few career counterintelligence officers. With the creation of the German Empire in 1871, however, intelligence, like other instruments of power, needed to expand and become institutionalized. Given the military origin of that empire, it is unsurprising that the armed forces took the lead in the new institutions.

This shift was neither sudden nor complete. In the two decades before 1914, German naval officer Gustav Steinhauer occupied a position somewhat analogous to that of Wilhelm Stieber. He had served as one of the kaiser's bodyguards at the 1901 funeral of Queen Victoria, and was thus well known to British Special Branch officers. That same year, however, Steinhauer became head of the British branch within the Nachrichten-Abteilung, the newly formed German naval intelligence service. His appointment may have been due in part to the kaiser's good opinion of the young officer, although Steinhauer, like his emperor spoke, English well. William Melville, a retired police superintendent and early counterintelligence agent in what became the British Security Service, was able to track Steinhauer's efforts to place agents and message drops in Britain. The easy identification and tracking of a known foreign security official contributed to the compromise of German spy networks at the outbreak of the war.[60]

Perhaps because the general staff was already a well-established institution, German army intelligence developed in a more conventional manner. In 1889, the General Staff in Berlin established Sektion IIIb, upgraded at the start of World War I to a full staff division or Abteilung IIIb. In the tradition of the Prussian General Staff, however, a small number of often junior-ranking officers manned IIIb both before and during the conflict. The division's head was usually a colonel, with officers as junior as captain acting as intelligence staff leaders for field armies. In addition to compiling enemy order-of-battle data and providing border security officers, IIIb also placed a limited number of agents, especially inside Russia.

This activity increased rapidly at the outbreak of war. Captain Friedrich Gempp, the intelligence officer for the German Eighth Army in East Prussia, managed to insert agents to track the opposing Russian army in the field as well as additional agents into Saint Petersburg who sought to bribe Russian generals. In 1915, Gempp expanded his efforts by training and releasing Russian POWs to influence public opinion in their homeland. He claimed to have encouraged Russian army demoralization and to have framed General Vladimir Sukhomlinov, the Russian war minister, as a spy, although in truth both Russian morale and Sukhomlinov were probably doomed without his interference.[61]

In January 1917, Abteilung IIIb underwent reorganization and expansion. As part of this shift, it added information operations to support domestic morale to its existing repertoire of counterintelligence, HUMINT, espionage, code breaking, and order of battle.

In November 1919, a year after the German defeat, German military intelligence re-emerged under the cover name of Abwehr, with Gempp as its first chief (1919–27). Given the political instability of Germany in 1919, the group's purpose was as much countersubversion and counterrevolution as counterespionage. Still, just as with MI5 and the SIS, severe budgetary cuts hampered the Abwehr's functions for the next fifteen years of its existence.[62]

German Intelligence Post-1933

During the 1930s, the Abwehr grew along with the rest of the armed forces. In 1937, the Abwehr was elevated into a group of departments and attached to the Oberkommando der Wehrmacht, the joint armed forces headquarters. In addition to counterintelligence and foreign order-of-battle information, the agency was also responsible for collecting information about foreign industry and economics.[63]

The Nazi regime brought with it more funds but less effectiveness. The Versailles Treaty restrictions on the size of the armed forces meant that Germany in the 1930s had a serious shortage of specialists in many areas of national security, including intelligence. The Nazi propensity for creating party units that duplicated government agencies not only compounded this shortage but created inefficiencies and rivalries in all aspects of the state. One should note in passing that Heinrich Himmler's Schutzstaffel (SS, literally "security squadron") began as a protection force for Hitler before expanding into a separate army and state. Himmler's rival Hermann Goering merged various entities to create a rival security structure, the Geheime Staatspolizei (Gestapo, General State Police).

Most of the espionage agents recruited by the Abwehr and its SS equivalent, the Security Service, or Sicherheitsdienst (SD), were ill prepared in terms of language abilities, tradecraft, and knowledge of their target countries. This facilitated the British ability to identify and turn German agents sent to the United Kingdom, allowing an elaborate deception operation (the Double-Cross System) whose effectiveness could be verified by ULTRA intercepts. Nor was this the only German failure. As Mark Hull, a professor of military history, observed about the twelve incompetent (and sometimes mentally unstable) agents sent to Ireland, the German intelligence services constituted "an organization so organically flawed that outside interference was almost incidental to its global ineffectiveness."[64]

Germany did have some successes, of course, including the Venlo incident of November 1939 in which SD officers, posing as German dissidents, decoyed two senior SIS agents to the Dutch-German border and then kidnapped them.[65] In general, Germany's counterintelligence and countersabotage agents had much more experience and success than its offensive HUMINT collection. In Belgium, for example, the Germans were able to intercept and either turn or imitate the radio transmissions of many agents sent by the British Special Operations Executive (SOE), a covert operations arm. This German equivalent of the Double-Cross System reached the point where SOE operations in Belgium were "no more than a mirage created by the Gestapo."[66]

Perhaps the most serious effect of Nazification was to distort the worldview of all of its government and party officials, imposing the Nazi ideology in a manner that prevented realistic intelligence analysis during and long after World War II. Even professional officers such as Admiral Wilhelm Canaris of the Abwehr and Major General Reinhard Gehlen, head of the Foreign Armies East (Fremde Heere Ost, FHO), General Staff section responsible for intelligence against the Soviet Union were misled by racial stereotypes concerning their opponents.[67] Like other German observers, FHO consistently underestimated the number of units that the Red Army could field. In addition, Gehlen was reluctant to recognize tactical indications that contradicted his strategic conception. In November 1942, for example, he believed that the Red Army was too weak to counterattack in the Stalingrad area, and therefore dismissed the activation of a new Don Front headquarters that presaged the encirclement of German Sixth Army.[68]

Hitler fired Canaris for suspected disloyalty in early 1944, after which Walter Schellenberg, an equally disloyal but more circumspect official of the SD, absorbed most of the Abwehr.[69] Relieved of duty in April 1945 for defeatism, Major General Gehlen survived the war and then offered FHO's remaining staff, files, and agents to the Allies. Seeking information about the Soviet Union at the dawn of the Cold War, the U.S. Army and later the CIA absorbed the so-called Gehlen

Organization.[70] Gehlen's subordinates had considerable knowledge concerning the Soviet bloc, but some became double agents who provided false information and betrayed genuine Western agents to the Soviet and East German authorities. Subsequently, fraudulent defectors from East Germany infiltrated the West German government, military, and intelligence structure.[71] Quite apart from this infiltration, Gehlen and his organization retained many of the prewar prejudices of the German military, including virulent anticommunism and racism, thereby unintentionally misleading their new allies.[72]

Imperial Russian Secret Police

It is a cliché to observe that Russian governments have used frequent foreign invasions to justify autocratic control and that those governments, in turn, require political policing to protect the autocracy. One might date this policing function to Ivan IV's Oprichnina (1565–72), but this private army functioned more as a means for mass terror than for selective investigation of the regime's foes.[73] During the 1600s and 1700s, the so-called Secret Chancery existed to investigate threats such as false claimants to the throne, with various tsars abolishing the office to win public approval and then reactivating it in private. More practically, in 1697 Peter I (the Great) established the Preobrazhensky Office to monitor the reliability of the imperial guard regiments, but this office did not prevent the involvement of those regiments in three coups between 1751 and 1801. Then the Decembrist Revolt of 1825 startled the regime with its first manifestation of Western reform ideas among the ruling elites of Russia. In 1826, Tsar Nicholas I established the Third Section of the Imperial Chancery as a staff for investigating subversion. He also created a uniformed organization, the Imperial Gendarmerie, as a network of enforcement throughout the empire.[74]

While these mechanisms might have provided internal security in ordinary times, they were insufficient to combat the terrorism that troubled Russia in the second half of the nineteenth century. The root causes of these attacks are beyond the scope of this study, but the leaders are easily identified. Imperial Russia had created a small group of intelligentsia: well-educated people whose modest social status excluded them from any influence in the government. With no other outlet for their ideas, the intelligentsia turned to violent conspiracies for various causes. These young people provided the core groups, sometimes augmented with other classes, and included anarchists, nihilists, Social Revolutionaries, and to a lesser extent Marxist communists. They turned to assassination to topple the regime, but also used bank robberies to finance their efforts. The preferred weapon for their attacks was an improvised bomb thrown by hand.

After multiple attempted assassinations between 1866 and 1880, Tsar Alexander II transferred both the Gendarmerie and the Third Section to a new Department of Police under the Ministry of Internal Affairs (MVD). Despite this reorganization, there was poor coordination between different police units, which allowed some radicals to elude surveillance. In 1881, the People's Will (Narodnaya Volya), a splinter of a larger populist movement, succeeded in assassinating Alexander with two bombs outside the Winter Palace in Saint Petersburg. Given Alexander's role in freeing the serfs in 1861, his murder only encouraged reactionary efforts to tighten control. Additional "Protective" or "Guard" sections appeared in major cities, eventually evolving into the Department for Protecting the Public Security and Order, known by its Russian acronym as the "Okhrana." Among those it caught was Lenin's older brother, who was executed in 1887 for attempted murder. Still, despite the government's best efforts, Social Revolutionaries continued their terror efforts, even murdering the head of the Okhrana in December 1883.[75] Moreover, beginning with the abortive revolution of 1905, Russian police had to reorient their efforts from thwarting individual terror plots to influencing broad-based social movements, a far more difficult task.

Within the empire, the Okhrana was a relatively small part of the police, with fewer than a thousand personnel overall. For purposes of this survey, its true significance lay in its activities outside Russia. Because so many would-be revolutionaries were in exile abroad, the Okhrana established major stations in Paris and Berlin. These stations used both formal liaison and illicit bribery to gather information about radicals from local police organizations. One of the most successful Okhrana officers was Peter Ivanovich Rachkovsky, who headed the Paris bureau from 1885 to 1902. In addition to collecting police reports, Rachkovsky inserted deep-cover agents into various groups including radical Jewish Russians in New York City, exiled Latvians and Poles in London, and revolutionaries in Bucharest. On several occasions, he passed information concerning radicals to the Swiss authorities, who then made the arrests. In 1890, one of Rachkovsky's agents arranged for a large meeting of would-be assassins in Paris, complete with weapons and written notes of their roles in the proposed plot, after which the Paris police were tipped off to arrest them all. In an effort to halt these penetrations, the exiled Social Revolutionaries organized their own counterintelligence bureau but had limited success.[76]

The Okhrana went to great lengths to recruit, train, and support such penetration agents. A number of Russian women spent years undercover; some were wives and sisters of male Okhrana officers while others were genuine radicals who were persuaded to defect. To preserve the cover of these agents inside Russia, they were arrested, sentenced to Siberia, and then allowed to "escape" abroad to become revolutionary leaders, where they again betrayed various conspiracies.[77]

While the Okhrana was ultimately unsuccessful in protecting the Romanov regime, it set two examples that endured long beyond the 1917 revolutions. First, the Bolsheviks, like other radical Russian groups, regarded the primary purpose of a government intelligence agency as being domestic countersubversion. Moreover, the Bolsheviks inherited the belief that it was acceptable and indeed necessary to violate the norms of international behavior by punishing or murdering its opponents in other countries.

As the civilian regime struggled against terrorism, the Imperial Russian Army had its own intelligence difficulties. Russia's defeat by Japan in 1905 prompted a renewed effort to improve both order-of-battle data and expertise on potential opponents. By 1914, Russian military intelligence had an excellent picture of Austro-Hungarian military capabilities and plans and was reasonably accurate in its assessment of the German military. During the war, Russians operating out of France and Switzerland developed several effective agent networks, some equivalent to the British train watchers in the west. At the outbreak of war, however, Russia, like the other belligerents, anticipated a short conflict and therefore dispersed its army intelligence staff to various nonintelligence tasks. It took two years to restore effective tactical intelligence functions, by which time the army was slowly collapsing.[78]

Russia's initial defeats of 1914–15 inspired a sense of betrayal and spy mania. In May 1916 a prominent counterintelligence officer, Colonel N. S. Batushin, was given almost unlimited powers to search for spies, including wiretaps, opening correspondence, and searching and detaining people without authorization. In addition to the ingrained anti-Semitism of the imperial state, "foreign" companies and banks appeared to be the enemies of Russia. While German intelligence may have contributed to this psychology, the ensuing witch hunts damaged both public morale and legitimacy of the tsarist regime that tolerated such behavior.[79]

Rise of the Chekists

The institutional paranoia of the late tsarist state only reinforced the natural tendencies of the communist revolutionaries. As a tiny faction that had exploited public discontent to seize control of a huge empire, the Bolsheviks were determined to ensure that no other group was able to overthrow them in the same manner. In December 1917, the new regime established the All-Russian Extraordinary Commission, known for its Cyrillic acronym as the "Cheka." After merging with the investigators of the Petrograd revolutionary committee, the Cheka then called upon other Soviets throughout the former Russian Empire to form their own local Cheka committees. From the beginning, this agency's purpose was to guard the Communist Party regime in Russia. This included domestic countersubversion, counterintelligence, and eventually foreign intelligence to support the party. Beginning in 1922, the organization underwent a long series of redesignations, becoming in succession the GPU, OGPU, NKVD, MVD, and MGB before emerging in 1954 as the immensely powerful Committee of State Security (KGB). Throughout the life of the USSR, however, the head of this organization was always a secret policeman rather than a foreign intelligence expert, and his officers proudly identified themselves as "Chekists" (Chekisty).[80]

For the first fifteen years of its corporate existence, this organization had much of which to be proud. By creating imaginary anti-Bolshevik conspiracies such as the "Trust," the Chekists misled and captured some of the most effective foreign agents. In Western Europe, master agents such as Dmitri Bystrolyotov rivaled the adventures of fictional spies, bribing officials, seducing female clerks, and stealing classified information across the continent.[81] As the Communist International (COMINTERN) expanded its influence worldwide, Soviet agents found local support in many quarters. Some well-educated leftists in Western countries bought into the propaganda of the Soviet workers' paradise. This allowed the OGPU/NKVD and its military counterpart, the General Staff Intelligence Directorate (eventually called the GRU), to recruit ideologically motivated spies such as the Cambridge Five and later scientists involved in the Manhattan Project. During World War II, when the USSR was allied with the United States and the United Kingdom, numerous well-intentioned people in the West saw no point in obeying security regulations that denied classified information to the Soviets.

Despite massive success in human intelligence collection, Soviet intelligence's core purpose remained the maintenance of the Communist Party in control of the Soviet Union. Joseph Stalin's paranoia was the ultimate cause of the great purges of the later 1930s, but successive OGPU/NKVD heads shared his concerns, amplifying that paranoia into a constant feedback loop. Once the purges began, both Russian leaders and foreign intelligence agencies found it relatively easy to frame individual Soviet officials for their own purposes.

The purges almost decapitated the military, intelligence, and governmental capacity of the USSR. The NKVD, as it was designated from 1934 to 1943, went through three chiefs in two years (1936–38) while thousands of its officers were themselves purged without trial. The losses were so heavy that in the 1970s, the KGB found that it had no coherent record of what its predecessor, the NKVD, had done in foreign intelligence during the 1930s. To make up for this deficiency, KGB officials encouraged a former agent, who had spent fifteen years in the Gulag, to write his own recollections of the era, which were then used as the basis to publicize the successes of Soviet intelligence.[82]

More significantly for Soviet national security, the intelligence agencies of the era—NKVD, GRU, and staff elements of COMINTERN—became heavily politicized at the same time they lost the institutional knowledge they needed to operate. For example, General Filipp Golikov, a line officer with little intelligence experience, became the seventh head of the GRU in five years when he took over that agency in mid-1940.[83] During the period leading up to the 1941 German invasion, such inexperience made it difficult for the Soviets to overcome the signal-to-noise issue (see chapter 3) or to identify German deceptions. The Soviet GRU, NKVD, and COMINTERN collected extensive indications of German preparations to invade but were unable to convince Stalin of the threat.

Like the rest of the Soviet armed forces, intelligence officers in the GRU had to learn painful lessons in 1941–42 concerning how to identify and counter German military techniques. During the first half of the war, the NKVD not only provided its own troop units to fight as infantry but also organized blocking detachments to return stragglers and deserters to their parent units. It also had considerable, if ill-defined, control over intelligence gathered by partisan units in the German rear areas. On April 14, 1943, however, a reorganization within the Defense Commissariat created a new Third Main Directorate for Counter-Intelligence, headed by Viktor S. Abakumov. This organization was in part intended to counterbalance the influence of NKVD chief Lavrentiy Beria, perhaps the most powerful person in the USSR after Stalin. The new Third Directorate re-emphasized political reliability of troops as well as counterintelligence and countersabotage; Stalin nicknamed it "Death to Spies" (Smert' Shpionam, often abbreviated as SMERSH). It is no coincidence that SMERSH came into being just as the Red Army began to reconquer lost territories; SMERSH detachments down to division level were instrumental both in dealing with German stay-behind agents and in ensuring the subjugation of what became the Soviet bloc of countries in Eastern Europe. SMERSH was a relatively small portion of the Soviet structure, with no more than eighteen thousand officers and guard troops in 1945. By this time, Soviet counterintelligence officers were sufficiently sophisticated that they could catch and "double" many German agents while exploiting the friction between Abwehr, the SD, and other German organizations.[84]

Immediately after the war, General Abakumov became the minister for state security, controlling most of the police of the Stalinist regime and thereby continuing his role as a bureaucratic counterweight to Beria. In the postwar period, Soviet security forces had to deal with significant insurgencies in Ukraine and the Baltic States while following Stalin's guidance to isolate Soviet-controlled populations from the West. In 1951, however, Abakumov was dismissed and eventually executed.[85]

Not only Stalin but also the men he chose to run his intelligence operations wasted other talents and opportunities. An experiment of merging MGB and GRU assets overseas failed. While the ideologically motivated spies of the prewar period continued to provide a flow of information, few new assets were developed in the later 1940s. Meanwhile the U.S. Army's SIGINT analysts had discovered the Achilles' heel of Soviet communications security: sloppy operators had reused codes that were intended for one-time use only, thereby allowing the army to slowly decrypt a backlog of previously indecipherable messages. These so-called VENONA intercepts eventually allowed the Americans and British to identify some of the most dangerous Soviet spies in their midst. In turn, these discoveries prompted the United States to pressure Britain about periodic security reinvestigations, a procedure that identified potential security leaks with long-term access to classified information.[86] Moreover, as time passed, the oppressive nature of the Soviet regime became apparent, which reduced the pool of potential recruits who would spy for ideological reasons. By the 1960s, worldwide dissatisfaction with the Soviet regime meant that most new agents could only be recruited by large sums of scarce foreign currencies. Overall, Soviet intelligence and counterintelligence capabilities declined during the Cold War.

Just as with the Nazi regime, Soviet leaders were prisoners of their own ideology, making it difficult for them to accept accurate intelligence estimates even when they received them. The Communist Party of the Soviet Union defined itself as the leader of an historically inevitable revolution; given that context, its senior officers found it difficult to believe that opponents represented anything other than mercenaries hired by the capitalists. In 1968, KGB field reports accurately described the dissatisfactions and goals of the reformers in Czechoslovakia. Yet the leaders in Moscow could not accept the idea of a revolutionary effort to replace a socialist regime. Instead, they believed that the movement was a Western and "Zionist" plot even after the West was obviously surprised by Soviet military action. To support this delusion, Yuri Andropov had the KGB plant and then report as fact allegations of CIA plots.[87]

Thus Soviet intelligence reports came to reflect the beliefs of both decision makers and senior intelligence officials. By the time Leonid Brezhnev became general secretary of the party in 1964, the politicization of intelligence reports had become so extreme that the KGB felt obliged to generate imaginary reports that fed Brezhnev's vanity.[88] Station chiefs used their budgets to pay foreign journalists and to fund public demonstrations that appeared to support Brezhnev's policies and speeches. In practice, of course, the non-Soviet world had little or no interest in such matters. By contrast, when those same agents obtained classified Japanese intelligence concerning foreign terrorism, "Moscow Centre" did not bother to translate the reports.[89] Even East German intelligence had to cater to the perceptions of communist leaders; insiders concealed their knowledge that NATO's war plans were purely defensive because Marxist doctrine and rhetoric assumed capitalistic aggression.[90]

In July 1975, veteran KGB agent Hugh Hambleton met secretly with KGB chairman Yuri Andropov, who became head of the Soviet Union seven years later. Seeking to use Hambleton's expertise, Andropov asked questions that showed a distorted view of the world, including asking about Jewish "persecution" in the United States and inquiring whether "progressive American youth" looked to the Soviet Union as the hope of the future.[91]

Andropov's ignorance, together with a natural belief in capitalist conspiracies, largely explain Project RYAN, the massive 1981–84 search for indications that President Ronald Reagan might launch a surprise attack on the USSR. Not only the KGB and GRU, but also the intelligence agencies of Soviet satellites took this search as their first priority. The urgent effort increased the opportunities for misunderstanding in any nuclear confrontation.[92]

Postcommunist Russia

The failed August coup of 1991 was the logical consequence of having an intelligence agency devoted to propping up the Communist Party. Vladimir Kryuchkov, whom Mikhail Gorbachev appointed to head the KGB in 1988, had been influenced by Andropov earlier in his career. Once in office, he manipulated information to create the sense of an emergency and then joined with other plotters in launching the coup. Most of Gorbachev's security guards remained loyal to him, however, which thwarted attempts to detain him.[93]

Soon after the coup failed, the KGB split up. Branches of the agency became the national services of the various republics that broke away from the Soviet Union. Russian president Boris Yeltsin, another intended victim of the coup, considered the KGB's functions to be necessary but sought to split those functions into weaker agencies. In December 1991, the First Chief Directorate became the Foreign Intelligence Service (SVR). Yeltsin split off various units such as communications and signals security and reduced the rump of the KGB into a counterintelligence service, which in 1995 became the Federal Security Service (FSB).[94]

Having been a career KGB officer (1975–91), Vladimir Putin was briefly head of the FSB in 1998–99 before becoming Yeltsin's prime minister and successor. Not surprisingly, he reversed the dismemberment of the FSB, which regained control of communications and border guards in 2003. Putin promoted former KGB officers into authority positions throughout his government while periodically reshuffling security forces to ensure his own control.[95] Outside of Russia, GRU and SVR actions have included cyber interference in German and American elections as well as the murder of various defectors such as Alexander Litvinenko. Clearly, the Putin regime follows the traditions of covert actions abroad to enforce its own control at home.

Summary

The institutional development of intelligence organizations varied considerably between European states, reflecting both national culture and the geopolitical situation. France and Russia viewed intelligence primarily as a police matter and Germany focused on defense issues, while Britain's agencies eventually reported to a committee in which the Foreign Office predominated.

In most instances, however, the internal security of the regime was the primary focus of the effort. Threatened by religious, nationalistic, and ideological extremists, the counterintelligence/countersubversion officials in each state turned their eyes abroad, collecting information and covertly attacking those extremists who used foreign sanctuaries.

Given this background, it was perhaps inevitable that governmental intelligence activities were often heavily partisan. Nazi Germany and the Soviet Union were the most extreme instances of this politicization, with both rulers and intelligence officers blinded by their own ideological prejudices.

There were partial exceptions to this generalization, of course. Despite a lack of parliamentary oversight, the British unwritten constitution gave the intelligence agencies there a sense of apolitical professionalism that tried to limit the partisan or illegal use of such agencies. Frequent regime changes in France had a similar result, pushing French police and intelligence agencies toward loyalty to the nation rather than to any specific administration or political hue. In that instance, however, French politicians responded with unreasoning suspicion of their own intelligence services. In the Third Republic, such politicians divulged cryptographic capabilities to foreigners for domestic reasons while in the Fifth they resorted to partisan covert operations run out of the presidential palace.

Regardless of differences in culture and history, European governments often failed to view their intelligence organs as sources of knowledgeable information about threats. Instead, they demanded and often got partisan agents who performed covert operations but might be hard-pressed to offer sophisticated and accurate analysis.

Chapter Five

The U.S. Intelligence Community, 1882–1961

Chapters 5 and 6 provide a brief history of the institutional evolution of the U.S. intelligence community (IC) and its relationships with political decision makers. Some of the same themes identified in European intelligence history will reappear in the course of this overview, but in intelligence, as in many other ways, the American story is sometimes different.

Some of the reasons for this variance appear obvious. For centuries, North America was geographically isolated from external threats and thus had little need for the national security structures of Europe. During the 1950s, this isolation deteriorated rapidly under the global threats of the Cold War, but prior to that point intelligence, counterintelligence, and countersubversion appeared to be necessary only during major conflicts. Closely related to this lack of threat was a federal government that was relatively small and weak in peacetime, with public attitudes that resisted large and intrusive regimes.

As remarked in chapter 1, American military commanders were expected to be their own intelligence officers. The Civil War was a partial exception to this rule, with the Pinkerton National Detective Agency providing effective counterespionage protection but incompetent intelligence collection and analysis. After Allan Pinkerton quit in 1862, the Union gradually developed not only a network of scouts and spies, but also ciphers and decryption for telegrams.[1]

More generally, wartime presidents such as Lincoln, Wilson, and Roosevelt expanded the executive branch into many areas of American life, including countersubversion. In the first two instances those large and intrusive (at least by American standards) government operations abated with the end of the conflict. Federal institutions, including intelligence groups, cut back drastically even in 1945–47, but the growing tensions of the Cold War led to the National Security Act of 1947 and other manifestations of a permanent federal executive.

Origins

During the nineteenth century, the tiny professional armed forces of the United States occasionally sent officers to Europe to study the military programs of the great powers, but there was little interest in intelligence per se. The year 1882 is the usual date cited for the origins of a permanent national-level intelligence service. In that year, the U.S. Navy Department created the Office of Naval Intelligence (ONI) and began to accredit permanent naval attachés.[2] The War Department followed suit, appointing the first military attachés after it established (1886) a tiny Military Information Division (MID) within the office of the adjutant general. Initially, the division had to appeal to the field for reports from officers who had visited foreign countries on leave.[3] The MID covertly reconnoitered Mexico in the 1890s and other countries beginning in 1905, using the data to prepare contingency files rather than current intelligence estimates.[4] When the Army organized a hierarchy of officer service schools after the Spanish-American War, these schools regularly translated open-source accounts of European military doctrine and developments.

In a sense, these actions were the intelligence corollaries to Frederick Jackson Turner's Frontier thesis: the idea that the closing of the American frontier, which had heretofore been a defining characteristic of the nation, meant that Americans were now more interested in world events and trade. One might also argue that collecting information about European military affairs and especially European technology was an implied task as the Army and Navy officer corps began to develop as professional bodies.

These halting steps were primarily concerned with collection of open-source and unclassified human intelligence. Although uniformed attachés and instructors undoubtedly used their professional judgment in writing their reports, ONI and MID had no specific authorization for intelligence analysis or prediction. Many flag officers would have objected strenuously to the idea that relatively junior officers could evaluate a military issue on their behalf. It might therefore be more appropriate to date American military intelligence to the Panama Canal controversy of 1903. At that time, the newly organized Army General Staff produced a detailed area study of Panama for governmental reference. In 1911, the General Staff wrote a contingency plan for Mexico with similar background information gathered from various U.S. consulates. Five years later, the State Department created its own tiny Bureau of Secret Intelligence, whose reports supplemented normal diplomatic cables.[5]

The decentralized nature of American government probably explains why domestic counterintelligence and countersubversion were even slower to develop. Nineteenth-century police agencies in major cities had to deal with extremist groups, including anarchists, radical socialists, and exile nationalist movements such as the Fenians from Ireland. Yet most of this police work was incidental to criminal investigations rather than the result of ongoing political surveillance. At the same time, state and national governments abetted the anti-union activities of the Pinkerton National Detective Agency, hired by businesses to infiltrate and discredit labor groups as well as to oppose strikes with violence.[6] Such activities became so blatant that in 1893 Congress passed the Anti-Pinkerton Act, which forbade the federal and District of Columbia governments from employing agents of Pinkerton or similar agencies.[7]

Periodically, genuine extremism or foreign espionage also came to the attention of the U.S. Justice Department and the Secret Service, and during the Spanish-American War the service tried briefly to search for Spanish spies.[8] The low priority of domestic security threats in peacetime may be illustrated by the fact that Congress only tasked the Secret Service with presidential protection in 1902, after three assassinations in thirty-six years. As late as 1915, the same agency had primary responsibility for counterintelligence, serving as the main investigative service of the federal government.

The third presidential assassination, that of William McKinley in 1901, was the work of a deranged anarchist. McKinley's successor, Theodore Roosevelt, wanted greater information about and control of radicals, a desire that led in 1908 to the formation of the Bureau of Investigation (later Federal Bureau of Investigation) under the Justice Department. Fearing a political surveillance force, the House of Representatives initially refused to fund any detectives for the Justice Department, so Roosevelt and his attorney general created the new bureau by administrative order while Congress was not in session.[9]

For a brief period in 1917–18, the U.S. Army and Navy frantically expanded intelligence activities, establishing organizations and procedures that paralleled those of their European allies. Army staffs not only formed a G2 (Intelligence) division parallel to the French Deuxième Bureau, but also learned the intricacies of aerial imagery, signals intelligence, and tactical order of battle from their French and British cobelligerents. In the War Department in Washington, what had once been the Military Information Division was attached to the Army War College, which in turn served as the plans division of the General Staff. This small intelligence section grew from three officers in April 1917 to a Military Intelligence Division of 282 officers at the time of the armistice, with offices in major cities. In addition to a "Positive Branch" concerned with collecting intelligence and liaison with the allies, MID included a "Negative Branch" dealing with counterintelligence, censorship, and protection of industry from sabotage. This last function alone included 372 employees nationwide.[10] Just as hundreds of amateur intelligence officers began to learn their trade, the war ended and soon thereafter MID underwent major reductions in size. The remaining staff of MID and ONI labored to update their intelligence files by collecting information from attachés and informants, especially in Mexico.[11] To continue monitoring radicals and other presumed threats to security, MID, like the Bureau of Investigation, used volunteers that in retrospect seem extremely biased: former members of the wartime American Protective League, private citizens so concerned about subversive movements that they would work for free.[12]

Interwar Period

The continued alarm about political radicals carried over into peacetime, bringing with it the first major instance of American countersubversion efforts. During the war, concerns about espionage, sabotage, and disloyalty had prompted the United States, like most other belligerents, to severely restrict personal liberties and arouse public awareness of such issues. Government officials, including many counterintelligence analysts, became conditioned to believe in a major threat of subversion. The legitimate dangers of espionage and sabotage developed under wartime psychological pressures into a major espionage scare of 1917–18.

The Bolshevik Revolution magnified American security concerns. Although there were no serious connections between that revolution and American unions, some American workers undoubtedly sympathized with their Russian counterparts. Wartime inflation was followed by a recession when the government canceled major contracts at the end of 1918. Despite this recession, in 1919 American unions launched a series of major strikes to improve their pay. American businessmen pushed back, alleging that the strikers were Bolsheviks in disguise. Anarchist bombings only reinforced the unreasoning suspicion of Italians, Jews, and other ethnic groups vaguely regarded as radical. Even the temperance movement became involved, equating alcohol consumption with disorderly conduct, German beer gardens, and anarchism. Public opinion therefore pressed for strong if undefined government action against this mass of vaguely perceived dangers.[13]

Attorney General A. Mitchell Palmer had failed to get a peacetime law to replace the Sedition Act that expired at the end of the war. In the summer of 1919, Palmer seized upon the "Red Scare" to gain momentum for his desired ends, persuading Congress to pass a special appropriation to investigate foreign threats. The tool to do this was a newly created General Intelligence Division—colloquially known as the Anti-Radical Division—within the Justice Department.[14] To head the division, Palmer selected J. Edgar Hoover, who had established anti-Bolshevik credentials while reviewing alien internment and deportation orders. Hoover built a bureaucracy of card files to track alleged radicals; he also told journalists that the Industrial Workers of the World and similar groups were using propaganda to stir up violence among African Americans. Southern congressmen agreed, unwilling to admit that African Americans had any grounds for grievance.[15]

Hoover and Palmer had difficulty documenting their suspicions, but that did not prevent them from launching a series of raids between November 1919 and January 1920, targeting leftist organizations in major cities. Because the Justice Department had relatively few agents of its own, it relied on local police and immigration authorities to make many of the arrests. This only increased the arbitrary and violent nature of the raids, which rounded up at least three thousand and perhaps as many as ten thousand people without any real evidence of criminal activity. Although the "Palmer Raids" led to 656 deportations, many more were eventually released without charges. The raids backfired on their perpetrators, however. President Wilson and the Department of Labor, which had authority for deportations, pushed back against Palmer. Unabashed, Hoover and the Bureau of Investigation proceeded to investigate any organization or person who opposed the raids—including the American Civil Liberties Union, future Supreme Court Justice Felix Frankfurter, and church groups—convinced they must be communist sympathizers.[16]

This search for subversives helped Hoover to become director of the Bureau of Investigation in 1924, although a reforming attorney general forbade the bureau from collecting domestic intelligence and limited it to investigating specific crimes. When in 1938 Franklin Roosevelt wanted to investigate pro-German propaganda, however, Hoover suggested he circumvent the 1924 rule legally by having the secretary of state *ask* the FBI for such an investigation. In 1939, FDR created an Interdepartmental Intelligence Conference (IIC) of the FBI, ONI, and MID. Despite its blatant exclusion, the State Department usually sent a representative to IIC meetings, which were preoccupied with counterintelligence and countersubversion.[17]

In the interim, the Supreme Court had ruled (*Olmstead v. U.S.*, 1928) that it was legal for Prohibition enforcers to place a wiretap on a suspect's telephone because that tap was not on the defendant's property. This decision, and the prospect of similar wiretaps by the FBI, prompted Congress to pass the Communications Act of 1934 that forbade such surveillance without a court order.[18] Despite this ruling, in 1940 President Roosevelt broadened Hoover's domestic intelligence actions, including authorizing warrantless wiretaps in national defense investigations. The FBI expanded its surveillance to any activity that Hoover considered subversive, including labor unions, Eleanor Roosevelt's liberal activism, and future presidential candidate Adlai Stevenson.[19]

One of the few American intelligence successes during the interwar years was in cryptology. When MID largely closed down at the end of the war, its head, Brig. Gen. Marlborough Churchill, urged that the cryptology branch, MI8, continue in peacetime. Jointly financed by the War and State Departments, a "black chamber" began operations in New York City with a cover story as a commercial code company. Herbert O. Yardley, the gifted amateur who had headed M.I.8 during the war, successfully cracked the codes of numerous foreign governments. Most significantly, in December 1919 Yardley solved the Japanese diplomatic code, enabling him to decipher the precise negotiating positions of the Japanese delegation to the Washington Naval Conference of 1921–22. This rare achievement gave American negotiators a great advantage at the conference, allowing them to pressure Japan until it agreed to its lowest acceptable terms: a ratio of six Japanese to ten U.S. and ten British in terms of battleship tonnage.[20]

Yardley's black chamber declined steadily after this success. Not only did budgets shrink, but he also found it increasingly difficult to obtain the coded messages from cable companies in violation of peacetime law. The U.S. Navy was able to intercept only a handful of encrypted Japanese radio messages for Yardley to analyze. In May 1929, the new secretary of state, Henry L. Stimson, ordered the black chamber shut down, allegedly remarking that "gentlemen do not read each other's mail." Fortunately for the future of American SIGINT, another pioneering cryptologist, William F. Friedman, continued work under the Army's chief signal officer. Friedman offered employment to Yardley's experts, although Yardley himself declined. The combined operations became the Signals Intelligence Service in late 1929.[21] Meanwhile, a trickle of Navy officers went to Japan to learn the language,[22] and a few Army officers assigned in China also studied their future opponents. A decade after he closed Yardley's black chamber, Stimson, by that time secretary of war, was much more amenable to reading decrypted Japanese intercepts.

On the eve of entering World War II in 1941, the American intelligence apparatus was an uncoordinated assortment of underresourced structures in the Navy, War, Justice, and State Departments. Given the shortages of qualified personnel and equipment, the U.S. Army and Navy communications intelligence offices focused on decrypting Japanese "Purple" code (diplomatic) messages, especially those related to ongoing negotiations in Washington. The two offices devoted relatively little effort to military or naval codes, on which they had less success. They shared the labor of Purple decryption, alternating days as to which branch worked on messages.[23] This apparent cooperation actually concealed a collective neglect of analysis. Given the division of labor and the restricted distribution list for the decrypted cables, very few individuals read all the messages available in context and in "real time." Nor was there a sure means of passing their decrypts to the president during evenings and weekends.[24] Unlike the Washington Naval Conference, this time the American advantage in signals intelligence did not assist decision makers.

The OSS

Wartime brought a proliferation of new intelligence organizations. In his usual way of managing people, FDR assigned different stakeholders to control different portions of a governmental function. Building on its prewar role in Mexico, the FBI got responsibility for all intelligence and counterintelligence in Latin America, creating a Special Intelligence Service to support civil attachés (later termed legal attachés) in American embassies there. Critics later argued that profit-motivated informants sold the FBI more rumors and fantasies than facts.[25] Meanwhile, military intelligence units proliferated, including everything from Army Air Force intelligence and counterintelligence to joint teams for the study of tides and terrain for amphibious landings.

Yet even before the Pearl Harbor surprise, Roosevelt had launched a radical departure from this model of fragmented, agency-specific collection with minimal analysis. On July 11, 1941, he ordered the formation of the Office of Coordinator of Information (COI), soon redesignated as the Office of Strategic Services (OSS). To head it, Roosevelt chose the Republican antithesis of the New Deal, William J. Donovan, a conservative Irish Catholic who had twice run for office in New York State. After earning the Army's three highest decorations during World War I, Donovan became a millionaire Wall Street attorney. Although his domestic politics were the opposite of the president's, the new COI/OSS director agreed completely with FDR on the need to defeat the Axis.[26]

The avowed purpose of Donovan's organization was to create a single agency as a focus for national intelligence analysis, with other agencies directed to provide copies of all raw information to it. Donovan recruited prominent historians, political scientists, anthropologists, and other academic experts for his Research and Analysis Branch. On paper, this was an excellent idea, but in reality it had two major flaws. First, the existing intelligence agencies resisted efforts to give their trained personnel or their classified intelligence to the OSS. More significantly, however, the analytical function of the OSS took a back seat to a broad spectrum of covert operations.

Both the president and his new spymaster were fascinated with the potential of insurgency, sabotage, subversion, and commandos. To some extent, this fascination came from the example of Winston Churchill's Britain, which had turned to such asymmetrical techniques to weaken victorious Nazi Germany and in the process bolster domestic morale. Churchill, Roosevelt, and Donovan all tended to exaggerate the potential of such techniques. One of Roosevelt's own sons, who had previously worked for Donovan, was also a convert. As executive officer of a Marine Raider battalion, James Roosevelt II landed on Makin Atoll in an August 1942 commando raid. Donovan tried to replicate this type of action many times over by inserting individual agents and three-man Jedburgh teams to organize resistance and disrupt Nazi rear areas.

While senior American military leaders resisted the intelligence functions of the OSS, they were more than happy to have Donovan undertake psychological, commando, and covert operations that would otherwise divert the armed services from their conventional missions.[27] To this end, military leaders persuaded the president to subordinate the OSS to the Joint Chiefs of Staff (JCS), although the military never had complete control over such a visible and controversial organization.

Colonel (later Major General) Donovan accomplished OSS unconventional operations through a combination of optimism, inspirational leadership, and improvisation. He used people whom the rest of the government considered unreliable, such as socialists and radicals of the Industrial Workers of the World to work with European unions. Left-wing veterans of the Abraham Lincoln Brigade in the Spanish Civil War led insurgent efforts in Italy, while progressive writers produced "black propaganda" to demoralize the enemy.[28]

The results of all this effort were mixed, with successes as well as failures. Both during and after the war, Donovan tried to build the public reputation of the OSS, even employing screenwriters to give Hollywood pro-OSS scripts.[29] Yet part of the OSS reputation was a disregard for procedures and hierarchy. Like their French counterparts, some of whom had served on OSS Jedburgh teams, many veterans of Donovan's organization displayed a cavalier attitude about following procedures and informing higher headquarters of their activities. Many of the later leaders of the CIA gained experience in these special operations in the OSS, foreshadowing similar issues after the war.[30]

Both the Jedburgh teams and single intelligence collectors usually infiltrated by air, either by small aircraft landings in northern France or parachute drops for deeper insertions. The population in occupied countries such as Norway or France was either neutral or pro-Allies, ensuring that these risky operations had some reasonable chance of success. Local Resistance teams often met and concealed the new arrivals, and a few such missions had considerable success in terms of human intelligence or insurgent resistance to the occupiers. Yet as one CIA historian later concluded, "black entry operations, in Europe at least, made only a peripheral contribution to the main war effort."[31]

This "cowboy" reputation of deep penetration operations and disregard for procedures helped doom the OSS. Beginning in 1943, General Donovan conducted a long bureaucratic campaign to ensure that an independent intelligence agency would survive the war. Each of the older intelligence and counterintelligence organizations wanted to have the lead role in postwar intelligence, but they all agreed on opposing any peacetime role for Donovan or the OSS. When FDR died in April 1945, Donovan's bureaucratic chances died with him.[32] Not only did President Harry Truman have a personality conflict with the patrician Republican Donovan, but also many officials advised the president to do away with the organization. In September 1945, Truman abruptly terminated the OSS. Most of its personnel returned to the armed services or peacetime academic positions. A rump group of analysts transferred to the State Department, while the War Department gained control of some OSS special operations personnel.

Truman soon recognized that he needed at least some of the functions that the OSS had performed, and on January 22, 1946, he formed a rudimentary intelligence organization called the Central Intelligence Group (CIG). Although conceived to provide analysis for the president, this organization eventually regained control over the surviving human intelligence capabilities of the defunct OSS.[33]

Forming the Central Intelligence Agency

The National Security Act (NSA) of 1947 reflected the belated recognition that the United States had to restructure its government for prolonged semimobilization in the Cold War.[34] The resulting organization, however, was in many ways a compromise between those who wanted a centralized, unified defense structure and those, primarily in the Navy Department, who sought to retain service independence by forming a loose confederation of agencies. In part, this disagreement arose from the fear that, as had happened in Britain in 1918, all naval aviation might be resubordinated to the newly independent U.S. Air Force. More generally, naval officers disliked the idea of centralized staffs dictating to commanders afloat, while State Department officials rightly feared that a strong Department of Defense would impinge on their authority in foreign affairs. As a result, NSA 1947 was a compromise in which the secretary of defense initially had little staff and only vaguely defined supervision over the Army, Navy, and Air Force departments that nominally reported to him.[35] The Defense Department itself did not exist by name under the original law. Only a series of amendments to the 1947 act, including significant reorganizations in 1949, 1958, and 1986, gradually gave the defense secretary his modern powers.

NSA 1947 reflected a similar resistance to centralization of intelligence. The Department of State, FBI, OSS, and even the CIG had all tried in vain to assert supremacy or at least coordination of authority over the intelligence staffs of the three service departments.[36] The services had genuine operational requirements for their own intelligence capabilities and therefore resisted any outside control. As a by-product of these disagreements, the 1947 law authorized a DCI who, like the defense secretary, had considerable responsibility but limited authority. As his title suggested, the DCI was supposed to coordinate all national intelligence efforts to provide the president and National Security Council with a coherent intelligence picture. The DCI's position, however, gave him no control over the budgets or activities of the growing number of intelligence agencies, especially those in the three service departments.[37] This position carried with it an additional handicap not shared with the defense secretary: the DCI had to manage and lead the expanding CIA while simultaneously attempting to coordinate the other agencies in the intelligence community. When on top of this a president expected the

DCI to brief him personally on a regular basis, the position of DCI often became impossible. Such structural weaknesses caused considerable bureaucratic inefficiency and friction within the executive branch of the government.

NSA 47 also gave the National Security Council authority to assign the FBI and the military intelligence branches to investigate domestic subversion. Although Congress later set tight criteria for persons who could be tracked for possible subversion and espionage, J. Edgar Hoover continued to maintain his large filing system, sometimes simply removing the records from central files so that the FBI could deny having files on specific people or groups. Even after these removals, by 1960 there were 432,000 such records in the headquarters files.[38]

Once NSA 47 regularized the DCI's existence, the early history of that office and of the CIA was mixed at best. The first two heads of the CIG, Rear Adm. Sidney Souers and Lt. Gen. Hoyt Vandenberg, were men of considerable political and organizational influence. Vandenberg in particular was the nephew of a U.S. senator and used the DCI position as a stepping-stone to become the Air Force chief of staff. By contrast, the first director under the 1947 act was Rear Adm. Roscoe Hillenkoetter, a relatively junior officer who could not represent his agency effectively in Washington politics. This was particularly true after Truman's political ally (and former DCI) Souers became secretary of the National Security Council, in effect supervising Hillenkoetter.[39] Whereas, Vandenberg, having previously been the Army's assistant chief of staff for intelligence, received a courtesy invitation for the new DCI to sit on the U.S. Communications Intelligence Board (USCIB) dominated by the armed services, it took Hillenkoetter months of bureaucratic effort to obtain even limited access to recurring SIGINT reports produced by the armed services.[40]

Given his weak bureaucratic position, Hillenkoetter tried to cooperate and compromise with the other members of the Intelligence Advisory Committee, the latest incarnation of the IIC. All the service intelligence chiefs on this committee were senior to him in military rank, while the FBI continued to insist upon its dominant intelligence role in Latin America.[41] Douglas MacArthur and other military leaders hampered CIA operations in Asia, and again Hillenkoetter lacked the influence to gain access for his agency.

Meanwhile the increasing pressure of the early Cold War prompted Truman administration officials to look for new tools to stem what they perceived as Soviet expansion. The first such tool was the covert financial support of moderate political parties in Europe, especially Italy. In 1948, the National Security Council expanded the CIA's responsibilities to include propaganda, economic warfare, sabotage, and assistance to insurgents.

Next, the influential George Kennan, director of policy planning at the State Department, advocated a small contingency capability for covert action. At the time, most of the government perceived the CIA as primarily an analytical organization, and Rear Admiral Hillenkoetter lost the ensuing bureaucratic negotiations concerning Kennan's new force. Most of the covert operations functions fell under the newly created Office of Policy Coordination (OPC), which was administratively housed in the CIA but responded to directions from the secretaries of state and defense.[42] This new entity inevitably caused friction with the Office of Special Operations (OSO), the existing human intelligence organization of the CIA. Each organization disparaged the qualifications of the other, and on occasion duplicated efforts.

Secretary of State George C. Marshall nominated the first head of the OPC, Frank Wisner, a product of the OSS, whose charismatic and iconoclastic leadership was in the Donovan style. Instead of a small contingency force, Wisner recruited other OSS veterans to launch special operations in many parts of the world. The effort had almost unlimited funds because Wisner gained access to the counterpart accounts used for administration of Marshall Plan aid to Europe. He soon established forty-seven overseas posts, resulting in both an OPC and an OSO station chief, neither of which was popular with conventional diplomats, in a number of American embassies. In the space of only four years (1948–52), the OPC expanded from 302 personnel and a budget of $4.7 million to 5,954 people and $82 million.[43] In effect, the government had re-created the OSS, and once again the covert operators gained a reputation for acting with few checks or controls.

More disturbing was the fact that a number of Wisner's operations were compromised, with volunteers either killed or doubled by their opponents. Soviet agents penetrated the refugee groups from which Wisner recruited, and double agent Harold ("Kim") Philby, assigned as the

British SIS liaison in Washington, betrayed other operations to Moscow. Once the Korean conflict began, the OPC proved equally ineffective there, sacrificing some 1,200 exiles in failed attempts to penetrate the north.[44] With little prospect of overthrowing their oppressors, local inhabitants were unwilling to aid the infiltrators, eliminating the favorable conditions that the OSS had experienced during World War II.

The heyday of such operations was in the early 1950s, when the CIA deposed a democratically elected government in Guatemala (1954) and helped the SIS do the same in Iran (1953), halting the nationalization of foreign oil assets and restoring the shah to power. In 1949 and again five years later, another ex-OSS officer of the OPC backed military coups that changed regimes in Syria. These events fueled conspiracy theorists, especially in the Middle East, to believe that the U.S. government was behind every violent change in government. Beginning in 1966, the long-running *Mission: Impossible* franchise in television and film fed the legend of CIA meddling, reflecting and contributing to anti-American attitudes in the Third World.[45]

As the OPC continued to expand in the late 1940s, Hillenkoetter's beleaguered agency was the subject of the first of many reform studies, conducted by three attorneys with experience in intelligence: Allen Dulles, William Jackson, and Mathias Correa. At the request of the National Security Council, the trio submitted a report on January 1, 1949.[46] Predictably, the report faulted the CIA for poor administration and inability to coordinate the intelligence community; it also recommended that the CIA have exclusive control of the OPC. The National Security Council set aside some of these recommendations but did insist that the DCI, not the service agencies, had final control over what went into national intelligence estimates.[47]

Despite this authority, Hillenkoetter either could not or would not assert himself with the intelligence community, and the CIA drifted as an organization. The admiral was on the way out as DCI even before a series of surprises in 1949–50—Soviet detonation of a nuclear device, North Korean invasion of the southern peninsula, and Chinese intervention in the conflict—made a change of leadership appear essential.

The next DCI had the administrative clout to succeed where Hillenkoetter had failed. Lt. Gen. Walter Bedell ("Beetle") Smith had worked his way up from private in the National Guard to become Dwight

Eisenhower's chief of staff in World War II and Truman's ambassador to Moscow from 1946 to 1949. Wracked by stress-related ulcers, Smith had twice declined offers to become DCI, but the crisis in Korea prompted him to finally accept the post in October 1950. When Truman demanded multiple intelligence estimates within twenty hours, Smith was able to coerce the other members of the IIC into cooperating in a system for rapid production and consensus building. He also told the Departments of State and Defense that their input for the OPC must pass directly through his office, and later required a similar reporting path for overseas reports from the OPC. This consolidated the DCI's control over the OPC as part of the Directorate of Plans, although for a time Wisner's group remained separate from the OSO.[48]

Lieutenant General Smith brought Allen Dulles, a senior official of the OSS during World War II, into the CIA. Smith selectively implemented Allen Dulles' recommendations, gradually merging all covert collection and action under Dulles as deputy director for plans. Smith himself remained skeptical of the huge expansion of covert operations. Like many career soldiers during World War II, he regarded OSS operations as wasteful and inefficient, while as DCI he believed that the CIA's primary function was to analyze all-source intelligence. He assigned wartime colleagues, such as Lt. Gen. Lucian Truscott, to review OPC operations in the field, and he canceled a number of those operations. Among these abortive plans was the recruitment of a group of former Hitler Youth who were paid and armed to prepare for resistance work if the USSR invaded the West. Instead, these recruits planned to assassinate moderate leaders of the new German government. The Truman administration, however, placed such emphasis on active measures that the agency continued to expand its covert role. In particular, Truman and the National Security Council (NSC) insisted on supporting ill-conceived attempts by the Nationalist Chinese to continue their fight against the communists inside China. In 1951, Dulles advanced to become deputy DCI, with Wisner as head of the plans directorate.[49]

Expanding the Intelligence Community

Even after HUMINT and covert action were subsumed under a single agency—the CIA—the armed services maintained separate signals intelligence organizations, although they made repeated attempts, such as cooperating on Purple code decryption, to avoid duplication of efforts. Before and during World War II, the services had focused on their perceived primary opponents, so that the U.S. Navy took the lead against Japanese codes while the U.S. Army cooperated with the British Government Code and Cypher School in the latter's efforts to decrypt German strategic communications. The United States provided early computational capability to speed ENIGMA decryption. Not only did this division between the services continue after 1945, but also the newly created U.S. Air Force formed its own signals security service. Each service tried to maintain independence in SIGINT matters to support its own requirements and ensure the secrecy of these efforts. Again, these requirements were entirely legitimate but the result involved inefficiencies and sometimes failure to share information.

In 1949, Secretary of Defense Louis Johnson formed an Armed Forces Security Agency in an effort to resolve the issue. Unfortunately, the new agency neither improved service cooperation nor addressed the SIGINT concerns of civilian intelligence entities such as the CIA, FBI, and State Department.[50] On November 4, 1952, President Truman issued an executive order instead creating the National Security Agency (NSA), although the services still retained considerable independence in their intercept operations.[51]

Lieutenant General Smith was able to ensure that the DCI was the chair of the USCIB. Still, the defense secretary remained the designated executive agent for signals intelligence, and the USCIB reported to a special committee of the National Security Council. The governing directive, NSC Intelligence Directive (NSCID) 9, effectively denied the DCI any authority over SIGINT.[52] The USCIB remained independent of both the DCI and the interagency Intelligence Advisory Committee until 1958.

The newly created NSA director position was supposed to centralize efforts in communications intelligence (COMINT) but could not prevent either the military services or the FBI from collecting and analyzing signals for their own purposes. The Navy and Air Force were particularly concerned with controlling noncommunications or electronics intelligence (ELINT). It was essential for air commanders to know the locations of air defense radars and similar emitters so as to visualize and control tactical operations.

Similar delays and limitations occurred in creating a centralized organization for imagery interpretation. During World War II, the U.S.

Army Air Forces and Navy had learned much about such interpretation from the British, who had pioneered stereo-vision interpretation of photographs to view targets in three dimensions. During the postwar period both American air services retained control over what was then termed photographic interpretation (PHOTINT), used for aerial target and bomb damage assessment. When the CIA took form in 1947, many of its employees had wartime experience in PHOTINT and suggested that the agency acquire its own capability in this area. Among the numerous reforms that Lieutenant General Smith brought to the CIA was the formation of a small Photo Intelligence Division in 1952. The development of the U-2 reconnaissance aircraft and later reconnaissance satellites provided sufficient demand for a large imagery interpretation organization, the National Photographic Interpretation Center, which President Eisenhower authorized just before he left office in 1961.[53] Within the Defense Department, a new National Reconnaissance Office began to manage and prioritize imagery collection missions.

Eisenhower Intelligence Reform

In 1953, Dwight Eisenhower took office, and his former chief of staff, Lieutenant General Smith, moved from DCI to undersecretary of state. This appointment was typical of Eisenhower, who tended to place military officers in major posts within his administration. The new president was aware that this trend might appear suspect to the general public, and so he deliberately chose a number of distinguished civilians for balance.[54] Among these was Allen Dulles, promoted to be the first civilian DCI in February 1953; his brother John Foster Dulles became secretary of state.

Whatever doubts Smith privately expressed to his former commander, covert action remained a major tool of the American state. Eisenhower and the Dulles brothers shared a moral certainty that caused them to regard any state that tried to remain neutral in the Cold War as a Soviet dupe. Yet Eisenhower and his new DCI inherited a disjointed CIA and intelligence community, possessed of enormous capabilities but prone to error and duplication. Over the course of his eight years in office, Eisenhower made a sustained effort that significantly improved the intelligence community as a whole.

More generally, the massive structural changes in the U.S. government between 1933 and the early 1950s prompted repeated efforts at intelligence reorganization. During the early years of the Eisenhower administration, three committees examined different aspects of the intelligence community: the Clark Task Force of the Hoover Commission, the Doolittle Committee on Covert Activities, and the Technological Capabilities Panel. Collectively, these three panels identified a pattern of problems, but they could not, because of their temporary nature, correct those problems. Such corrections would be the focus of a sustained effort at intelligence reorganization that dominated Eisenhower's second term.

At the request of Harry Truman, between 1948 and 1955 former President Herbert Hoover presided over two successive attempts to make government smaller and more efficient. The Commission on Organization of the Executive Branch generated an estimated 3.3 million words of reports, including 314 major recommendations to improve government operations.[55]

One portion of the Second Hoover Commission was a panel on intelligence activities, chaired from 1953 to 1955 by Gen. Mark Clark.[56] The classified recommendations of this "task force" included dozens of proposals, ranging from raising the rank of each service's staff intelligence head to restricting clandestine operations by the armed forces to standardizing the reference numbers for all military maps.[57] Some of these recommendations failed because they conflicted with long-standing organizational norms, such as the belief that the intelligence staff was less significant than the operations staff at any given headquarters level and therefore should not be increased in stature. Clark's task force also recommended adding the director of the NSA to the Intelligence Advisory Committee and eventually merging that committee with the USCIB, but the armed services stonewalled such ideas.[58] Other proposals, such as those on clandestine operations, became the topic of recurring discussions for the remainder of the Eisenhower administration.

The task force's unclassified conclusions about Allen Dulles as a manager were polite but openly critical: "We are convinced, however, that in his enthusiasm he has taken upon himself too many burdensome duties and responsibilities on the operational side of CIA's activities. The task force feels that certain administrative flaws have developed in the CIA."[59] The panel recommended restructuring CIA management to facilitate the DCI's coordination responsibilities, but such suggestions had already been overtaken by another committee.

Even before General Clark's panel rendered its report, Eisenhower was aware of the issue of management within the CIA. While serving as DCI, Smith had become concerned about the handling of covert operations by Dulles and the man who succeeded Dulles as deputy director for plans, Frank Wisner.[60] Smith apparently concluded that, while gifted at field operations, both men were negligent concerning security, records keeping, and authorization for covert actions. In fact, Smith had been reluctant to allow Dulles to succeed him as DCI, fearing that without supervision, Dulles' enthusiasm might lead him to an ill-considered adventure.[61] Smith apparently communicated these concerns to his former chief, the new president, who valued Dulles' expertise but soon had his own questions about the DCI.

On July 26, 1954, Eisenhower appointed Lt. Gen. James Doolittle to chair a "Panel of Consultants on Covert Activities" and asked Doolittle and Clark, both of whom were his former subordinates, to "avoid unnecessary duplication of work as between you."[62] Clearly, the president wished to downplay the CIA management issue in Clark's findings to Congress; he specified that Doolittle's report be classified Top Secret and delivered directly to him.

Two months later, the committee rendered its conclusions, arguing for extreme measures in covert operations because the United States faced "an implacable enemy whose avowed objective is world domination. . . . There are no rules in such a game."[63] Yet the Doolittle committee found a poorly organized CIA that was unprepared for its task. The agency had grown so rapidly that it had not even completed security background investigations on several hundred employees and was losing potential recruits because of prolonged delays in said investigations. Nor were the current employees the best available; the committee concluded that "[d]ead wood exists at virtually all levels" such that the agency could cut 10 percent of its workforce without adverse effect on its performance.[64] Security procedures were frequently violated without consequences to the individuals. The agency had developed excellent training in languages and covert operations, but these facilities were underutilized. Moreover, the agency staff was scattered among forty-three buildings, making coordination difficult within the agency, let alone with other intelligence organizations.

The Doolittle Report was particularly critical of the DCI and his subordinate leaders. It urged that "the present elaborate staff structure of the Deputy Director for Plans" be simplified and observed that the agency "suffered from lack of continuity in policy and direction."[65]

When the committee met the president in person, its verbal criticisms were if anything more scathing than the written report. Doolittle acknowledged that Dulles was uniquely knowledgeable and dedicated, but he remarked that the CIA "grew like a topsy, sloppy organization" with "more loyalty than competence."[66] The committee described Dulles as so protective of his staff that he became emotional about criticism, while "Frank Wisner is a chap of great promise but not a good organizer."[67] The implication of such remarks was that, as a general officer, Doolittle considered the civilian leaders of the CIA to be incompetent managers. By contrast, Eisenhower defended Dulles' performance, believing that "no military man could do the job." Yet even he admitted that he was "astonished" at the lack of good administrators in government.[68]

The Doolittle Report made a thorough list of suggestions to tighten the administration of the CIA, including organization, security, training, and budgetary processes. Yet no brief investigation could provide the sustained effort necessary to transform the agency, so the report had no immediate consequences.

Eisenhower continued to push for greater integration and reduced duplication in government, even when that meant overruling the preferences of the armed services from which he came. Eisenhower used general staff procedures to run his administration but was by no means blind to the civilian nuances of his task. If anything, Eisenhower was too hesitant to coerce Dulles and other leaders to implement his reforms.

As for Dulles himself, even his critics acknowledged that he had phenomenal expertise in covert operations, immense dedication, and the fierce loyalty of his subordinates. Yet he was uninterested in administration and institutional politics and rarely exerted himself in the field that had stymied his predecessors: coordination of the IC. In this larger arena, he apparently relied on his brother John Foster Dulles, the secretary of state, to insulate him from challenges. Only sustained pressure forced the DCI to address the institutional problems of the community.

The Technological Capabilities Panel

One aspect of the ongoing controversy concerning the perceived Soviet advantage in nuclear delivery systems—the alleged "bomber gap" and later "missile gap"[69]—was a pervasive government and public concern about the possibility of surprise attack, of some form of "nuclear Pearl Harbor." President Eisenhower cast a broad net to find solutions to this problem, and he welcomed advice from an unusual source: the Technological Capabilities Panel (TCP) of 1954–55.

In early 1954, Leo Dulbridge, chair of the Science Advisory Committee in the Office of Defense Mobilization, assembled what became the TCP under the chairmanship of James R. Killian, president of the Massachusetts Institute of Technology.[70] Killian was an administrator rather than a research scientist, and he brought a practical approach to solving organizational problems within the executive branch. He was also determined to show the government the value of scientific advice. Eisenhower came to rely on Killian's opinions for a wide variety of subjects, including not only weapons and reconnaissance but also expanded scholarships and research grants for science.[71]

The TCP described the risks of nuclear surprise attack. It also recommended priorities for the development of intermediate and intercontinental ballistic missiles, improved radars and communications, and other factors in the strategic arms race. Edwin Land, inventor of the Polaroid camera, served on an intelligence section of the TCP that made significant recommendations concerning imagery intelligence, the key to determining the true number of Soviet delivery systems. While urging the long-term development of imagery satellites, Killian and Land seized upon the proposal of Kelly Johnson to build the U-2 reconnaissance aircraft as an interim solution. The two men convinced the president to approve this design, already rejected by the Air Force, and place it under the CIA.[72]

The TCP was so successful that the administration convened another such group, chaired by Rowan Gaither but including Killian, in 1957. The resulting report, "Deterrence and Survival in the Nuclear Age," warned of U.S. vulnerabilities to surprise attack; its publication a month after the launch of the first Soviet artificial satellite made it highly controversial.[73] The Gaither Report encouraged the development of additional radars and antiballistic missiles, as well as dispersal and other precautions for the Strategic Air Command.

Forming the President's Board

After the Doolittle investigation, staff members of both the NSC and the CIA had suggested that such a committee become permanent. The

Clark task force had gone even further, proposing the creation of two oversight bodies for intelligence: a bipartisan joint committee of Congress and a committee of private citizens to report periodically to the president.[74] Dulles, who preferred that congressional leaders turn a blind eye to covert activities, was dismayed by the possibility of congressional oversight of intelligence, as was the president. They therefore decided to form a presidential board in hopes of pre-empting Sen. Mike Mansfield, a frequent critic, from forming a congressional committee.[75]

Dulles wrote out a proposal for the board and discussed it with the president in November 1955. On January 13, 1956, Eisenhower created the President's Board of Consultants on Foreign Intelligence Activities (PBCFIA) with Killian as chair, instructing him to consider all foreign intelligence activities but concentrate on the CIA and other key elements.[76] The remainder of the board consisted of men with wide experience in government and the military, if not in the field of intelligence. In addition to General Doolittle, the board included Gen. John Hull, former vice chief of staff of the Army; Robert Lovett, former undersecretary of state and secretary of defense; Benjamin Fairless, former president of U.S. Steel; and, in a gesture of bipartisanship, Ambassador Joseph Kennedy. It also had an experienced official of the NSC as full-time staff director.[77] When Killian stepped down in 1958 upon becoming Eisenhower's science advisor, he remained on the board while General Hull assumed the chair of the PBCFIA.

Although it was expected to convene only a few times a year, the PBCFIA met frequently and traveled to various headquarters throughout the spring and summer of 1956, interviewing the heads of most of the government's intelligence units. In addition to numerous suggestions given directly to the agencies involved, between 1956 and 1961 the PBCFIA rendered six formal reports to the president—reports that included more than thirty major recommendations.[78] In almost every instance, the president endorsed these recommendations and forwarded them through channels for action by the relevant agencies, in some cases requiring periodic progress reports.[79] At the time of the first PBCFIA report in late 1956, both the DCI and the director of the budget tried to answer the new set of requirements with brief, simplistic responses.[80] This did not satisfy the president, and thereafter a considerable correspondence arose concerning the various recommendations. By 1960, Eisenhower's last national security assistant, Gordon Gray, had learned that the president's default reaction to any response that fell short of full compliance, and indeed almost any report having to do with intelligence, was to refer the matter back to the PBCFIA.[81]

Institutionalizing the Intelligence Community

During Eisenhower's second term, the PBCFIA pursued a number of intelligence issues. These topics included making the DCI into the leader of an integrated intelligence community, increasing control over covert actions, improving strategic warning, integrating signals intelligence with other sources, and reducing duplication of effort throughout the IC. Many of these changes, such as an institutionalized system of communications and indicators for strategic warning, endured for decades (see chapter 7). For purposes of this discussion, however, the most significant efforts concerned the role of the DCI, the management of covert operations, and greater integration of signals intelligence.

The first recommendation presented by the PBCFIA returned to the issue identified by the Clark and Doolittle panels: enhancing the leadership role of the DCI in coordinating the government's intelligence efforts. The board recommended that the DCI "be encouraged to exercise a more comprehensive and positive coordinating responsibility" to improve integration and reduce duplication.[82] Specifically, the board urged Dulles to appoint a chief of staff or executive director to supervise the internal workings of the CIA so that Dulles as DCI could focus on his broader responsibilities. Dulles, however, placed such emphasis on CIA operations that he repeatedly reversed this proposal, trying to delegate his IC responsibilities to a subordinate so that he could concentrate on his own agency.

The first step in this process was to appoint Lucian Truscott to the newly created post of deputy director for coordination. When Dulles told the president of this plan, Eisenhower replied that he understood the proposal to be the reverse—that it was the DCI rather than a subordinate who must perform the community coordination.[83] The DCI appointed Truscott to the new position anyway and later claimed presidential approval. Although Killian agreed that Truscott had helped in the coordination effort, the PBCFIA repeatedly recommended that the DCI create a true executive director to run the agency under him.[84]

In a later attempt to delegate his IC functions, Dulles expanded the responsibilities of Lyman Kirkpatrick, the agency inspector general, who had frequently acted as the CIA point of contact to the various reform committees.[85] Although Eisenhower recognized the need to create an executive director and repeatedly remonstrated with the DCI, he was unwilling to coerce compliance. In a February 2, 1960, meeting with General Hull, the president finally acknowledged that "he would have to make a choice either to keep Mr. Dulles without such a Deputy or relieve him in order to carry out the reorganization," and he concluded that Dulles was too valuable to replace.[86] Despite this perception of failure, in practice the accumulated recommendations of the PBCFIA pressured Dulles into much greater efforts to coordinate and integrate the IC.

Nowhere was this pressure more evident than in persistent PBCFIA efforts to improve control and management of covert collection and action, the twin areas that were Allen Dulles' primary focus. In March 1954, President Eisenhower had approved National Security Council Directive 5412/2 on such operations, superseding previous regulations. This directive created a "Special Group" of senior officials, often referred to as the "5412 Committee," but initially this committee was intended more for coordination than for formal approval of proposed covert operations. The Special Group consisted of the undersecretary of state, an assistant secretary of defense, and the president's special assistant for national security affairs.[87] Given the subject matter, the DCI was also ex officio a member. Under various names, this group functioned for decades.

Both the Doolittle Committee and the PBCFIA suspected that the CIA did not always consult the Special Group as required, and that in any event the staff of the deputy director for plans (DD/P) tended to conduct covert operations without considering all the risks involved. In its first report, the PBCFIA urged that NSC 5412/2 procedures be regularized and that all proposals "receive the benefit of proper joint staffing and formalized approval," in addition to requiring the CIA to keep the Special Group informed of later developments in each operation.[88]

The administration's immediate response to this proposal was the issuance of Annex C to NSC 5412/2, which required the CIA to inform the Departments of State and Defense of how it implemented programs discussed in the Special Group. Approval for highly sensitive proposals that did not involve military actions was delegated to the secretary of state.[89] This limited change, however, did not address the staffing issue. When the PBCFIA raised the question again in late 1958, Eisenhower directed that the Special Group should meet on a weekly basis unless there was no issue to discuss. He was concerned about secrecy of such activities and specified that all records should be maintained either by the CIA or in sealed envelopes in his own safe. Prompted by the PBCFIA recommendations, the president further directed that the Special Group must evaluate as well as approve all covert operations.[90] His national security assistant, Gray, wrote to the other group members observing that Eisenhower "takes very seriously, not only the Special Group, but also the Hull Board [PBCFIA]."[91] Gray emphasized the need for the group to perform as the president expected and asked each participant to contribute one staff person to maintain records and administration.

The PBCFIA recommendations went much further than just the Special Group, however. With General Doolittle on the board, it is no surprise that the group continued to pressure the DCI to reorganize the functions of the DD/P. In its third report (October 30, 1958), the PBCFIA observed, "From evidence we have seen, it is our feeling that . . . the Plans Group (for the Agency) may be incapable of making objective appraisals of its own intelligence information as well as of its own operations when it is engaged in Cold War activities which are the subjects of its own reports."[92] Instead the board recommended that the dual functions of intelligence assessment and mission evaluation be reassigned elsewhere within the CIA. Even in the CIA, operators needed to be separated from their intelligence analysts to improve objectivity.

Coming on top of previous criticisms of the DD/P, this recommendation, backed by the president, finally pressured Dulles to undertake a reorganization of the Clandestine Service in 1958–59. He made his inspector general, Kirkpatrick, responsible for mission evaluation and gave Richard Bissell, the OSS veteran and economist who had supervised the U-2 project, a new post as assistant deputy director for plans.[93] Bissell soon replaced Wisner as DD/P and brought more order to the covert operations planning of the agency. This success was so marked that Bissell was considered a likely candidate to succeed Dulles as DCI.[94] Dulles also assured the president and the board that "DD/P actions are taken only after necessary policy guidance has been obtained from the

Special NSC 5412 Committee."[95] While acknowledging improvements, the PBCFIA remained skeptical, even in 1961, that CIA covert operations were worth their cost, especially since they appeared to be at the expense of intelligence collection.[96]

It may appear incongruous to speak of improvements in covert action planning in the CIA during the period leading up to the Bay of Pigs disaster. A full examination of that event would be so voluminous that it would divert the focus of this study from the major trends of the period. Nonetheless, a few observations are appropriate. By his own admission, while working on the U-2 Bissell had developed an aversion to the military style of planning.[97] As a result, and contrary to the intent of the reform recommendations, Bissell largely excluded the military from the Cuban exile invasion. The risky invasion plan was caught in the vacuum between the Eisenhower and Kennedy administrations, with JCS concerns ignored and the new president demanding ill-considered, last-minute changes.[98] The resulting failure should be compared to more effective CIA operations of the same era, notably in Laos, which suggest the beginnings of a more cautious approach to covert efforts.

COMINT, ELINT, and the Intelligence Community

As previously described, when Eisenhower and Dulles took office the IC was a confederation of independent entities, loosely coordinated by two overlapping panels: the IAC and the USCIB. Although the DCI chaired both entities, he had relatively little control, especially over the signals intelligence activities of the different armed services, each of which was represented on both panels. This divided structure was an obvious target for both a president and an advisory board dedicated to increased intelligence integration through a stronger DCI.

In its first set of recommendations, the PBCFIA noted that the IAC appeared functional only in situations short of war and requested that the DCI review the structure of this committee and report to the president. The same report noted that the DCI had no control over intelligence operations outside the CIA, with each department placing its own intelligence needs ahead of those of the rest of the IC.[99] While Allen Dulles' opinion of this recommendation is unknown, he apparently considered major organizational change to be unlikely to occur and thus not worth significant effort on his part. A year later, therefore, the third set of recommendations of the PBCFIA was much blunter, suggesting that the two boards be merged into a single U.S. Intelligence Board (USIB) chaired by the DCI and including a National Indications Center for warning purposes.[100]

This proposal provoked bureaucratic outrage, especially among the intelligence branches of the armed services, who considered control of SIGINT to be essential to their functions.[101] Seeking to reach consensus about the proposal, Allen Dulles assigned General Truscott to interview each member of the USCIB separately. Only the three civilian members—the Atomic Energy Commission (AEC), the Department of State, and the CIA—were in favor of the merger, and even Dulles thought that any change should be delayed until the implementation of other ongoing innovations. On January 22, 1958, the USCIB voted overwhelmingly against its own abolition.

Meanwhile, however, Killian had persuaded Eisenhower to appoint a special group, similar to the highly successful TCP, to review the scientific aspects of COMINT. William Baker of Bell Telephone Laboratories, at that time the leading center of electronics research, chaired this group, producing the so-called Baker Report in late 1957. This report emphasized the importance of integrating all forms of signals intelligence into the overall intelligence picture and recommended creation of a research institute to deal with the scientific problems of SIGINT. Given his wartime experience with ULTRA decrypts, Eisenhower endorsed the thrust of Baker's report, which he cited as another argument for centralized control of SIGINT.[102]

After Killian had prepared the ground in this manner, President Eisenhower was unimpressed with protests against the merger of the USCIB with the ISC. On March 12, 1958, he overruled the armed services and approved the merger, directing that a new NSCID 1 be written within twelve months to implement the change. In one stroke, more than a decade of service independence in SIGINT was severely weakened.[103]

Of course, this reorganization did not give Allen Dulles anything like untrammeled power within the IC. It did, however, continue the efforts of both Eisenhower and the PBCFIA to make the DCI into a leader of the interagency effort. This in turn facilitated Dulles' ongoing task to satisfy another PBCFIA recommendation by revising all the NSCIDs, which governed the IC. By the end of the president's second term, Dulles was signing some NSCID correspondence as chairman of the USIB rather than as DCI.[104]

Although the inclusion of COMINT into the IC was a significant institutional step, it did not ensure complete integration of signals intelligence. The PBCFIA was less successful in its persistent efforts to place ELINT, the noncommunications aspect of SIGINT, under the control of the national security agency director (DIRNSA). At the same time that the PBCFIA advocated merger of the two intelligence panels, it had also urged the inclusion of ELINT as a significant source of intelligence information. The president agreed to this in a January 15, 1959, meeting, and DIRNSA soon became a member of the USIB.[105]

Nonetheless, the armed services, especially the Strategic Air Command (SAC), insisted on their need for ELINT information for operational purposes, such as planning electronic countermeasures against Soviet air defenses. This question became even more prominent when, only two months after the U-2 incident of May 1960, Soviet air defense shot down a SAC RB-47 aircraft collecting ELINT over the Barents Sea.[106] After study by the Joint Staff, the secretary of defense and DCI recommended that certain ELINT activities be delegated to the commanders of unified and specified commands, including SAC, provided that the Joint Staff monitored it to avoid duplicating collection efforts.[107]

To facilitate SIGINT centralization, the board also recommended that the position of DIRNSA should not be treated like other joint flag officer positions; that is, the position should not be filled by a simple rotation between the services, but should be open to a broader pool of nominees, with the successful candidate remaining in the position for at least four years. Pressured by the Joint Chiefs, Secretary of Defense Thomas Gates diplomatically insisted that it was important for all the military services to share in this important national position.[108] The president did not overrule Gates, and the DIRNSA position continued to rotate between the armed services, but the occupant was far more influential than equivalent three-star officers elsewhere in the armed services. Fifty years later, as noted in chapter 1, the DIRNSA became a four-star command with extended tenure of office.

Security Concerns

Although McCarthyism is often portrayed as a politically motivated witch hunt, after 1945 the West faced a genuine threat from Soviet espionage, which recruited highly placed agents largely through ideology.[109] For practical as well as partisan political reasons, the Eisenhower administration sought to shore up its procedures concerning personnel and document security. The very first letter to the president from the PBCFIA alluded to the need to stop information leaks concerning atomic weapons and COMINT.[110]

Repeated congressional allegations of security breaches added urgency to administration issues. In April 1956, the NSC Planning Board recommended uniform systems of security investigations for both federal employees and contractors. J. Edgar Hoover seized on this proposal as a justification for increasing the FBI budget, calculating that fingerprint checks for 250,000 contract employees for the Defense Department alone would require $645,000 in additional funds by 1958.[111] The NSC proposal went to the Interdepartmental Committee on Internal Security (ICIS), which concluded that the various departments already had procedures for their employees but needed a better process for contractors. The ICIS noted, however, that dismissing a government employee for security reasons would violate the guarantees of the Civil Service Act, which permitted an employee to demand that the government show cause for dismissal in open court.[112] This remained an issue until the Reagan administration.

Assessment

A century after Allan Pinkerton allegedly saved Abraham Lincoln from possible assassination in Baltimore, the FBI had become not only a national criminal investigation service but also a political police, watching anyone whose actions offended J. Edgar Hoover. The preoccupation with alleged communist subversion was about to become even worse during the 1960s, as the next chapter will discuss.

Meanwhile, the foreign intelligence community had developed most of the elements necessary to reduce uncertainty and advise national leaders during the Cold War. Still, Eisenhower was convinced that he had failed in his efforts to create a more effective IC. As his cabinet continued trying to implement intelligence reforms during his final days in office, he observed that he "had suffered an eight-year defeat on this question [of efficient, integrated intelligence] but would leave a legacy of ashes for his successor."[113]

In one sense, the president was correct: changing the culture and functions of a vast, disjointed bureaucracy is a difficult task that rarely succeeds rapidly or completely. The members of the IC, especially the armed services, retained much of their independence even in 1961. This frustrated Eisenhower, who believed that the CIA should provide all national-level intelligence. In a conversation with his national security assistant, Eisenhower asserted that the JCS should also have only one intelligence organ rather than dealing with the three service intelligence branches.[114] He clearly agreed with PBCFIA suggestions that individual departments were placing their own priorities ahead of national requirements, and he objected to the inclusion in the revised NSCIDs of a vaguely defined "joint intelligence,"[115] when he wanted the Joint Chiefs and unified commanders to receive integrated intelligence support.

Although forced into a wider community role, Allen Dulles was neither able nor willing to control the IC completely. With presidential backing, Lt. Gen. Ralph Canine, the first DIRNSA, made considerable progress within his agency but still dealt with independent service intelligence branches.[116] The 1958 Amendment to NSA 47 gave the secretary of defense control over departmental budgets, allowing limited progress in this regard. At the instigation of the PBCFIA, by 1960 the secretary's assistant for special operations held an annual budgetary review of the SIGINT activities of the three services plus that of the NSA, identifying duplications in expenditures and operations.[117]

The Eisenhower reformers were neither completely successful nor omniscient. On numerous occasions, Killian, Hull, Doolittle, and others urged the president to take risks and increase U-2 reconnaissance to determine the extent of Soviet strategic delivery systems. In retrospect, these conversations have an ominous tone, with Eisenhower repeatedly noting the negative consequences of losing an aircraft.[118]

Despite these failings, the PBCFIA's contribution to developing American intelligence capabilities and integration was noteworthy. As previously mentioned, the 1961 establishment of centralized imagery tasking (the National Reconnaissance Office) and interpretation (the National Photographic Interpretation Center) rounded out the intelligence community for the next several decades. Designations and procedures changed over time, but many of Eisenhower's ideas, including the PBCFIA, endured under other names.

Chapter Six

The U.S. Intelligence Community since 1961

The reform efforts of the Eisenhower administration carried over into the early Kennedy administration. Thereafter, the government and with it the intelligence community became increasingly involved in Vietnam. When that issue convulsed the nation at home, government surveillance of domestic opposition also ramped up, leading to a well-intentioned reform movement that hamstrung later efforts at counterterrorism. The pendulum swung back to increasing HUMINT and covert operations during the 1980s, only to meet further reductions and restrictions after the end of the Cold War. This reduced intelligence capacity then had to grapple with nonstate actors and religious extremism in the new century.

Continuity in Change

The President's Board of Consultants on Foreign Intelligence Activities (PBCFIA) ceased to exist along with the rest of the Eisenhower administration in January 1961. Despite significant improvements in intelligence integration, the CIA under Allen Dulles continued on its independent path, especially regarding covert action. Two developments prompted the new Kennedy administration to resume the reform efforts of its predecessor.

First, as noted in chapter 5, the Bay of Pigs invasion caused a major re-examination of covert actions, particularly since it came on top of previous failures in Tibet and Indonesia. The careers of Allen Dulles and his deputy director of plans, Richard Bissell, were blighted. Dulles became the designated scapegoat for the Cuban invasion and was succeeded by the chair of the AEC, John McCone. Bissell moved briefly to the National Reconnaissance Office and then to a think tank; he was succeeded in the CIA by Richard Helms, an Office of Special Operations human intelligence officer rather than a covert operator. The OSS special operations tradition was by no means dead, but for some time the government was more cautious in its clandestine efforts.

President Kennedy tried a number of different solutions, including reviving the PBCFIA under another name. On May 4, 1961, he established the President's Foreign Intelligence Advisory Board (PFIAB), with James Killian again serving as chairman.[1] Patrick Coyne also resumed his role as staff director.

Simultaneously, the new defense secretary, Robert McNamara, entered office with a clear agenda to increase his control over the department and to improve efficiency. This agenda included controversial concepts such as a department-wide capabilities and budgeting process, computer-driven data analysis, and a unified Defense Logistics Agency. For purposes of this discussion, the most significant of McNamara's ideas was a Defense Intelligence Agency (DIA).

When McNamara first instructed the JCS to plan such an agency, their response was a loosely confederated "Military" Intelligence Agency under JCS control. The director of this agency would be little more than a figurehead who chaired a board that included the service intelligence chiefs, the Joint Staff Intelligence chief (J2), and the director of the NSA. As McNamara continued his centralizing efforts, it became clear that such a proposal would not satisfy him.[2] In an amended proposal of April 21, 1961, the JCS cited Eisenhower's final reform study, the 1960 Joint Study Group Report, and the 1958 revisions of the NSCIDs in their advice to the secretary on forming the DIA.[3] When McNamara formally proposed this new entity to Kennedy, the secretary in turn cited both the Joint Study Group and Killian's endorsement.[4] McNamara described this new agency as providing military intelligence to the Joint Chiefs, the unified commanders, and the USIB the same audience that Eisenhower had envisioned. Once again, a major intelligence organ was a product of executive fiat rather than legislative authorization.

Congress and the services expressed uneasiness because the DIA represented yet more increases in McNamara's authority as defense secretary. To ease acceptance of the new agency, its first leaders were balanced between the services with an Air Force director, an Army deputy, and a Navy chief of staff. Two years later, the JCS gave up even the intelligence staff functions of their J2 section, which was replaced by DIA personnel.[5] Over time, the development of civilian analysts within the DIA tended to balance the presence of uniformed officers assigned from the services.

The existence of the DIA also contributed to further integration of the IC. In March 1964, the military service representatives lost their voting rights in the USIB, with only the DIA and NSA representing the Defense Department. Moreover, DCI McCone added his deputy director to the board to represent the CIA, symbolically satisfying the recurring demand that the DCI distance himself from his agency in order to run the community. The resulting USIB therefore consisted of the DCI as chair, plus representatives of six intelligence agencies: CIA, DIA, NSA, Department of State INR, AEC, and FBI.[6] By the time McCone did that, however, the CIA was deeply involved in another major challenge.

The CIA in Vietnam

In May 1954, the Viet Minh defeated the French Army at Dien Bien Phu, leading in a few months to the Geneva agreement that partitioned Southeast Asia between Laos, Cambodia, and the two Vietnamese states. Even before the French surrendered, the Dulles brothers sent Col. Edward Lansdale, a U.S. Air Force officer who had helped defeat the Hukbalahap insurgency in the Philippines, to Saigon. Lansdale had been assigned to the Office of Policy Coordination and therefore maintained that he was not employed by the CIA, a distinction without a difference. Once in Saigon, he set to work sabotaging Viet Minh operations and spreading propaganda to discredit Ho Chi Minh's regime. This propaganda encouraged Christian residents of northern Vietnam to move to the south as refugees, a movement permitted by the Geneva agreement. Additionally, Lansdale began to support Ngo Dinh Diem, a nationalist of some credibility who eventually maneuvered himself from premier to president of the new government of [South] Vietnam. For two years (1954–56), Lansdale operated a special station reporting directly to Allen Dulles and separate from the official (OSO) CIA station in Saigon.[7]

The twin CIA stations were heavily involved both in reporting on challenges to Diem's leadership and in assisting him to block his noncommunist opponents. For much of the 1950s, Diem and his brother Ngo Dinh Nhu communicated with the U.S. government through the CIA rather than through ambassadors. Lansdale provided CIA funds that allowed Diem to purchase the support of the armed Cao Dai sect, and then persuaded the Vietnamese leader to use his army to begin pacification programs in the countryside. In April 1955, both CIA stations supplied information that the DCI used to persuade the secretary of state and President Eisenhower that the United States should support Diem against an attempted coup by the Binh Xuyen gang, another semiautonomous armed group. At the time, France and the nominal emperor of Vietnam, Bao Dai, both sought to depose the beleaguered premier, but the CIA stations ensured that the United States remained steadfast. Thereafter, Lansdale convinced the often passive Diem to organize a national referendum on whether he or the emperor should be head of state. Despite some ballot stuffing in the major cities, Diem had genuine popular support, leading him to a lopsided victory in the referendum of October 23, 1955.[8]

Despite these contributions, Diem resisted the efforts of Lansdale and other Americans to help him develop an effective government, including intelligence organs. The CIA provided support to the southern government's efforts at human intelligence against the north, only to discover that these efforts were largely illusions conducted by corrupt officials who diverted the intelligence funds given to them. Diem was willing to accept American aid but not American guidance or partnership, instead concentrating on repressing the surviving communist sympathizers in the south. By 1959, this repression had provoked a renewed insurgency against the Saigon government, and the CIA found itself lacking even basic information about North Vietnam's domestic security apparatus. The agency was thus unprepared when John Kennedy became president in 1961 and immediately demanded the initiation of an anticommunist resistance movement in the north.[9]

The Saigon chief of station at the time was William Colby, a legendary OSS officer who had parachuted behind enemy lines twice during World War II, once with a Jedburgh team in France and the second time with a larger group in Norway. He provided training and equipment for the Saigon government to insert a total of eight single intelligence agents and twenty-eight guerrilla or sabotage teams into North Vietnam between December 1960 and January 1964. The agents involved were from a variety of Southeast Asian nationalities. Moonlit aerial insertions and supply drops alternated with coastal raids during the dark of the moon. Yet the entire process was sacrificial: virtually all of the agents sent to North Vietnam were caught or captured within weeks of arrival, after which their captors tortured the survivors into sending false radio reports. Many of the teams landed near where their relatives lived, but even this did not increase survival rates. While the CIA was skeptical about many of the false reports that came back, Colby and his successors continued resupply missions rather than allow genuine agents to starve.[10]

The Kennedy and, later, Johnson administrations provided conflicting guidance. On the one hand, these insertions operated under frequent restrictions, especially a prohibition against endangering the 1962 neutralization of Laos by entering North Vietnamese airspace by way of its neighbor. On the other, President Kennedy, Secretary of Defense McNamara, and Secretary of State Dean Rusk all pressured the CIA to expand its efforts so as to make Hanoi pay a higher cost for its own infiltrations into the south. Ultimately, in 1964 the Defense Department took the program over. Thereafter, the Military Assistance Command, Vietnam (MACV) operated a similar program under its Special Operations Group but had no more success than had the CIA. Just as in Eastern Europe, China, Tibet, and North Korea, covert operations into areas with no chance of liberation and without reliable welcoming parties were a well-intentioned failure.[11]

While the CIA helped Vietnamese infiltration efforts, the Diem regime continued its independent path. The full story of the regime is beyond the scope of this work.[12] By 1963, Diem had alienated much of his own populace, as well as the administration in Washington, with his repressive actions and self-defeating efforts at counterinsurgency. Even if President Diem retained some credibility, his brother Nhu had become a lightning rod for opponents, especially when the administration forcibly interfered with worship by the Buddhist majority of the country. The final outrage came on August 21, 1963, when Nhu engineered attacks on Buddhist temples, killing dozens if not hundreds of civilians.[13]

The Kennedy administration wanted to demand that Diem dismiss his brother, but they soon realized that Diem would only balk, so they decided to pass the demand directly to the South Vietnamese generals to force the change. This led to the Americans actively cooperating in a coup plot at the end of August, but miscommunications caused the participants to pause and rethink the situation. The influential American ambassador Henry Cabot Lodge was much more aggressive about regime change than either the head of the military assistance command or the CIA station chief, both of whom reflected the hesitation they sensed in Washington. When the crisis subsided, the United States contented itself with halting funding for the Vietnamese special forces that Nhu had used against the Buddhists. Lodge also suspended CIA meetings with Nhu, which had the unintended effect of reducing intelligence reporting on the situation.[14]

Two months later, however, the Diem government remained paralyzed while both the generals and the Kennedy administration became more committed to replacing the Ngo brothers. A CIA officer, Lucien Conein, was the plotters' preferred contact with the American government because they had known him as an OSS officer in 1945 and as a Lansdale station officer a decade later. Ambassador Lodge told the plotters that the United States would not oppose a change of government that promised more effective prosecution of the war. Yet neither side was specific about the fate of Diem and Nhu or the future form of government in Saigon. On November 1–2, 1963, the plotters overthrew and then murdered the Ngo brothers. The United States soon realized that it had sacrificed Diem's popularity and legitimacy, however limited, without any corresponding improvement in the war effort.[15] For the remainder of the conflict, the United States and South Vietnamese struggled with this handicap.

American Intelligence in Vietnam

During the Second Indochinese War (1959–75), American military forces made a number of innovations in intelligence as well as fire support. The U.S. Army had its own dedicated aircraft (OV-1 series) to detect both infrared and moving target indicators at long ranges. The services also employed futuristic ground sensors that, when properly interpreted, could track enemy supply and troop movements with considerable accuracy. At great risk to themselves, small American patrols observed North Vietnamese supply routes to permit focused aerial attack. Under the cover name of radio research companies, the Army Security Agency had considerable success in tactical signals collection against a sophisticated foe, although the strict security procedures for signals intelligence often limited distribution of this data to tactical commanders.

American military intelligence operated under a number of handicaps in Southeast Asia. All the armed forces were hard-pressed to provide experienced leaders for their units, a problem that was especially acute for field intelligence collection and analysis. In previous wars, combat arms officers, sometimes without specific training, had functioned as unit intelligence officers and then moved to command when the opportunity arose. That practice continued in Vietnam, but in 1962 a separate intelligence and security branch came into being for the Army. With few experienced senior leaders, the new branch had to learn how to operate under the unusual requirements of counterinsurgency.

The most serious such requirement (and handicap) was the difficult task of evaluating progress in a war that lacked the traditional measurements such as territory captured. Contrary to legend, American commanders did not blindly rely on a simplistic and often exaggerated "body count" of the enemy. Sophisticated leaders in the armed services and CIA recognized that there was no simple way to quantify will, social development, and political orientation. This was especially true of a society in which both the nominal government and the well-equipped opposition struggled for the loyalty—or at least control—of the population. Secretary McNamara's emphasis on quantitative measurement, however, tended to stress the collection of data over the effective analysis of the results.[16] Perhaps the most judicious conclusion is that the opposing side was at least as uninformed as the United States was about the state of "hearts and minds" in rural Vietnam, as evidenced by the repeated failure of the Vietnamese people to rise up in rebellion when called upon to do so in 1968, 1972, and 1975.

The Johnson administration as well as MACV sought to apply a sophisticated understanding of the nature of counterinsurgency to the methodology used in pacification. A group of reform-minded officials, notably Robert W. Komer, urged that the war effort include economic and political alternatives to the communist message. Komer eventually persuaded President Johnson that all pacification efforts must be integrated under a single manager who would in turn be subordinate to Gen. William

Westmoreland, head of MACV from 1964 to 1968. In May 1967, Komer as a civilian became Westmoreland's deputy for pacification, heading the interagency Civil Operations and Revolutionary Development Support (CORDS). CORDS unified all Americans involved in nonmilitary operations and eventually won the support of the Saigon government as well. William Colby returned to Vietnam as Komer's deputy and, in late 1968, his successor. Both men led strenuous and sophisticated efforts to develop popular support for the Republic of Vietnam.[17]

Komer also developed what became known as the Phoenix (Phung Huong) program, which evolved in December 1967. Phoenix is often portrayed as a rogue assassination program that allowed Vietnamese officials to eliminate their personal opponents. In actuality, the program sought to arrest and convict the Viet Cong infrastructure agents who controlled the population in each village. Once again, there was a fine line between fighting genuine subversion and abusing government power. Provincial heads of Phoenix were sometimes corrupt and torture undoubtedly occurred, yet the program had some successes. Between 1968 and 1972, the program reportedly "neutralized" 81,740 VC, of whom 26,369 were killed, often by conventional military forces rather than by Phoenix agents. Live suspects produced more intelligence than dead ones, and even Hanoi officials acknowledged that Phoenix contributed to success in some pacification of rural areas.[18]

The North Vietnamese decision to sacrifice many southern resistance soldiers in the 1968 offensive also significantly weakened the southern insurgency, leaving the regular People's Army of [North] Vietnam to carry the main war effort thereafter. Yet all of these efforts at pacification and countersubversion took time, which was soon in short supply for the South Vietnamese defenders. Moreover, weakening the insurgent infrastructure did not necessarily mean increasing popular support for the Saigon government. As the war grew, so too did the opportunities for corruption within the Army of the Republic of Vietnam and its government.

Domestic Surveillance Encore

While Americans and their South Vietnamese allies sought victory on the battlefield, the United States also endured years of civil strife in the form of civil rights activism, urban violence against a repressive police, and antiwar demonstrations. Only the latter were in fact related to international events, and the peace activists were well-intentioned opponents of foreign policy rather than conscious tools of nefarious foreign powers. Nonetheless, for many conservatives such as J. Edgar Hoover, all such activists were domestic manifestations of the international threat of communism; any protest or disorder appeared to be subversion or rebellion. In a misguided effort to reduce crime and maintain public order, the Johnson and Nixon administrations began to equip police forces with military-grade weapons and eventually to divert social service funds to policing and prisons.[19]

The repressive approach to civil disorders was by no means universal. For example, the regular Army—as opposed to National Guardsmen obeying orders from state authorities—usually avoided extremes of violence on those occasions, such as Detroit in 1967 and Washington in 1967 and 1968, when it confronted public demonstrations and disorders.[20] Antiwar demonstrators may have felt frustrated at the Pentagon in 1967, but the Army generally respected their rights.

This does not mean that the Army was immune from the burdens of domestic surveillance and repression during the 1960s. At the time, many major cities had small detachments of Army counterintelligence (CI) agents usually engaged in routine tasks such as investigating the background of recruits seeking security clearances. These CI agents dressed in civilian clothes and had a youthful appearance, since they were often younger than FBI agents. Beginning with the Little Rock, Arkansas, civil rights confrontation in 1957, counterintelligence agents reconnoitered sites and coordinated with local police before the arrival of federal troops in the area. They were often the only military assets available on the ground when such crises began. The Department of the Army recognized the risks of domestic surveillance, and in 1960 revised its rules to require presidential approval for CI investigations within a civilian jurisdiction. Yet the crises of the 1960s seemed to justify such investigations; once federal troops intervened to help integrate the University of Mississippi in the fall of 1962, several CI agents went undercover to monitor local sentiment about that intervention.[21]

Collecting tactical information about violent disorders was one thing, but surveillance of legitimate dissent was quite another. In 1964, Lyndon Johnson directed the FBI to investigate the origins of urban riots, emphasizing the potential role of black militants and Marxists. By 1967,

Johnson had come to agree with J. Edgar Hoover that communist agents were behind antiwar protests. Attorney General Ramsey Clark instructed the Army's CI agents, along with the National Security Agency, to support the FBI in investigating what Johnson believed was an attempt to overthrow the government.[22] A significant number of CI agents were members of minority groups and/or appeared to be of college age, making it easier for them to infiltrate various protest movements. For three years under Johnson and especially under Nixon, CI agents provided thousands of reports on protest activity to the FBI. Fortunately for the integrity of the Army and the society, one military intelligence officer took action to publicize the policy. In January 1970, Capt. Christopher Pyle, a former instructor at the counterintelligence school, revealed the role of Army CI in domestic surveillance in the first of several articles appearing in the *Washington Monthly*.[23] This publicity eventually brought about a moratorium on CI agents operating in civil society, followed by severe restrictions on any military intelligence collection on American territory.[24]

The CI agents were only one aspect of the much larger domestic surveillance effort. Under Hoover, the FBI maintained files such as the Rabble Rouser Index for those allegedly fomenting racial discord, and the Counterintelligence Program–New Left for antiwar activists. Without search warrants, the FBI broke into various offices looking for evidence of such activity.[25] The White House also directed the CIA to conduct Operation Chaos, aimed at locating the supposed foreign links behind racial, antiwar, and other protests. In 1970, Nixon staffer Tom Charles Huston was asked to find ways to improve intelligence coordination. He recommended wiretaps and telephone intercepts as well as lowering the age of informants from twenty-one to eighteen. Fortunately, this so-called Huston Plan was never approved.[26]

In 1966, the Supreme Court heard a case involving the illegal FBI bugging of a Washington lobbyist. Hoover had argued against disclosing the FBI's conduct in this case. Unfortunately for him, the solicitor general who appeared before the court was Thurgood Marshall, himself a long-time target of FBI surveillance. To avoid poor publicity, Hoover ordered an end to break-ins, illegal wiretaps, and opening of first-class mail. Without these tools, the FBI had little success in identifying genuine spies in the United States. Yet the secret surveillance of domestic dissent continued on a limited scale for several more years.[27]

The Church Committee

The men who broke into the Democratic Party offices in the Watergate Hotel were paid by the (Republican) Committee to Re-elect the President, although most of them had previously worked for the CIA and other intelligence agencies. Still, the Watergate scandal, in conjunction with the opaque prosecution of the Vietnam conflict, caused such a fundamental distrust of government that it finally brought about public reconsideration of domestic surveillance. Four months after Richard Nixon resigned, investigative journalist Seymour Hersh published a major article on intelligence surveillance of domestic dissent.[28]

President Gerald Ford appointed his vice president, Nelson Rockefeller, to chair an investigative commission that included Ronald Reagan and retired general Lyman Lemnitzer. The commission reasserted individual rights but generally downplayed reports of violations and said that its five-month tenure had left insufficient time to investigate allegations of CIA assassinations abroad. It recommended both an amendment to the 1947 National Security Act and an executive order to restrict CIA actions inside the United States. The commission also suggested three forms of oversight. The PFIAB should assume an explicit oversight role for the CIA, Congress should create a joint committee on the matter, and the CIA inspector general's status should be upgraded.[29] In effect, the Rockefeller Commission had a narrow charter and appeared to be one more effort to clean up after the Nixon era.

Previously, Congress had avoided any significant oversight of the intelligence agencies. Many members considered intelligence and covert action to be necessary evils and saw no electoral benefit in investing their time on such a topic. The political consequences of accidentally disclosing classified information also deterred involvement in the subject. When the House of Representatives first created an intelligence committee, the chamber as a whole ignored what that committee learned and did. Moreover, the House committee became involved in a confrontation with the administration about classified information. Once the committee began to publish classified documents, the administration responded by redacting the documents it provided. Secretary of State Henry Kissinger blocked subordinates from testifying and refused to transfer documents.[30]

The Senate intelligence committee had a different outcome, due in large measure to its chairman, Frank F. Church (D-ID). In 1975, Church sought to build a nonpartisan consensus within his committee while educating the public about the realities of intelligence. The Senate committee published most of its findings, including such dubious activities as the Huston Plan and CIA involvement in the overthrow of Chilean leader Salvador Allende. Church's exhaustive hearings explored both covert actions and domestic surveillance, and when the process ended many of his committee staff members found work with a subsequent, standing oversight committee.[31]

Church's contribution was matched by the DCI at the time, William Colby. During his confirmation hearings, he had hinted at some of the irregularities conducted by the agency, and when the Hersh article appeared, the Ford administration did not include Colby in its policy meetings concerning a response. Colby was an honorable man who felt that Congress had a right to information. He gave the committee most of what it requested, often without clearing the information transfer with the administration, an action that irritated Kissinger. While the reports of both congressional committees indicted the Nixon-Ford administration, once again the DCI became a scapegoat. On November 1, 1975, the president dismissed Colby, although the DCI continued to function until George H. W. Bush returned from China to assume the post three months later.[32]

Of the many consequences of these revelations, perhaps the most obvious was the Foreign Intelligence Surveillance Act (FISA) of 1978. This act limited intelligence searches and electronic wiretapping warrants within the United States to those circumstances where the primary purpose of the investigation was to obtain information concerning foreign intelligence organizations.[33] Even under those circumstances, such surveillance had to be approved by designated U.S. district judges. The rare exceptions authorized by the act required that the attorney general deposit certifications of compliance with the FISA court.[34] Although FISA records were classified, there is no indication that these additional requirements hampered legitimate counterintelligence efforts.

Beyond that, the set of executive orders and regulations erected as a result of the Church Committee investigations were intended to restrict FBI domestic surveillance while completely precluding such surveillance by any other intelligence agency, such as Army counterintelligence. This was a well-intentioned effort to prevent the kind of unauthorized surveillance that had gone on for decades. These rules, however, divided the intelligence community into two unequal pieces: the FBI and all the foreign intelligence agencies. The latter were forbidden to possess any records, even names, of U.S. persons, which made it difficult for the FBI to pass any warning information to them even if the bureau were willing to imperil a developing court case by doing so. The foreign intelligence agencies followed terrorists and other threats abroad, but only the FBI was permitted to track suspects once they entered the United States. As they crossed the U.S. border in either direction suspects would in effect appear to one agency and disappear from another. Counterintelligence and counterterrorism were not the primary mission of the FBI, and work in these fields was not considered career-enhancing.[35] Moreover, the justifiable concern about political surveillance meant that the FBI was unable to collect information about any organization unless it knew of a probable crime. In 1993, it took a decision from Attorney General Janet Reno to force the FBI to share foreign terrorism information with even a few officials of the National Security Council. By the same token, the CIA was reportedly slow to share information about al Qaeda with the FBI.[36] While by no means the only reason for the surprise of September 11, 2001, this division was a key factor in permitting that surprise.

Executive Order 12036, issued in 1978, was a major statement of the new restrictions on intelligence. It forbade most collection of intelligence within the United States except by the FBI and severely limited maintenance of any intelligence collection or records about American citizens or corporations. It also explicitly forbade assassination of foreign leaders, reflecting a general disdain for special operations.[37] The 1980 Intelligence Oversight Act required the president to determine that an intelligence collection effort was important to national security and to so inform congressional intelligence committees. Carter's choice for DCI, Stansfield Turner, dismissed as many as two hundred covert operators and eight hundred human intelligence case officers.[38]

Some of these intelligence "reforms" reflected the Carter administration's efforts to reduce spending in government. As part of reorganizing the White House staff, Carter abolished the president's intelligence advisory board, arguing that the reorganized National Security Council could perform the same functions. The Intelligence Oversight Board became two high-level committees of the NSC, renamed Policy Review and Covert Operations. Like Ford, Carter was interested in controlling intelligence rather than getting independent advice on the subject. The Iranian hostage crisis prompted a review of both the CIA cutbacks and the necessity of an advisory board.[39]

Because the CIA had almost no HUMINT resources inside Iran, the Defense Department improvised its own covert reconnaissance prior to the failed attempt (Operation Eagle Claw) to rescue the hostages in Tehran. For example, Army Special Forces included a concealed unit, Detachment A, that had existed for decades inside West Berlin with the mission of disrupting any Soviet takeover. Prior to the Eagle Claw attempt, two members of Detachment A reconnoitered the Ministry of Foreign Affairs in Tehran, where the U.S. chargé d'affaires and two other diplomats were held separately from the other hostages. This reconnaissance found much heavier security than the Joint Task Forces had anticipated, forcing a major revision of the plan.[40]

After the hostage crisis, the chief of staff of the Army decided to retain this limited HUMINT capability, known as the Intelligence Support Activity (ISA). Quite apart from the controversial use of counterintelligence agents in domestic surveillance, Army HUMINT had a mixed record but improved in the early 1980s. The CIA Directorate of Operations (DO) was displeased by the existence of the ISA, and considerable friction ensued. By the later 1980s, relationships between the ISA and DO improved somewhat, although the Army general officer assigned to the DO as liaison had little ability to influence CIA clandestine case officers concerning specific Army needs. In 1995, the descendant of the ISA was included in a unified Defense Human Intelligence Service under DIA. While HUMINT relations followed this meandering path, the relationships between the DO's covert operators and Army Special Forces continued to be more fruitful.[41]

The Reagan Years

As in other fields, the Reagan administration attempted to reverse the intelligence policies of Jimmy Carter. The new administration reduced some of the restrictions in E.O. 12036, resisted requirements to inform Congress on sensitive operations, and revived the PFIAB in a weaker form. The White House cited examples of communist spies caught in the United States to justify increased human intelligence collection.[42] Although intelligence expenditures were classified, they appeared to follow the same trajectory as those for defense. From a low of $3 billion in 1973, the IC budget reached $13 billion by the time Carter left office and peaked at an estimated $30 billion in 1990.[43]

The new administration was genuinely concerned about the communist threat, and certainly the Soviet Union and its allies—especially Cuba—had become more aggressive after the American withdrawal from Vietnam. Reagan was convinced that the Caribbean region was under constant threat of Marxist expansionism. Although he used the conventional military to overthrow a Marxist regime in Grenada (Operation Urgent Fury, 1983) and to deter the Sandinista invasion of Honduras (Operation Golden Pheasant, 1987), Reagan also turned to covert action as a preferred instrument of power, especially with regard to the Sandinista regime in Nicaragua.

A key figure in such actions was William Casey, DCI from 1981 until his death in 1987. Casey had been a senior official of the OSS during World War II, and thereafter held various roles in Republican governments, but his only postwar intelligence position was a single year on the PFIAB under Ford. Even when Casey formed a counterterrorism center in 1986, its focus was on covert operations against terrorists rather than understanding the threat.[44] Working with Secretary of State Alexander Haig, Casey exaggerated the extent of foreign support given to the Sandinistas. As mentioned in chapter 1, Casey's deputy DCI, Adm. Bobby Ray Inman, resigned when he concluded that Casey was misrepresenting foreign arms shipments to Nicaragua.[45]

During the 1980s insurgencies in Nicaragua and El Salvador, pro- and anti-Marxist forces both committed serious human rights violations, but it was the anti-Marxists—especially the Contras who opposed the Sandinista regime in Nicaragua—who got the most publicity for their crimes. In 1981, Reagan issued a presidential finding to support the Contras, but for three successive years (1982–84) Congress passed the so-called Boland Amendment that forbade any intelligence spending to support these rebels.[46] This led to two interrelated administration efforts, both of them apparently guided or at least inspired by DCI Casey.

First, Casey contributed to the creation of a program that crossed the line from public information to manipulation of domestic political opinion. Reagan and Casey apparently believed that North Vietnamese and Soviet disinformation had misled the American people concerning Vietnam, so the administration set out to counter such efforts with respect to Central America through National Security Decision Directive 77 of 1983.[47] The State Department's Office of Public Diplomacy for Latin America and the Caribbean (S/LPD) used Army psychological operations officers and others to burnish the freedom-fighting credentials of the Contras while emphasizing both actual and imaginary crimes of the Sandinistas. In the lead-up to Reagan's re-election in 1984, a series of government "background" briefings created the public impression that Moscow was about to supply Nicaragua with MiG-21 fighter planes; two years later, CIA analysts concluded that no such weapons had arrived, nor would such an arrival have changed the regional balance of power anyway. Otto Reich of S/LPD lobbied journalists and their bureau chiefs against reporting critically of the administration's policies. The Government Accountability Office later concluded that S/LPD efforts qualified as prohibited propaganda. Conservatives and foreigners alike paid for apparently independent media entities to generate pro-Contra opinion and news pieces.[48]

Second, Casey handed off Contra support to the staff of the National Security Council (NSC), thereby respecting the letter but not the intent of the Boland Amendment because the NSC was not an intelligence agency. Two successive national security advisors, Robert McFarlane and John Poindexter, oversaw this effort, although its most famous action officer was Lt. Col. Oliver North, detailed to the NSC staff from the Marine Corps. North used funds from various sources, including Saudi Arabia, to finance both propaganda efforts and support for the Contras.[49] Some participants may have been unaware of the various actions involved, including the full extent of the infamous Iran-Contra affair, yet the president at least supported private fundraising to circumvent Congress.

In 1984, an Iranian arms dealer approached a former CIA officer claiming that Prime Minister Akbar Hashemi Rafsanjani was willing to reopen talks with the United States, including exchanging new Soviet equipment in Iranian hands for antitank and air defense missiles that Iran needed for its prolonged war with Iraq. The next year, the government of Israel offered for its own reasons to be an arms intermediary, and McFarlane persuaded Casey to back the effort; the president was apparently willing to initiate contact, vaguely hoping to save American hostages held in Lebanon. The original plan was that Israel would transfer American weapons from its stockpiles, to be replaced by additional shipments from the United States. Other intermediaries, including Saudi arms dealer Adnan Khashoggi, were also involved. The original Iranian arms dealer then raised his profit margin on these shipments, while Lieutenant Colonel North proposed using the proceeds to augment other funds going to the Contras. Hard-line elements inside the Iranian regime decided to weaken Rafsanjani by leaking news of the deal. The entire conspiracy collapsed when a Lebanese journal publicized the arms-for-hostages arrangement on November 3, 1986.[50]

This affair thus involved three different offenses, each of which violated U.S. policies or laws. The NSC staff negotiated with Iran at a time when the government officially refused to negotiate with the Islamic Republic; to free the hostages, the administration sold weapons, including parts for Hawk antiaircraft missiles and TOW antitank missiles, disposing of U.S. property without congressional authorization; and it transferred the resulting funds to the Contras in violation of congressional mandates. Ultimately, only three American hostages regained their freedom, while a frustrated Hezbollah with its Iranian backers kidnapped six more after the deal collapsed. The scheme resulted in a dark, humorless farce in which McFarlane attempted suicide and the secretaries of state and defense had to resign for an operation run out of the White House, yet Reagan evaded blame and his DCI died of an unrelated illness. Once again, covert operations failed to meet the partisan expectations of decision makers.

Counterintelligence

The 1980s were also notable for the discovery of foreign spies operating inside the United States. At least sixty-two Americans were arrested for espionage during the decade, of which almost half were caught in the period from 1984 to 1986. The NSA, CIA, and armed services all found traitors within, including the family of John Walker, whose betrayal of codes gave the Soviet Union access to most encrypted naval communications. Those apprehended included Larry Wu-tai Chin, who had spied for China since at least 1952. Coincidentally, in 1984 Ana Montes began a career of spying for Cuba while working for the DIA, although she was not detected until 2001.[51]

Particularly galling for the IC was the apprehension of Jonathan J. Pollard, a civilian analyst for the Department of the Navy, who sold thousands of documents to Israel. Although Israel had spied extensively on the United States during the 1940s and 1950s, by the time Pollard was caught the CIA and Mossad had few secrets from each other. Moreover, persistent Israeli pleas that Pollard had done nothing really wrong encouraged unjustified suspicions concerning the loyalty of other American citizens of Jewish ethnicity.[52]

The End of the Cold War

The U.S. intelligence community consistently overestimated the strength and resilience of the Soviet Union and was generally surprised by its rapid collapse. The same could be said of the Soviet leadership, however, because both American analysts and Soviet politicians were often looking at the same distorted data.

The command-directed Soviet economy placed great emphasis on meeting numerical production quotas, while the quality of what was produced often suffered. Worse still, production and budgetary figures were misleading, chosen for propaganda value rather than accuracy. Managers at every level reported meeting or exceeding production goals, regardless of the true figures. In the mid-1980s, the Soviet government officials believed that the armed forces had a total of 39,000 tactical and strategic nuclear warheads, until the Defense Ministry's head of logistics reported that the actual figure was closer to 43,000. For decades, the Soviet regime quoted its defense budget as being only 4.6 percent of the total state expenditure, an absurdly low figure that reflected only military personnel costs of the conscript armed forces; all weapons and supplies were concealed in the budgets of other ministries. At Mikhail Gorbachev's behest, Central Committee Secretary Vadim Medvedev calculated total defense spending to be at least 16 percent of domestic product, and he suspected that the true cost of defense might be 25 percent.[53] With misleading data such as this, Gorbachev had difficulty making rational national security decisions, and American analysts could be equally wrong. This was an unavoidable limitation of human intelligence; knowing what your adversary believes has limited value if that adversary is factually misinformed. Both sides knew that the USSR was under considerable political, social, and economic strain, but not how close it was to the breaking point.

One senior Soviet analyst in the DIA did predict the August 1991 coup against Gorbachev. Yet it would have required a crystal ball to predict that Gorbachev would emerge from the coup still nominally in charge but with much of his legitimacy transferred to the combative Boris Yeltsin, who ended the year controlling both the Kremlin and Soviet nuclear weapons.

Much of the attention of U.S. collection systems, analysts, and decision makers was diverted to Iraq for a critical nine months in 1990–91. Just as with military forces, the collection systems and analysts so painstakingly built up during the previous decades performed well despite the inevitable disconnects and miscommunications associated with any war. The different armed service intelligence organizations still insisted on their own wording in DIA intelligence estimates. Not coincidentally, the commander-in-chief, Central Command, Gen. Norman Schwarzkopf, acknowledged that he had received excellent intelligence support, but he grumbled that the intelligence assessments were often so caveated as to be useless to him. Some disconnects were simple misunderstandings. For example, the undermanned Air Force intelligence analysts in Saudi Arabia were not told about the target planning conducted by the "Black Hole Gang" and as a result did not respond in a timely manner to what this secretive group of targeteers requested, which resulted in considerable friction.[54]

With the defeat of Iraq and the collapse of the Soviet Union, a drive to downsize the national security establishment was inevitable. For the sixth time in ninety years, the United States demobilized after a war with little thought for the future needs of defense. James Woolsey, the DCI from 1993 to 1995, delayed the drawdown by asking for additional intelligence funds, but even he eventually had to acquiesce. His successors, John Deutch and George Tenet, had limited influence in the Clinton administration. Overall, IC spending declined from an estimated $29 billion in 1992 to $20 billion six years later, with concomitant reductions in HUMINT field collectors.[55] Coming forty years after the initial expansion of the IC during the Korean conflict, this drawdown hastened the retirement of an entire generation of analysts and collectors. Defense

Department intelligence activities also suffered. The armed services had already been short by up to one-third of authorized career intelligence officers who, having entered the service in the 1970s and early 1980s, were now poised to provide experienced leadership in the new decade. On top of these shortages, large numbers of such officers left active duty in 1992 as the services reduced their personnel strengths by up to 40 percent. In retrospect, cutting defense readiness after the Cold War should have been counterbalanced by more intelligence capability, not less, to reduce risks. In practice, however, the services and agencies generally cut all activities by an equal percentage and then encouraged those who were eligible to retire early. In the case of intelligence, this meant eating the seed corn needed for future conflicts. Only Soviet foreign area officers had to remain on active duty, briefly, to verify various arms reduction agreements.

While the resources of the IC shrank noticeably, ideas of how to organize and employ the remaining resources proliferated. Some of these ideas were well worth trying, including Woolsey's efforts to increase cooperation between the Directorates of Operations (collectors) and Intelligence (analysts). Typical of such broad ideas was William Clinton's July 14, 1995, speech at CIA headquarters. Among the priorities the president wanted to see addressed were (1) intelligence support to the military, (2) knowledge of hostile countries and WMD, and (3) knowledge of transnational threats including nonproliferation, terrorism, drug smuggling, and organized crime.[56] The IC could and did work on these and other topics, although the FBI seized upon international organized crime as a reason to expand its network of legal attachés overseas. Unfortunately, unlike Soviet communism, the transnational threats involved complex parameters of analysis without clear-cut policy solutions.

Congressional and administration demands that the IC provide better support to the military were not new. In 1983, for example, the alleged intelligence shortcomings of the Grenada intervention and the Beirut bombings seemed to argue for greater use of the CIA and other capabilities to assist the armed forces. This blossomed under Clinton into a robust interaction between the CIA and DoD headquarters and schools at various levels. The designated chief of this developing structure was the agency's associate director of military affairs. Yet, as noted in chapter 2, focusing limited collection capabilities on one intelligence problem almost inevitably means neglecting other, equally important issues. Lacking a clear distinction between tactical and strategic intelligence, the Clinton and subsequent administrations unwittingly reduced support to policy makers by increasing support to field commanders.[57]

Weapons proliferation was particularly frustrating. Chapter 3 has already discussed the multiple issues posed by Iraq. In 1998, the CIA was blindsided when India conducted a series of nuclear tests.[58] In addition, Pakistan's Abdul Qadeer Khan crisscrossed the Middle East and Africa, gaining financial assistance from Libya, uranium hexafluoride from Niger, and export and production facilities in various locations. Initially trading stolen centrifuge designs for other aid, Khan eventually assembled a group of exporters who, by the late 1990s, offered complete enrichment plants for purchase by Iran and Libya.[59] Khan also aided North Korea's nuclear program by trading with other states, including Iraq, gaining radioactive materials in return for Pyongyang's missile designs.

While Iraq got most of the headlines during the 1990s, Iran and North Korea posed equal problems in the arena of nonproliferation. These closed societies, especially North Korea, had always made intelligence collection difficult. Moreover, the two regimes built hardened facilities that almost precluded destruction of their programs by kinetic means. Subconsciously, some officials aggravated by intractable proliferation issues may have transferred their frustration into dissatisfaction with the IC that analyzed those issues.

Three successive administrations largely disregarded intelligence concerning Pyongyang's programs. Focused on the Soviet Union, the Reagan administration showed little concern for North Korean violations of nuclear rules; Pyongyang procrastinated for years about completing the detailed application to join the nuclear safeguards agreement of the International Atomic Energy Agency (IAEA). George H. W. Bush finally got the agreement completed in early 1992, but only at the cost of the U.S. publicly withdrawing all ground- and sea-launched tactical nuclear weapons from the peninsula. Yet Pyongyang's declarations of nuclear materials frequently varied from the truth, and it began to impede or block IAEA inspections. North Korean intransigence led to a formal withdrawal from the nonproliferation agreements in June 1994. The Clinton administration substituted the "Agreed Framework," by which the North Koreans promised to freeze their nuclear program in return for two proliferation-resistant nuclear power reactors. Neither side honored this deal.[60]

The loss of IAEA inspections reduced the amount of technical information available to the IC, but the CIA and other agencies repeatedly estimated that Pyongyang was on the road to developing nuclear devices; by the mid-1990s, the IC judged that the North Koreans probably had one or two nuclear weapons in hand. Decision makers appeared reluctant to acknowledge such warnings. The Clinton administration, in particular, was more invested in maintaining the Agreed Framework than in dealing with the reality of North Korean nuclear weapons.[61] Diplomacy often involves accepting risks in hopes of a long-term improvement.

Counterterrorism Wars

The end of the Cold War also unleashed a number of regional powers and nonstate actors to pursue their own objectives. Terrorist groups posed similar problems to those presented by proliferators. It was difficult for any intelligence service to infiltrate collectors into closely knit, fanatical organizations. Thus, although counterterrorism experts frequently identified an increase in "chatter" that might presage a significant attack, the place, time, and method of such an attack were rarely if ever clear.

Combating state-supported terrorism was simpler in terms of both collection and response, as illustrated by the Reagan administration's duel with Muammar Gaddafi of Libya. In March 1986, a U.S. Navy show of force off the Libyan coast failed to intimidate the dictator; while the Navy was still maneuvering on his doorstep, he sent instructions to some thirty embassies to conduct further terrorist attacks.[62]

U.S. SIGINT determined the targets of these orders, and local governments prevented several of the attacks. Regrettably, warning of an attack in West Berlin arrived too late. At 1:49 a.m. on April 5, 1986, a bomb exploded in a dance club, killing 3 and wounding 229, of whom 2 dead and 79 wounded were Americans. Gaddafi tried to deny responsibility, unaware of the NSA intercepts.[63] The U.S. response was Operation El Dorado Canyon, a significant bombing raid that at least made the dictator more cautious. Perhaps, in fact, the seeming success of El Dorado Canyon, as well as the Clinton administration's attacks on Iraq during the 1990s, contributed to the George W. Bush administration's belief that invading Iraq in 2003 was a reasonable response to the 9/11 attacks.

In the 1990s, however, the terrorist threats were mostly nonstate actors, especially al Qaeda. By definition these nonstate actors lacked identifiable pressure points that could be threatened or targeted to discourage future attacks.

On June 25, 1996, a bomb largely destroyed an apartment building near Khobar, Saudi Arabia; the building had housed coalition personnel involved in the Operation Southern Watch aerial patrols over Iraq. Nineteen U.S. Air Force personnel died and almost five hundred of various nationalities were wounded. The U.S. government and courts blamed Iran for the attack, probably because the Saudi government had no wish to acknowledge the culpability of Osama bin Laden and other Saudi nationals. Two years later, on August 7, 1998, truck bombs exploded outside the U.S. embassies in Nairobi, Kenya, and Dar es Salaam, Tanzania, killing 224 and wounding 4,500, mostly local residents.[64] This time the United States correctly identified Osama bin Laden and his lieutenant, Muhammad Atef, as the planners of the attack, but only apprehended a few lesser figures. Bin Laden may have chosen the August date as the eighth anniversary of the U.S. decision to send troops to Saudi Arabia. The Clinton administration used precision-guided munitions against suspected terrorist targets in Sudan and Afghanistan, but again had no means of striking a decisive blow directly at the terrorists.

The Defense Department considered the use of special operations troops against these targets to be too risky. The CIA, having been criticized for previous covert operations that failed, was equally reluctant, as the terrorism coordinator at the time, Richard Clarke, noted bitterly and perhaps unfairly,

> CIA's career management saw my proposal to aid the Northern Alliance [in Afghanistan] as a risk to CIA. For those who had spent fifteen, twenty, or more years in CIA, there was a clear pattern. Whoever was in the White House would get worked up over the cause du jour. He would be unable to get the rest of the government to produce results, so he would turn to the CIA. He would push the CIA to do risky, potentially controversial things.

> Later, after things went badly, the White House people would be gone and CIA would get the blame.[65]

Thus, even before an al Qaeda suicide team damaged the USS *Cole* in October 2000, the IC was fully aware of the threat and struggling to anticipate the next attack. The IC knew that the port of Aden was a vulnerable anchorage. More generally, two months before the 9/11 attack, DCI Tenet told the national security advisor, Condoleezza Rice, that another al Qaeda attack was imminent, possibly in the United States.[66] Still, the inherent difficulty of predicting terrorist incidents *precisely*, compounded by the legal barriers between the FBI and the rest of the IC, led to a situation that was condemned as an intelligence failure.

Once the 9/11 attacks occurred, the administration of George W. Bush was understandably focused not on intelligence but on action, including covert operations. CIA paramilitary officers led the American intrusion into Afghanistan, performing brilliantly in cooperation with the Northern Alliance to overthrow the Taliban government. Unfortunately, the short-term success of this "light footprint" of American forces in Afghanistan encouraged a false analogy that similar means would suffice to maintain long-term stability in that country and in Iraq.

In 2002, while the administration moved toward war with Iraq (see chapter 3), two national intelligence reports cautioned about the instability of a post-Saddam Iraq. These reports pointed out obvious problems: the difficulty of building a government in a country that had more disgruntled people than democratic traditions and the regional power vacuum that might well follow regime change.[67] The projections proved remarkably accurate, as the administration underestimated both the social control of the Ba'ath regime and the eagerness of Shi'a as well as Sunni groups to expel foreigners.[68] Having used intelligence as a lever to justify intervention in Iraq, the Bush administration felt forced to continue the war long after Saddam was overthrown. By 2007, the sustained conflict in Iraq was straining the military capacities and public will of the United States, allowing the Taliban and other resistance forces to reassert themselves in Afghanistan. Rather than an intelligence system, armed UAVs became an economy of force measure to limit the damage in Afghanistan.[69]

Meanwhile the harsh interrogation techniques used by CIA officers and contractors raised serious questions of legality and morality. By a narrow, precise reading of Geneva Convention III, attorneys in the Bush administration concluded that only qualified prisoners of war, not including "unlawful combatants," had the right to be protected under the convention. This contradicted U.S. Army intelligence doctrine, which extended Geneva protections and fair treatment to all detainees, although some military personnel imitated CIA methodology. Unfortunately, these harsh interrogation techniques, including so-called "waterboarding," were patterned to a large extent after the techniques that the military had used to train American personnel to resist enemy torture (survival, evasion, resistance, and escape, or SERE). In turn, that torture was based on Chinese communist interrogations during the Korean War. These interrogations were *not* concerned with obtaining valid intelligence data but rather with extorting false propaganda statements from prisoners. Thus the harsh interrogation techniques were not only of questionable legality and morality, but also known to be ineffective in their intended purpose. When news of those techniques became public, that reveal not only discouraged American public support for the conflict, but also motivated additional "foreign fighters" to travel to Iraq and fight the Americans.[70]

Subsequent congressional investigation confirmed the use of SERE techniques and found that the CIA and contractor personnel involved, including psychologists, had no prior experience in interrogation as well as inadequate linguistic and analytical support. Prior to 9/11, in fact, the CIA had already concluded that such atrocious techniques would produce false reports but no real intelligence. Worse still, no one had briefed President Bush on the specific techniques used until April 2006, while the officials involved consistently obstructed and misled oversight by Congress, the White House, the Department of Justice, and the agency's own inspector general.[71] The administration may have deliberately failed to brief the president in order to give him deniability about the matter.[72]

The "War against Terror" meant a sudden demand for analysts, Arab linguists, and other specialists whom the IC had laid off during the 1990s. Several thousand military reservists, many of them veterans of the Cold War and 1991 conflict, provided an initial transfusion of talent during the first twelve to eighteen months after 9/11. Yet after a decade of drawdown, most of these people had developed separate careers to which they wished to return. Moreover, while Congress appropriated large sums of money for the problem, it was reluctant to authorize permanent increases in civilian or military personnel end-strength, either for the Defense Department or the IC. Thus, to make up for the intelligence strength lost during the 1990s, the IC had little choice except to use contractors.[73] Some contractors were retirees with long experience in the field, but inevitably the different agencies hired unqualified "interrogators" as well as some outsiders who for ill-considered reasons leaked classified information.

Wartime once again brought concerns about domestic subversion, which led to questionable collection methods. In an era where terrorists used the internet to locate and communicate with each other, increased surveillance of electronic communications was an unavoidable necessity. The PATRIOT Act of October 2001 reversed some of the safeguards of the 1978 FISA law, reducing court oversight with regard to the monitoring of e-mails, voicemails, and the internet. A related response to 9/11 was to give the FBI more power to surveil and investigate.[74] Even before the PATRIOT Act became law, however, the Bush administration authorized NSA collection of electronic communications involving al Qaeda. Although the order was couched in terms of collecting only against non-U.S. persons, and the administration later cited Franklin Roosevelt's 1940 warrantless wiretap order under similar circumstances, in practice it was virtually impossible not to violate FISA.[75] A series of scandals ensued.

Some of this electronic surveillance was dubious if not clearly illegal. That said, some commentators appeared uninformed about the processes used to analyze such data. One article concluded that only 1.8 percent of terrorism cases filed were clearly linked to bulk data collection by NSA.[76] Yet that data was vital for the basic SIGINT technique known as traffic analysis. Consider a hypothetical situation in which a known terrorist telephone number (or internet IP address) A frequently contacts numbers B, C, and D, and number B in turn often contacts numbers X and Y at about the same time as it was in communication with A. These conversations by themselves may be completely unrelated and innocent, but they may justify further investigation, including FISA warrants, of communications between B, X, and Y. Simply because the bulk data does not appear in the final case does not mean that data is unnecessary; it may well have provided the initial leads for subsequent warranted investigations.

Yet More Reform

Information sharing between the FBI and the rest of the IC increased significantly after the 9/11 attacks, although various agencies still placed "caveats" on their information to limit dissemination. Meanwhile, a series of laws directed the most significant reorganization of the federal government since 1947. While well-intentioned, some of these actions actually increased the complexity of coordination problems. The Homeland Security Act of 2002 (implemented by appropriations in 2004) moved various agencies including the Coast Guard, Federal Emergency Management Agency, and Secret Service into a new Department of Homeland Security, which added yet another intelligence entity to the community. The same act also created a separate National Homeland Security Council, although President Barack Obama eventually merged the staff of this new council with that of the National Security Council so that the two councils were effectively interchangeable.[77]

The Intelligence Reform and Terrorism Prevention Act of 2004, in turn, created the DNI. Again, this separation of the coordination function from the head of the CIA was overdue by half a century. The new office (ODNI) at least began the process of increasing coordination and standardization, especially concerning the logic and procedures of analysis. In turn, the DCI's title changed to "director, CIA," allowing him or her to focus on this complex task. Although the new head of the IC no longer had to manage the internal workings of the CIA, that also meant that he or she lost some of the administrative clout that came from operating that agency.[78] Additionally, the DNI still faced the daunting tasks of advising the president on intelligence while trying to integrate three different cultures: military intelligence, civilian intelligence, and FBI criminal investigation.[79] Moreover, to begin operations the ODNI had to appropriate buildings and borrow personnel from other agencies, causing some friction. Finally, as noted in chapter 1, the DNI position has often been as politicized and controversial as the preceding DCI slot.

Even before the creation of the DNI, in 2003 Secretary of Defense Donald Rumsfeld moved to create a single undersecretary of defense for intelligence, who supervised the vast majority of the intelligence community including the DIA, NSA, National Geospatial-Intelligence Agency, and National Reconnaissance Office. This position helped simplify the labyrinth of defense intelligence operations, although until the DNI took over the post it only added to the difficulties a DCI experienced in trying to coordinate the IC.[80] The position eventually came to include a separate title as director of defense intelligence within ODNI.

Politicizing Intelligence

The Trump administration was not the first to politicize intelligence, although no other administration went to such extremes with those who disagreed. Allen Dulles and William Casey agreed fully with their administrations about the perceived struggle with Marxism, devoting themselves more to questionable covert operations than to IC integration. The last DCI, George Tenet, dissented when the Israeli government insisted that Jonathan Pollard be released in return for a security agreement. In effect, Tenet was implementing Huntington's third requirement for a profession (see chapter 1): that it discipline members who fail to maintain standards, and that there is no standard in the intelligence profession more important than protecting classified information. Tenet believed, correctly, that Israel would make the deal without Pollard, but he had to stand firm on resigning if Pollard were freed.[81]

Several early DNIs—John Negroponte, Michael McConnell, and James Clapper—were apparently successful in representing and coordinating the IC, probably because they all had distinguished national security careers prior to appointment; this is a welcome reminder that most interactions between intelligence leaders and politicians are *not* plagued by distrust and misunderstanding. Again, however, when choosing a DNI there is no substitute for hiring an experienced intelligence professional instead of a skillful political appointee.

Of the early DNIs, only Dennis Blair (2009–10) resigned after disagreements with the administration. After the tenure of James Clapper (2010–17), however, the position became a revolving door where incumbents were dismissed whenever they attempted to provide nonpartisan intelligence.

Despite the many changes in American intelligence organization, chapters 5 and 6 reflect several constant factors. The growing power of the federal government has been accompanied by frequent forays into domestic surveillance. Some of this surveillance was justified, especially during periods of war or other external threats. There really were German spies and saboteurs inside the United States during both world wars, and the Soviet Union did indeed pose a major security threat to America. Unfortunately, once the instrument of surveillance was forged for legitimate purposes, bureaucratic inertia as well as the natural bias of the party in power encouraged agents and executives to regard any political opposition or agitation, even peaceful First Amendment protests, as inherently wrong and suspect. As with minority rights, the need to protect the privacy of citizens is constant.

Chapter Seven

The Paradox of Warning

The ultimate test both of an intelligence structure and of its relationship with decision makers is warning of a surprise attack or other unexpected threat to national security. While reviewing the classic examples of strategic warning failure, this chapter will of necessity reiterate some information from earlier chapters. And, as already noted, in some instances, strategic surprise is a product of the same type of preconceived notions and operator dominance explored in chapter 3.

Three Basic Thoughts on Surprise and Warning

First, in the long run, surprise is unavoidable.[1] The intelligence community can and does strive to eliminate surprise, but there are too many opportunities for deception (including self-deception) and misunderstanding, especially when adversaries have different cultural and doctrinal norms. Eliminating *all* surprise is an impossible standard, equivalent in complexity and improbability to Ronald Reagan's goal of stopping every single inbound nuclear warhead with his Strategic Defense Initiative. No nuclear detonation and no strategic surprise are indeed the appropriate goals. In each instance, however, a single "leaker"—a single failure to detect and counter a major threat—would prompt many to condemn the entire system as worthless.

Second, our knowledge of this topic is based almost entirely on its failures. This means we have a biased sample of cases to investigate, in which the indications that "should" have led to warning appear blindingly obvious, but only in hindsight.[2] Successful strategic warnings—and many have undoubtedly occurred—rarely see the light of day. Moreover, in some instances the intelligence community did, in fact, identify a developing situation but failed in the ultimate step of convincing the decision maker to accept that interpretation of events. If the decision maker misunderstands or rejects what the intelligence officer is trying to convey, the former will blame the latter for the consequences, believing sincerely that the analyst rather than the operator caused the misunderstanding. As Thomas Fingar wryly observed, "I learned something a long time ago in this town [Washington]. There are only two possibilities [in a given situation or initiative]: policy success and intelligence failure."[3]

Third is the "Paradox of Warning," one of numerous paradoxes in this field. If an intelligence officer or agency does everything correctly—collects information in a timely manner, correctly interprets that information, and convinces the decision maker to act decisively—then the predicted event *never* occurs, and the intelligence officer/agency becomes the boy who cried wolf.[4] *The very fact that the intelligence system succeeds causes it to look like a failure.* Even if the initial warning were incorrect—and because friendly action changes the situation, it is often impossible to be certain after the fact—that warning may have the same effect as a failure in dulling the vigilance and open-mindedness of the decision maker.[5] In May 1973, for example, Israeli intelligence concluded that the Arab states were preparing to attack. Whether or not that warning was accurate, it prompted Israel to launch an expensive mobilization of its reservists for an eventuality that did not occur. Six months later, in the actual lead-up to the Yom Kippur/Ramadan War, the Israeli government was reluctant to mobilize again, especially with an election imminent.[6]

Forms of Surprise and Warning

Intelligence failure is not always the cause of strategic surprise. In a 2008 article, former CIA intelligence analyst John Gentry delineated six types of government failure that involve surprise: (1) failure to warn of a threat; (2) failure of the government to respond to intelligence warning with effective policies; (3) failure to warn of an opportunity for government action; (4) failure of the government to respond effectively to an opportunity warning; (5) failure to identify a vulnerability of the state or society; and (6) failure to ameliorate such a vulnerability once it has been identified. Of these six variations, only (1) and (3) represent purely intelligence failures, whereas the others are wholly or partially the responsibility of the rest of the government.[7]

Although identifying opportunities is a valid goal for intelligence analysts, there have been few studies of the matter.[8] If governments are reluctant to admit that they suffered a warning failure, they are even less likely to acknowledge that they missed opportunities. Consider an example of an apparent "opportunity failure" that will probably never be open for scholarly examination: the October 26, 1979, death of Park Chung-hee, dictator of the Republic of Korea (ROK) since 1963. Park's murder created a power vacuum in Seoul that lasted for more than a year. Eventually, a group of 1955 classmates from the Korean Military Academy violently repressed student demonstrations in Kwangju (or Gwangju), put thousands of citizens in re-education camps, and installed one of their number, Major General Chun Doo-hwan, as the president of the republic from 1980 to 1988.[9]

Although assassinations are inherently unpredictable, Park's death, at the hands of his own chief of intelligence, occurred after years of public disorders, including a failed 1974 assassination attempt that claimed the life of his wife.[10] It was therefore prudent to consider in advance the possibility that Park might lose his life or power suddenly and plunge his country into disorder. Yet the assassination surprised the ROK's bitter adversary, the [North] Korean People's Republic of Kim Il-sung, as much as it did the administration of President Carter. The ensuing power vacuum, in conjunction with Carter's previous reduction of troops on the peninsula, seemed to offer Kim an opportunity to seize the south. During 1980–81, Pyongyang increased attempts to infiltrate agents and guerrillas into the ROK but was clearly unprepared to exploit the situation. Pyongyang's subsequent behavior, including military exercises and the 1983 attempted assassination of President Chun when he visited Rangoon, suggest that Kim tried to prepare for and then re-create an opportunity that he had missed the first time.[11] However, missed opportunities, like strategic surprise, are often unrecoverable.

With regard to intelligence, therefore, let us focus only on the first of Gentry's six government failures: a failure of warning. There are generally three types of explanations for such failures. The first group of explanations is the procedural or structural type, in which the intelligence community of the surprised government either processes indications of attack incorrectly or has a structural impediment to processing and analysis. Such errors are indeed significant but are rarely the sole cause of failure.

The second group of explanations is what Abraham Ben-Zvi has termed analytical-revisionist studies. These explanations, which were especially popular during the decade after World War II; effectively deny that strategic surprise even occurred, substituting a secret scheme that tempts the attacker into action to serve the long-term goals of the not-so-surprised government. Thus Franklin Roosevelt and his advisors allegedly *wanted* Japan to attack Pearl Harbor to provide a pretext for the United States to enter World War II, or the Truman administration used South Korea as a pawn to justify the sacrifices of long-term containment of the communist bloc; or, more recently, Defense Minister Moshe Dayan's repeated denials that war was imminent in 1973 were supposedly intended to lure the Arab states into attacking so that Israel could defeat them again.[12] The widely held Arab belief that the 9/11 attacks were actually an American or Israeli deception reflect similar suspicions of conspiracy or duplicity.

Such arguments make three implausible contentions. They assume that democratically elected leaders are (1) so sociopathic that they willingly sacrifice thousands of their citizens just to achieve a policy advantage, but at the same time are (2) so foolhardy that they deliberately jeopardize and lose large portions of the armed forces they supposedly wanted to use for their nefarious purposes. Moreover, such arguments display a profound misunderstanding of government by believing that (3) the subordinates of the Machiavellian leader will neither take defensive action nor ever report their betrayal. Even in a Soviet Union wracked by Stalin's purges, the commanders of the Odessa Naval District and the Kiev Military District defied specific orders and alerted their forces on the eve of the German attack in 1941.[13] Conspiracy theories permit their authors to vent their anguish about an event that caused great suffering, but those theories lack explanatory or predictive value for serious students of history or intelligence.

The remaining school of thought regarding failures of warning is what Ben-Zvi labeled the cognitive-cybernetic one, which looks for reasons why analysts and decision makers would fail to draw appropriate conclusions from the available indications of surprise attack. Such reasons include but are not limited to Wohlstetter's signal-to-noise ratio, deliberate deception by the adversary (or self-deception by one's own government), preconceived notions, or confirmation bias, each of which has already been discussed in this study. These three categories of explanations, in conjunction with procedural and structural handicaps, provide the bulk of reasons for strategic warning failures in the cases that follow in this chapter.

One final caveat: for a policy maker, accepting and acting upon an intelligence warning is rarely a no-cost or low-cost decision. As already suggested, such a decision may involve adverse consequences such as the political and budgetary cost of mobilizing or the personal cost of modifying or abandoning a cherished policy. Thus even when the decision maker is not the prisoner of his or her misconceptions, that official may be tempted to risk surprise when the warning appears to be ambiguous or uncertain. Once again, the leader's poor opinion of his or her intelligence services can adversely affect the efficacy of warning from intelligence organs. The same issue reinforces the necessity of the analyst being clear and persuasive.

Indications and Warning Methodology

This chapter does not pretend to be a detailed study of the issues of strategic warning. Indeed, many of the classic examples of intelligence failure occurred before formal procedures for warning were developed. A brief description of the American procedure, however, may be useful before considering the case studies.

Beginning in 1949, and with a major impetus after the two Korean "surprises" of 1950 (see below), the U.S. intelligence community evolved a joint committee to monitor emerging threats. Weekly committee meetings and eventually standing organizations attempted, with varying degrees of success, to identify threats and provide warning to policy makers.[14]

Throughout the 1950s, the IC struggled to overcome internal differences and develop analytical processes for warning. The indications and warning (I&W) procedures that emerged were the central mechanism of current intelligence analysis and warning efforts for half a century. At its core, the I&W methodology first attempted to identify a series of possible threat events, referred to as "warning problems," such as hostilities between country A and country B; within each problem, in turn, there might be various possible eventualities, ranging from accidental clashes to surprise attack to gradual escalation. For each such problem, then, one can project various events or preparations that might occur prior to the threat event, and then try to define visible intelligence indicators that those events or preparations have occurred. Such indicators might include heightened propaganda, increased infiltration of armed agents, movement of troops to specific attack positions, or a maintenance stand-down to bring armed forces to a high state of readiness. Detecting evidence of each such event can be termed an *indication* that a particular *indicator* is active; dozens or perhaps hundreds of indicators, whether political/diplomatic, military, economic, or information, may be involved in any given warning problem. Rather than waiting for a single, unambiguous sign of aggressive intent, the cumulative impression of multiple such indications should help analysts and leaders alike to gauge the likelihood of attack.

As described in chapter 5, the President's Board of Consultants on Foreign Intelligence Activities (PBCFIA) under Eisenhower provided the bureaucratic impetus to implement this methodology. At the same time, the board hastened the development of procedures to prioritize warning communications related to the indicators.[15] NSCID 7 assigned to the Defense Department the task of creating a worldwide system to pass critical intelligence rapidly, but the president explicitly wanted DCI Allen Dulles to coordinate the effort. The Intelligence Advisory Committee therefore established a subcommittee on critical communications to develop the system.[16] After much debate, the so-called CRITIC system went into effect in July 1958. Officially, CRITIC was a message address group to dispatch warnings to operational and intelligence agencies.[17] In practice, however, the term "CRITIC" came to be regarded as a designation for intelligence reports that would receive the highest priority in a crowded communications system.

Urged on by the president, the Defense Department, working with the DCI, conducted tests to ensure rapid transmission of CRITICs. Not surprisingly, these tests indicated that messages transmitted over dedicated signals intelligence channels were much faster than those sent through the general communications system; one 1959 test found that the average transmission time for the former was 40 minutes, while for the latter it was 173 minutes. Both times were too slow in an era of intercontinental missiles. To expedite matters, the Defense Department began to replace its teletypes at all major nodes with newer machines that worked at the then-impressive rate of one hundred words per minute.[18]

While every intelligence analyst should be alert for warning indications, some intelligence agencies experimented with designating specific individuals to focus on the possibility of surprise. There was even a designated national intelligence officer for warning from 1979 to 2011.

There are obvious limitations with this or any I&W system, which sought to institutionalize an approach to unforeseen events—the logical equivalent of trying to establish bureaucratic procedures to ensure creativity and spontaneity. A threat might be so unusual that it was not identified and codified as a warning problem. In an era of potential nuclear annihilation, achieving speed in the transmission of indications also meant accepting the possibility of false alarms. To make the system function, junior special security and intelligence officers had to take the initiative, sending out raw reports that sometimes proved to be erroneous. Those who worked in the intelligence community during the Cold War can easily recall such false alarms, which necessitated considerable explanations to decision makers.

Moreover, the I&W methodology worked best for traditional warning of surprise attack between states, whereas recent instances of radical terrorism are much more difficult to predict. Above all, neither this nor any other warning system can work if the decision makers do not listen to the agencies or the evidence. Of course those decision makers have other sources of information as well as their own judgment, but the best analysts in the world may sometimes fail to convey warning to an unreceptive audience. Nevertheless, despite its limitations, this methodology offers a useful framework for examining the events leading to a crisis.

Operation Barbarossa, June 22, 1941

In August 1939, Germany and the Soviet Union signed the Molotov-Ribbentrop Pact, a series of agreements that in effect divided Eastern Europe into spheres of influence. After years of rhetoric against German aggression, Joseph Stalin and his government concluded that Britain,

France, and Poland were still unwilling to ally with the USSR against Adolf Hitler. Therefore, Moscow agreed to a temporary arrangement with Berlin. Stalin anticipated that continued German expansionism would lead to a prolonged struggle in the west—a struggle that would both weaken and delay the eventual German confrontation with the Soviet Union.[19] Much to Stalin's surprise, however, Germany defeated France and the Low Countries in less than sixty days during May–June 1940. Only Great Britain, weak and isolated, remained at war with Hitler, and the threat to the USSR reappeared with a vengeance less than a year after the Molotov-Ribbentrop Pact had supposedly defused the issue.

Despite the great purges of the later 1930s, the Soviet intelligence apparatus was neither deaf nor blind to this threat nor to the preparations leading up to Barbarossa. Based solely on Western sources, Barton Whaley identified eighty-four "warnings"—most of which were really groups of intelligence indications—of German preparation to invade. Just one of these "warnings" included more than three hundred reconnaissance overflights of Soviet territory. Soviet border troops reported a rising tide of line crossers and agent infiltrations.[20] Since Whaley's landmark study in 1973, access to Soviet archives has documented additional indications. Between July 1940 and June 1941, the German armed forces generated, and Soviet intelligence structures gathered, hundreds of indications of the coming offensive. Based on reports from communists who worked on German railroads, the transport directorate of the Soviet Internal Affairs Commissariat (NKVD) collected numerous instances of German railway movements concentrating troops and supplies opposite the USSR. Working from Soviet embassies throughout Europe, the military and political intelligence (GRU and NKVD) residents identified many indications of German preparations and intent to invade.[21] Using stolen codebooks, Soviet intelligence decrypted the communications of various European governments, although diplomatic messages rarely indicated the true intentions of an aggressive power.[22] Clearly, then, the Soviet intelligence failure lay not in the collection of indications but rather in their interpretation.

There were several weaknesses in Soviet interpretation. First, the great purges had emasculated Soviet intelligence organizations, imprisoning or executing experienced analysts and leaders.[23] General Filipp Golikov, a line officer with little intelligence experience, became the seventh head of the GRU in five years when he took over that agency in mid-1940.[24] Such inexperience made it difficult for the Soviets to overcome the signal-to-noise issue. Germany also propagated several deception stories to explain its troop concentration in the east. The most prominent such legend was that Germany was training troops in the east, beyond the range of British reconnaissance flights, for the coming invasion of the United Kingdom (Operation Sea Lion). Alternative cover narratives included German precautions against Soviet attack and the possibility that these troop concentrations were to support an ultimatum demanding limited concessions from Moscow.[25]

In addition to deliberate deceptions, genuine indications often provided "noise" that confused the defenders. The German invasion of the Balkans delayed Barbarossa from its original date of May 15, so that warnings that included that date were discredited when it passed without incident.[26] Britain, the United States, and other governments attempted to warn Moscow of the impending German attack, but Joseph Stalin rightly suspected those governments of trying to get the USSR involved in a war with Germany.[27]

Indeed, the principal reason for Soviet intelligence failure was Stalin. Contrary to legend, Stalin was far too paranoid to trust Nazi Germany's promises in the 1939 Molotov-Ribbentrop Pact; he knew that in the long run, conflict was inevitable, although he had expected that France would delay and weaken Hitler for years. The Soviet dictator was generally aware of the damage that his purges had done to the armed forces, and he desperately sought to delay the confrontation until he could rebuild those forces. He reasoned that the Red Army would be much better prepared to fight in 1942 than in 1941.

Under such circumstances, Stalin apparently convinced himself that Hitler was too rational to attack the USSR before he had defeated Britain. Therefore, Soviet policy avoided confrontation while continuing to provide Germany with vital raw materials. Given Stalin's tendency literally to "shoot the messenger," General Golikov and other officials often shaded their reports, emphasizing alternative explanations that were more in keeping with the dictator's hopes. These officials failed at the last and most difficult step in strategic warning: convincing the decision maker to act. Viewed in this manner, Stalin's refusal to react to German provocations and his instructions to avoid confrontation make more sense, although ultimately he was tragically wrong.[28] The Soviet dictator was not the only government head to mistakenly assume that Hitler was a completely rational actor.

Pearl Harbor, December 7, 1941

Because of the inherent differences between naval and land warfare, the Japanese preparations to attack Pearl Harbor provided fewer operational and tactical indications than the German invasion of the USSR. No troop concentrations were necessary to attack Hawaii, and indeed the marshaling of Japanese amphibious units appeared to be in preparation for landings in Southeast Asia, not an attack on the United States. The American-British imposition of trade sanctions in July 1941 sharply reduced the number of Western vessels traveling to Japan and thereby limited opportunities for foreign civilians to collect information there. In mid-October, the U.S. Navy sought to avoid provocation by rerouting shipping to the South Pacific, which meant that the Japanese carrier task force (Kido Butai) encountered no one as it approached Hawaii from the northwest.[29] Traveling under radio listening silence behind a storm front, that task force offered no indications of its movement. In fact, because the Japanese navy changed its radio call signs on November 1 and again on December 1, American traffic analysts had not yet reidentified individual vessels by December 7. In any event, previous instances of listening silence had heralded the movement of Kido Butai southward to strike Indochina.[30] Even if the United States had possessed highly placed sources within the Tokyo government, Japanese operational security was so thorough that only the units directly involved received instructions concerning the nature of the attack on Hawaii.[31]

At the tactical level, American staff officers misunderstood the state of strategic alert, dismissing radar detection of the airstrike as it approached. When the destroyer USS *Ward* sank a midget submarine at the mouth of Pearl Harbor seventy minutes before the air attack, the peacetime naval procedures and communications could not alert other vessels in time.[32]

Under such circumstances, warning of the Japanese attack depended solely on the collection and interpretation of strategic indications, especially those provided by signals intelligence. But these messages had to first be intercepted, then forwarded (often by mail) to Washington, D.C., and finally translated, decrypted, and analyzed. By 1941, the United States had achieved only limited decryption of Japanese diplomatic messages, such as the Purple code, and even less success working with the Japanese naval operations code, which the U.S. Navy referred to as "JN-25b." Given the shortages of qualified personnel and equipment, the U.S. Army and Navy communications intelligence offices focused on decrypting Purple code messages, especially those related to ongoing negotiations in Washington, and devoted little effort to military codes.[33] The two offices shared the Purple decryption, alternating days as to which branch worked on messages. This, in combination with the restricted distribution list for their work, meant that few individuals read all the messages available in context and in "real time." It also meant that commanders in Hawaii received only intermittent notice of what such messages suggested. American leaders were aware that their negotiations with Japan had reached a stalemate in November, but even the Purple messages to destroy codebooks (the last to be decrypted on December 7) did not seem as dire at the time as they do in retrospect.

Apart from a few Japanese language experts, U.S. intelligence organizations resembled their Soviet counterparts in the inexperience of their leaders, who were often line officers seconded to intelligence late in their careers. The G2 staff officer in the Hawaiian Department headquarters had so little knowledge of the situation that he declined offers of intelligence reports from his counterpart in the War Department.[34] In October 1941, Rear Adm. Theodore S. Wilkinson, who had no previous experience in his new field, became the third head of ONI within a year.[35]

Under these circumstances, it fell to American political leaders, already distracted by the undeclared naval war in the Atlantic, to recognize that Japan was about to attack the Pacific Fleet. Like Stalin earlier that year, President Franklin Roosevelt engaged in "mirror-imaging" of his foe and concluded that Tokyo would seek to avoid an unwinnable war with the United States. The president thought of the forward deployment of the Pacific Fleet from San Diego to Hawaii as a deterrent rather than a vulnerability. He and his advisors concluded that Japan might, in fact, strike the Dutch East Indies or Malaya, and on November 27 the War and Navy Departments issued "war warnings" that focused on such options.[36]

Upon receipt of this message, Adm. Husband Kimmel, commander-in-chief of the U.S. Pacific Fleet, took what he considered to be appropriate precautions. He conferred with his aircraft carrier commander, Vice Adm. William Halsey, and his Army counterpart, Lt. Gen. Walter Short. They agreed to heighten the alert status for the forces in Pearl Harbor while two aircraft carriers ferried aircraft to reinforce Midway and Wake Islands, which appeared to be likely Japanese targets. The third fleet carrier in the Pacific was already en route to the west coast of the United States for maintenance.[37] Thus, again contrary to legend, the carriers were absent from Hawaii not by chance but precisely because the U.S. Navy was aware of a general threat. As for Hawaii itself, based on previous alerts Lieutenant General Short believed that sabotage was a more likely threat than direct enemy attack. Kimmel was already conducting defensive air reconnaissance, but he did not expand that reconnaissance northward. In short, the defenders took significant precautions, but anticipated the wrong type of attack at the wrong locations.

South Korea, June 25, 1950

The Japanese decision to surrender in August 1945 led to a scramble to occupy parts of its empire. On the Korean peninsula, the Soviet 25th Army occupied the northern half while the U.S. XXIV Corps moved into the south; the 38th parallel (38 degrees north longitude) became the arbitrary dividing line between the two zones. These great power forces gradually withdrew during 1947–49, leaving behind the pro-Soviet government of Kim Il-sung in the north and the more independent Republic of Korea (ROK) of Syngman Rhee (Yi Sung-man) in the south. Each was aggressively nationalistic and sought to unify the peninsula by force. Indeed, the United States deliberately limited the supply of heavy weapons to the ROK for fear that Syngman Rhee might attack the north.[38]

Beginning in April 1948 and continuing for the next two years, the ROK was torn apart by a bitter communist insurgency that cost the lives of 7,225 ROK soldiers and policemen, at least 30,000 civilians, and 3 American advisors.[39] Pyongyang not only supported this insurgency but also launched border raids of increasing frequency and size. The [North] Korean People's Army (NKPA) doubled in size between November 1949 and May 1950, acquiring propeller fighters and T-34 tanks from the Soviet Union while Red China transferred two veteran divisions of ethnic Koreans. The U.S. embassy and advisors in the ROK were aware of most of this increase but were divided on its meaning.[40]

Unlike the classic warning failures of 1941 and 1973, the invasion of South Korea was not a bolt from the blue but rather a gradual rise in tension and foreboding. In Japan, Douglas MacArthur's intelligence officer, Maj. Gen. Charles Willoughby, was incurably optimistic about the possibility of attack or invasion. Yet the strong possibility of war was evident.

The Truman administration was surprised for two reasons that had little to do with intelligence indications. First, most officials assumed that Moscow controlled the Pyongyang regime, and they saw no reason why Joseph Stalin would risk a war over an insignificant portion of Asia. Stalin did, in fact, retain a veto over the decision to go to war, but in reality Kim Il-sung had his own policy objectives and eventually persuaded Stalin and Mao Zedong to concur.[41]

Both sides during the Cold War frequently made this mistake of attributing greater control over allies than either superpower enjoyed. In the case of Korea, this misconception was compounded by the fact that the Truman administration was still trying to adjust to the strange geopolitics of the Cold War. That administration had concluded, correctly, that in a general war scenario any forces needed to defend Korea would be better used elsewhere. Yet general war had become too costly in the nuclear age, leaving unsettled the question of Korea's political significance in a limited conflict of the type that would dominate the new era. The Truman administration had not yet thought the implications through. In retrospect, Truman not only believed in the principle of stopping aggression, but also could not afford politically to let Korea fall after his critics had blamed him for "losing China" the previous year.[42]

Second, one may still contend that the nascent American intelligence community failed to provide unambiguous strategic warning to policy makers. Yet even if the national IC had been unhindered by MacArthur and Willoughby filtering tactical data, it is doubtful whether analysts could have persuaded political leaders to regard the possibility of an invasion as grounds to make a major policy shift.[43]

After the Great Depression and World War II, the Truman administration, and indeed the general public, wanted fewer expenditures and commitments overseas. The United States gave the ROK only limited economic and military aid as well as general expressions of support.

It would be unfair to blame such policies for encouraging North Korean aggression, but certainly the administration gave no indication that it would respond forcefully when Pyongyang invaded the ROK, because the administration had apparently never contemplated that eventuality. The real surprise of June 1950 was not the invasion of the ROK but the American response to that invasion—a response that startled both sides.

Chinese Intervention, November 1950

The ill-prepared U.S. and other UN forces suffered heavily during the first months of the Korean conflict and were almost pushed off the peninsula. In the process, however, the NKPA became overextended. On September 15, MacArthur cut off the NKPA supply lines by landing at Inchon on the west coast. This operation completely reversed the situation, and by early October MacArthur's UN forces were approaching the 38th parallel while the NKPA was in full retreat.

The original American objective had been to restore the previous dividing line, but tactical victory encouraged a desire to eliminate the threat by consolidating Korea under one government. Both Syngman Rhee and General MacArthur wanted to continue the advance, and so the UN force spread out across the much larger expanse of North Korea. If the Truman administration had learned the concept of a limited war, its Far East commander had not; MacArthur broadcast radio demands that the North Korean regime surrender unconditionally.

Traditional explanations of the resulting confrontation generally focus on what political scientists Alexander George and Richard Smoke have termed "a double failure of deterrence."[44] In this interpretation, each side tried to warn the other of the consequences of intervening in North Korea; China in particular is supposed to have attacked because U.S. and other UN forces ignored its diplomatic messages by approaching the Chinese border. The Truman administration thought it could avert Chinese concerns by repeated assurances that it would not cross the Yalu River, but that did not satisfy Beijing.[45] Although this makes sense in terms of deterrence theory, it ignores the reality that Mao Zedong wanted to intervene as soon as the United States involved itself in the conflict.[46]

From Mao's viewpoint, the United States had already interfered in the Chinese revolutionary conflict by preventing the final defeat of the nationalist Chinese on Formosa/Taiwan. Now the United States had intruded into the *Korean* revolutionary civil war; success in that war might embolden the United States throughout East Asia, endangering Chinese national security. Moreover, Mao believed that Chinese intervention in Korea would improve the standing of his revolutionary state as the dominant power in the region. Thus, on July 7, 1950, at a time when the United States was retreating southward in front of the NKPA, the Chinese Military Commission ordered the assembly of 255,000 troops on the Manchurian-Korean border. Several hundred thousand additional troops joined them later. This was far more than a precautionary measure; the Beijing regime assigned captured former nationalist officers, who had received military training from American advisors during World War II, to join that border force and teach it how the American Army fought.[47] All this happened *before* the Inchon landing made it possible for the United States to invade North Korea and threaten the Manchurian border.

Given that Mao was prepared to intervene, why did he delay so long? Three different factors, two of which were hidden at the time, caused him to stay his hand. First, much of the collective leadership of the Chinese Communist Party was dismayed by the prospect of a new war so soon after they had finished their own decades-long civil conflict. Therefore, Mao had to convince his colleagues that he had tried all reasonable alternatives before attacking. He eventually adopted the transparent fiction that the huge intervention force was not part of the Chinese army but had rather "volunteered" en masse to fight in Korea. Second, while by no means a Soviet puppet, Mao understandably wanted Stalin's weapons and aid to support such a war. In early October, the Soviet dictator had second thoughts about the risks of a confrontation in Korea. On October 12, Mao paused the infiltration of troops into North Korea, both to appease his politburo and to put pressure on Moscow. Two days later, Stalin agreed to dispatch sixteen air regiments with combat veteran pilots to Manchuria, although he still restricted their use to North Korean airspace. Only after this Soviet decision did Mao commit the assembled frontier force to move across the Yalu River.[48]

The third factor is based on conjecture but offers the best explanation of the sequence of events. Throughout the Chinese Civil War, the communist strength of popular support from the people had to compensate for a severe weakness in logistics. Although the Red Chinese Army possessed and used a considerable number of trucks (which the UN air forces attacked as soon as they entered Korea), that army lacked the robust logistical support necessary to project power outside of areas where it had popular support to provide not only food, but also care of the wounded and oxcarts for tactical transport. Much of this support was missing in Korea, and indeed Chinese logistical weakness was a principal reason why the Chinese "volunteers," like the NKPA before them, had insufficient combat power to push their opponents off the peninsula. Moreover, once the Chinese advanced beyond the limited air umbrella provided by the Soviet and Chinese air forces, their tenuous supply lines would be vulnerable to air interdiction, even if not as vulnerable as Westernized transport might have been.

In the conventional, Western-oriented minds of MacArthur and his subordinates, any Chinese intervention should have occurred as far south as possible, to permit the Chinese to maneuver and expel the invaders. To apply that logic to the hybrid Chinese communist supply system was an instance of mirror-imaging, however; the closer the invaders came to the Yalu River, the easier communist logistics would become.

Thus, the opposing sides looked past each other. MacArthur's focus on absolute victory eventually dragged the U.S. government along with him; once committed to that vision, the Truman administration was unwilling to abandon it, and in fact did not do so even when the Chinese attacked.[49] No amount of strategic intelligence warning could have overcome that single-minded focus on a settled policy.

At the operational and tactical levels, there was still ample opportunity for intelligence warning to minimize the exposure of scattered UN forces. The first Chinese attacks, focused against ROK units because they were weaker, came on October 25, 1950, four weeks before the main "Chinese intervention" finally got strategic attention. The 6th ROK Division lost most of its combat power in five days. On November 1–6, elements of multiple Chinese divisions also struck the U.S. 1st Cavalry and 7th Infantry Divisions. While some have argued that this was a final "warning" from Beijing, it is more likely that the Chinese commander intended to give the invaders a bloody nose, causing them to pause while the rest of the Chinese forces entered Korea. Having attacked suddenly, these troops disappeared just as abruptly after November 6. Yet captured prisoners made no secret of their units or locations in Korea; by November 4 these prisoners had identified sixteen different divisions.[50] MacArthur and his G2, Willoughby, failed to draw the correct conclusion and take precautions against the coming assault.

Cuba, September–October 1962, and Tet, January 1968

Two other Cold War events, where the extent of surprise and intelligence failure are debated, deserve consideration. The roots of the Cuban Missile Crisis lie not only in the failed landing at the Bay of Pigs but also in the struggling Soviet missile program. Despite the propaganda success of launching the first satellite (Sputnik) in October 1957, the Soviets soon lagged behind the Americans in developing reliable intercontinental ballistic missiles (ICBMs). On October 24, 1960, an experimental R-16 ICBM exploded on its launchpad in Kazakhstan, killing most of the missile design team as well as the commander of Strategic Rocket Forces.[51] Nikita Khrushchev had reduced the conventional armed forces and tied his hopes for greater consumer goods to strategic missiles for deterrence, but his ICBM program was a failure. By early 1962, Khrushchev faced two problems: how to protect communist Cuba from American attack and how to build a nuclear deterrent until his engineers could develop a reliable ICBM.

Based on U-2 and other imagery, the National Photographic Interpretation Center (NPIC) was well aware of the deficiencies of Soviet missiles. Yet the American intelligence community had little to guide it to Khrushchev's solution to his problems, although in retrospect that solution was obvious. Shorter-range weapons, known as intermediate- or medium-range ballistic missiles, were relatively simple to design and build; by basing IRBMs and MRBMs in Cuba, Khrushchev thought he could both protect the Castro regime and create an effective substitute for ICBMs.[52] In his mind, this basing was equivalent to the U.S. deployment of Jupiter MRBMs in Turkey in 1961, although the Kennedy administration illogically considered the Cuban deployment much more provocative. Khrushchev expected to present President Kennedy with a fait accompli, apparently not caring that such a humiliation would force the young president to react strongly to the Soviet move.[53]

Prior to this point, the Soviet Union had never deployed strategic weapons outside of its own borders, so Khrushchev's plan challenged the "collective wisdom" of the IC. Hundreds of Cuban exile reports spoke of the movement of large missiles within the island, but analysts noted that to the untrained eye an air defense missile would look very similar to an IRBM. The IC as a whole was therefore reluctant to cry wolf about the unlikely eventuality of nuclear-tipped missiles appearing on America's doorstep.[54]

This preconception, plus the distraction caused by the September 30 violent demonstrations against integrating the University of Mississippi, may explain why the U.S. government became aware of the Cuban threat in two distinct halves. The first half was the Defense Department. On September 29, 1962, naval surveillance of Soviet freighters suggested that Il-28 medium bombers, which in some configurations could carry nuclear weapons, were being shipped to Cuba. The next day, a U-2 mission over western Cuba noted the presence of eight SA-2 firing batteries as well as a partially completed missile site near San Cristóbal. On October 1, 1962, Secretary McNamara and the JCS heard this information as part of their weekly meeting. An NPIC interpreter argued that the latter site had the same layout used in offensive missile sites within the USSR, even though no missiles were yet visible. McNamara recognized the offensive potential raised by this site as well as by the Il-28s. He instructed the Joint Chiefs to prepare for a number of contingencies, ranging from blockade to air strikes to invasion. The next day, he followed up with a detailed memorandum listing six possible developments that might require military action against Cuba; one of these contingencies was the presence of Soviet offensive weapons on the island. Without ordering any specific operation, McNamara's directives placed the military on notice to prepare for war within the next three weeks.[55]

As a result of McNamara's decisions, the Department of Defense began a major buildup in Florida, Georgia, and at sea near Cuba. Two weeks later, on October 14, another U-2 overflight showed completed IRBM and MRBM sites, at which point the White House began the intensive planning and negotiations that are usually described as the Cuban missile crisis. Most studies of intelligence in 1962 focus on this second iteration, two weeks after the Defense Department began to mobilize, as evidence of an intelligence failure. Instead, the fact that the Defense Department was operating on a different schedule with different, warlike guidance from McNamara—guidance that was not formally canceled—goes far to explain the alleged "warmongering" of the Joint Chiefs of Staff during the crisis.[56]

More than five years later, the United States was deeply involved in Vietnam, stuck in an apparent stalemate with North Vietnam. The older generation of Vietnamese communists, including Ho Chi Minh and Vo Nguyen Giap, counseled caution, but the actual leader in the north was Le Duan, who believed correctly that the United States could not sustain its effort indefinitely with so much domestic dissent. Le Duan pushed his concept of a major southern uprising through the party and government hierarchy.[57] In retrospect, Le Duan's belief that the South Vietnamese would rise up in this way was if anything more unrealistic than the American assessment of the war, but his failed attempt had significant consequences.

In the fall of 1967, captured documents gave the United States and its allies considerable indications of an impending communist offensive of unprecedented scope. Party guidance to cadre members seemed to be reaching for a new level of complexity regarding the integration of different arms and headquarters. General Westmoreland was sufficiently concerned about the possibility of such an offensive that he accompanied the Vietnamese chief of staff to ask President Nguyen Van Thieu for cancellation of the traditional Vietnamese stand-down during the Tet religious new year of 1968; Westmoreland had already canceled the truce for American forces.[58]

To this extent, then, intelligence convinced the field commander to take some precautions. Nonetheless, Westmoreland was caught out at the operational level. He was successfully distracted by the North Vietnamese siege of Khe Sanh, which functioned as a major diversion to draw troops away from Saigon. By contrast, one of his corps commanders, Gen. Fred Weyand, was convinced by enemy shifts in boundaries that the United States needed to concentrate in the Saigon area.[59]

The real problem was at the strategic level, where the Johnson administration sought to convince the American public that the war was developing in the correct direction. Westmoreland, who believed that journalists had distorted recent developments in South Vietnam, tried to counter these journalists. He therefore cooperated with the administration in making optimistic public statements in late 1967, trying to reassure America (the famous phrase, "light at the end of the tunnel"). It was the contrast between such optimism and the unexpected urban offensive of Tet that caused the Johnson administration itself, more than the American public, to overreact politically to an offensive that was actually a military failure for Hanoi.[60] Westmoreland's well-intentioned public speeches contributed to a strategic surprise despite tactical warning.

Yom Kippur War, October 6, 1973

Israel's surprise at the start of the 1973 conflict had its roots in the Six-Day War of 1967. Gamal Abdel Nasser had provoked Israeli attack by a number of ill-considered gestures, most obviously a demand that the UN remove its Sinai buffer force that had separated the two antagonists since late 1956. Because the Egyptian Air Force launched its aircraft early each morning as a precaution, on June 5, 1967, the Israel Air Force (IAF) waited until 7:45 a.m. local time to attack the Egyptian air bases, catching their aircraft on the ground for refueling. Having seized the initiative and achieved air superiority, Israel was then able to exploit Egyptian command errors and win the war rapidly.

This set the metric for victory for both sides. Israel understandably felt an immense level of confidence in fighting the Arab states, not recognizing that those states would do better, and Israel worse, in a conflict where the Arabs rather than the Israelis held the initiative. Having never experienced operational surprise, the Israel Defense Forces (IDF) confidently expected to get advance warning of attack and, failing that, to absorb and respond to any surprise.[61] As previously noted, Israeli analysts and military leaders had a preconceived notion, sometimes known as "the conception," that "Egypt would not launch war against Israel before she had first ensured sufficient air power to attack Israel in depth and in particular Israel's principal airfields, so as to paralyse the Israel air force."[62]

This conception was part of a larger problem of mirror-imaging, assuming that the Arabs would analyze the situation in strictly Western terms and not attack unless they could win total victory by Israeli definitions. Yet the Arab states could survive losing another war while Israel could not.[63] Given Tel Aviv's refusal to withdraw from the occupied territories until a complete peace was negotiated, Anwar Sadat and other Egyptians began to consider a limited war that, even if it ended in another defeat, would strike a psychological blow while demonstrating that Israel could not continue to occupy those territories indefinitely.[64]

In 1971, the British Joint Intelligence Committee staff produced a prescient analysis, proposing that Sadat might bring diplomatic pressure on the United States, and through it on Israel, by conducting a limited military action, under cover of the integrated air defense envelope established over the Suez Canal with Soviet-supplied missiles. Two years later, the British defense attaché in Cairo suggested that the Egyptians might only advance twelve kilometers east of the Suez Canal as a means of forcing negotiations. In the United States, State Department INR and National Security Council staffers also thought, more vaguely, that the Egyptian ruler would risk a war to break the diplomatic stalemate.[65] Overall, however, most Western officials and analysts deferred to their Israeli counterparts about likely Arab actions. Perhaps the single greatest factor in causing surprise was that almost all analysts had bought into the preconceived ideas of senior Israeli leaders. At the very least, such assumptions needed to be explicit rather than implicit. This is yet another illustration of the dangers of intelligence analysts identifying themselves too closely with the operators and decision makers. One Israeli commentator later noted that the 1973 warning failure "vividly illustrates the disastrous consequences that excessive domination by the political leadership can have."[66]

The Israeli "conception," in combination with contempt for its foes, also meant that soldiers and analysts underestimated Egyptian capabilities. Measured against the impossibly high standard of an Arab total victory over Israel and the low performance of the Arab armies in 1967, it was easy to believe that the Egyptians were incapable of operating their newly acquired Soviet weapons at any level. Israel estimated that Egyptian engineers would take twice as long as they actually needed to bridge the Suez Canal. In this respect, Sadat's expulsion of Soviet advisors in July 1971 seemed to make Egypt less ready for war, on the assumption that the Egyptians were incapable of fighting without foreign experts. In fact, the expulsion eliminated any Soviet control over the Arab state.[67]

In fairness to Israeli leaders, one must recognize a major diplomatic factor that hampered their perceptions in 1973. Having been the immediate initiator of war in 1956 and 1967, the Tel Aviv government feared that a third pre-emptive attack, however justified it might be, would cost it the support of the United States and other Western states. Thus Israeli concerns about war focused not on the possibility of their military defeat but rather on the risks of overreaction and escalation.[68] As previously noted, the warning crisis in the late spring of 1973 also made Israeli leaders reluctant to mobilize again in October. This is illustrated by the fact that Defense Minister Moshe Dayan put all Israeli regular forces on their highest state of alert on October 5, at a time when intelligence estimates rated the possibility of war as very low, but the next day the cabinet still hesitated about full mobilization, and Prime Minister Golda Meir forbade preemptive air strikes.[69] It is easy for an analyst or academic to agree with strategic theory expert Michael Handel that when in doubt one should always mobilize as a precaution.[70] In the real world, however, the economic, political, and diplomatic costs of such a reaction will encourage decision makers to accept risks and delay even when analysts present a clear case for warning.

The 1967 defeat gave Egypt the political impetus to do what Israel avoided. At enormous expense to the Egyptian economy, the government operated on a semiwartime footing from 1967 onward, notably improving the quality and cohesion of Egyptian military units.[71] Serious self-examination prompted many Arab military and political leaders to rethink their methods of planning and operation. The prolonged state of near war also permitted the Egyptians to desensitize Israeli observers by constant alerts that came to nothing. In the months leading up to the attack, the Egyptians held numerous exercises and twenty-two reserve mobilizations.[72] These apparent false alarms played into the conventional wisdom of Western intelligence agencies that Arab governments often engaged in heightened rhetoric but did little to implement that rhetoric.[73]

In terms of intelligence indications, in early October a few analysts in the IDF Northern and Southern Commands were quite concerned about the possibility of attack, while the national-level Directorate of Military Intelligence (DMI) was trapped in the labyrinth of the "conception." Yet even the career intelligence analysts did not re-evaluate their assumptions. Of equal seriousness is the fact that the nonintelligence line officer who headed DMI thought it was his responsibility to be the final arbiter on all intelligence estimates and sought to avoid troubling the chief of staff with complex or uncertain estimates. As a result, he did not acknowledge that war was imminent until 4:30 a.m. on the fatal day of October 6, 1973.[74] Even then, he projected, based on what made sense for the Egyptian front, that the attack would occur at 6:00 p.m. that day, giving Egypt the hours of darkness for bridge building. In reality, the Syrian and Egyptian planners had compromised on the unusual time of 2:00 p.m., halfway between their two preferred options of morning attack for Syria and evening for Egypt. Israeli commanders were still in final meetings when Arab artillery began firing.

There is an often-abused cliché to the effect that successful militaries prepare to fight the last war, while defeated armies are forced to reconsider the way they fight. That was largely the case in 1973, when mirror-imaging by decision makers and analysts alike meant that Arab capabilities and intentions were misunderstood. Once again, a supposed failure of intelligence was "not due to any dearth of information but to an incorrect evaluation of the available information."[75] In this instance, at any rate, only a minority of Western intelligence analysts identified the actual Arab course of action, and even they were largely ignored.

Assessment

This chapter paints a dismal track record of failing to identify and warn of coming strategic attacks. While intelligence analysts were by no means blameless, they often were unable to assemble the indications necessary to overcome preconceptions and convince the decision makers. In the case of Pearl Harbor, no one except the national decision makers saw all portions of the evidence in a timely manner, and those men lacked the time and the knowledge to interpret that evidence. Since then, the institutional development of intelligence has heightened the possibility that trained minds will be able to collect and interpolate the information, but that growth has been unable to overcome the preconceptions, mirror-imaging, enemy deceptions, and other barriers to warning. In this respect, chapter 6 has already argued that in the case of the 9/11 attacks, the intelligence community did notify decision makers of the strong probability of strategic surprise attack. Yet for reasons of both the inherent difficulty of collection against nonstate actors and the congressional barriers to all-source analysis of scattered data, the IC was unable to assemble indications that, *in retrospect*, would appear to clearly identify the place and methodology of attack. Indeed, the more radical an enemy course of action might be, such as the 1973 limited attack by Egypt, the more difficult it is for the defenders to correctly identify the enemy intent. In yet another paradox, the riskier an attack appears to the defender, the easier it is for that defender to overlook or misinterpret evidence that such an attack is imminent *because it seems so improbable*. The attacker who takes such a huge risk is more likely to achieve surprise than if he or she chooses a more cautious course of action.[76]

In summary, strategic warning represents the most serious and perhaps most difficult subproblem in the ongoing development of the operator-analyst relationship. When the IC successfully predicts and warns, the result is a nonevent. When, on the other hand, the government as a whole is surprised, the IC bears much of the responsibility, but that responsibility only contributes to decision maker distrust and disregard of the analysts in future assessments.

Chapter Eight

Conclusions

Operators and Analysts

The vast majority of interactions between intelligence and policy makers experience no more friction and misunderstandings than are typical of any group endeavor. Particularly in a democracy, most leaders understand the importance of building consensus and tolerating disagreement. In this regard, the American intelligence community has reached a level of professionalism and institutional maturity that enables it to perform its mission superbly under normal circumstances. Moreover, in those instances where the IC fails to convince a policy maker of the correctness of an intelligence assessment, the analyst must accept a fair share of responsibility for any resulting surprise or failure.

Nonetheless, a sudden ascension of an outsider to the summit of a government can have adverse effects on all those involved. This is particularly true when an incoming administration recruits its policy makers from areas outside of the executive branches of national and state government. Most newly installed presidents, cabinet secretaries, or governors of large states try to adjust to their new positions without being, as some might put it, "co-opted by the bureaucracy." Regardless of their experience in legislatures, law offices, or businesses, few of these decision makers have developed the organizational leadership skills necessary to operate a large federal department or a state such as California, let alone the entire federal government. They are accustomed to seeing every major document that enters or leaves their office and to making every important decision either by themselves or in a restricted meeting with their partners. Donald Trump was surely not the first federal executive to be angered when he discovered that in the multifaceted government of a world power, even mid-level civilians and field-grade military officers simply must make decisions on their own authority, sometimes catching their superiors off guard despite efforts to keep those superiors informed. This has been true of the U.S. government since at least the 1860s, when the federal system expanded to conduct the Civil War and never completely returned to its previous size.

The so-called "deep state"[1] is not a partisan conspiracy to thwart the executive but rather a collection of talented and experienced individuals dedicated to defending the Constitution and executing the laws without partisanship or prejudice. These individuals have personal opinions about certain policies and may attempt to defend their agency's bureaucratic turf, but they sincerely believe that they are acting in the national interest, and they usually are. This is especially true when they feel required by law or the national interest to act in a manner that they know may anger their politically appointed or elected superiors.

Nowhere is this disconnect between private and public endeavors more apparent than in the intelligence community, where the flood of raw information threatens to overwhelm even the analysts who look at it twelve to fourteen hours each day—a flood that is largely invisible to the rest of the government. After a century of development, the IC is still striving for greater integration and reliability, but its efforts, however imperfect, usually provide a valuable perspective on the world and how U.S. policies may interact with that world. Whatever it may look like to outsiders, the finished products of the IC are not just "CNN with secrets" or "connecting the dots."

Enter the preconceived notion, or what Matthew Wahlert termed "motivated bias." It is human nature to resist contrarian evaluations of events and expect that your preferred course of action will succeed. Closely related to that expectation is a desire to have positive feedback—to have those around you enthusiastically support both you and the mission as you have defined it. It is a commonplace occurrence for business managers and military leaders to demand that once a decision is made, all dissent cease and everyone work to implement the decision. Yet to insist upon that change in attitude from intelligence, to pressure the IC into conceding that the manager "could" be correct, defeats the purpose of having professional intelligence to begin with. It is entirely appropriate to ask analysts to explain their reasoning in detail, which is yet another reason not to have senior managers conducting daily briefings to their principals! It is a completely different and inappropriate action to tell the analysts, "You're wrong; go try again," rejecting their assessments out of hand.

Intelligence analysts, like other government officials, need to understand the decision maker's policies and goals, but understanding is not the same as embracing those policies and goals. Blindly accepting the assumptions and worldview of the leader leads to biased intelligence, such as the Soviet misinterpretations of Germany in 1941 or the Israeli mirror-imaging of Egypt in 1973.

Subversion and Special Operations

Even if the analysts avoid "drinking the Kool-Aid" of an administration's belief system, the history of intelligence institutions both in Europe and America indicates strong tendencies toward partisanship, seeking to suppress subversion at home and conduct covert actions to "punish" opponents abroad. This is another instance where the decision maker or operator identifies so closely with his or her policy as to regard opposition to that policy as a threat to the state. Because of the distorting power of being in office, responsible leaders must approach both countersubversion and foreign covert action with great caution.

Externally, covert and special operations are a necessary option in the toolbox of any state, but simply possessing the capability for such operations offers a constant temptation to substitute a "simple, quick" covert operation for more complicated, expensive, and appropriate efforts using diplomatic, informational, economic, and military power (in roughly that order of preference). Continuing the toolbox analogy, let us recall the cliché that "when all you have is a hammer, every problem looks like a nail." Whether spending money to influence a foreign election or deploying special operators to attack terrorists, such actions risk serious negative outcomes while diverting part of the intelligence community from its primary mission of reducing uncertainty through informed analysis. Oftentimes, the "hammer" of covert action, like the even larger hammer of military intervention, is simply the wrong tool for the task at hand. Before using that or any other tool, the cautious executive seeks a multitude of input. Senior intelligence leaders, along with diplomatic and military experts, can offer valuable context and identify the pitfalls of a particular action. Wise decision makers should strive to keep such expert advice untainted by preconceived notions and partisan support for a particular policy or course of action.

A government also needs the capability to identify and thwart espionage, sabotage, and subversion within its borders. Historically, much of this subversion was based on radical ideologies—religion, socialism, republicanism, anarchism, Marxism, and secessionist nationalism—that gave those in power the perception that such ideologies were an existential threat to their state and society. While sometimes necessary, countering such threats often jeopardizes the civil liberties the government is supposed to protect. Because of these factors, domestic surveillance requires oversight by inspectors-general as well as by Congress and the judiciary.

Politicization and Professionalism

Effective government *always* needs a sophisticated analysis of the capabilities and intentions of other actors. Such analysis is particularly valuable when it is irksome, when it identifies dangers and opportunities in a manner that does not accord with the decision maker's own view of the situation. A leader who wants a Greek chorus that always agrees with him or her should look to political followers rather than to the intelligence arm, although even campaign managers often impart unpleasant truths.

There is a link, perhaps unconscious, between politicizing intelligence executives and relying on intelligence assets to achieve domestic and foreign policy goals. The conscientious intelligence executive seeks to present his or her decision maker with analysis that is not only accurate and useful but also persuasive. Yet such a presentation may become an exercise in frustration, confronting the leader with an intractable, complex issue that lacks clear-cut solutions. The natural tendency on both sides is to think of ways that the existing intelligence capability, which has such a sophisticated understanding of an issue, might also help solve that issue. Sometimes such a solution is necessary and appropriate, but frequent decisions of this kind move the intelligence organization from the role of dispassionate analyst to that of partisan operator, whose view of reality is tied to a hoped-for outcome. Such a result is at best a slippery slope if not a looming abyss, leading to the German SD or Soviet KGB model where the intelligence structure becomes too biased to be effective at interpreting and predicting its opponents.

An unethical intelligence manager such as J. Edgar Hoover makes the situation even worse. The FBI director famously manipulated the "information" he presented to attorneys general and presidents as well as what he leaked to the press. Then, when a president authorized questionable domestic surveillance of specific foreign groups, Hoover abused that authority to collect against other parts of the population engaged in legitimate dissent.[2] Only concern for the FBI's public reputation caused him to curb his crimes. This admittedly extreme example should provide sufficient justification to discourage responsible decision makers from wanting their intelligence leaders to become partisan politicians and thereby risk violating their oaths to the Constitution.

The leader has both the prerogative and the responsibility of deciding what version of reality is most accurate. Nonetheless, common sense suggests that such a leader should seriously consider a dissenting analysis presented by a staff group that is *not* invested in the success of a particular government policy. Insisting that the intelligence analysts must "get on the team" and "support our policy"—or still less become personally loyal to the boss—displays a fundamental misunderstanding of what intelligence can bring to the table. This is the logical equivalent of Joseph Stalin, Mao Zedong, and Big Brother, who, not content to control the destiny of their states, demanded that their defeated prisoners must recant and confess their intellectual errors, acknowledging that the dictator was always correct. Perhaps, in fact, this was another subconscious connection in the George W. Bush administration, this time between its enthusiasm for creating confirmation-biased "intelligence" and using the ineffective and immoral "interrogation" techniques of the Chinese communists to brainwash their radical adversaries.

To return to the Huntington model: For decades, the U.S. intelligence community has been ready to function as a profession in the sense of (1) conducting critical work on behalf of the nation using (2) an extensive body of education and experience while (3) holding its own members to high standards of ethics, performance, and security. In order for intelligence to function in this manner the civilian leaders of the government should recognize intelligence work as a profession, including appointing career members of the profession to head agencies and act as inspectors general and DNI. This does not eliminate the need for congressional and judicial oversight, of course, especially in matters of domestic surveillance that have a particular potential for legal or partisan abuse. Nonetheless, even in such instances, FBI agents and other counterintelligence officers have generally maintained very high standards of professionalism and respect for rights. Selectively auditing intelligence professionals while trusting them to do the right thing is far more effective in defending individual rights and collective security than is any system that tries to prohibit an entire class of action that might be necessary to anticipate enemy attack. "Trust" is the key word, and it comes back to Huntington's first concept: that society delegates to a group of dedicated professionals the responsibility of performing an important function on its behalf.

Notes

Chapter One. Professions and Professionalism

1. Quoted in Frank J. Smist Jr., *Congress Oversees the United States Intelligence Community, 1947–1989* (Knoxville: University of Tennessee Press, 1990), 100.
2. Robert Hutchinson, *German Foreign Intelligence from Hitler's War to the Cold War: Flawed Assumptions and Faulty Analysis* (Lawrence: University Press of Kansas, 2019), esp. 2–4, 66–75.
3. U.S. Department of the Army, Field Manual 30-5, *Combat Intelligence* (Washington: Government Printing Office, 1973), 2–1.
4. Samuel P. Huntington, *The Soldier and the State: The Theory and Politics of Civil-Military Relations* paperback ed. (New York: Vintage/Random House, 1957), 8–10.
5. Rear Admiral John H. Godfrey, the British director of naval intelligence 1939–42, concluded that as a practical matter, intelligence work required the skills of civilians rather than those of regular navy officers. Christopher Andrew, *Secret Service: The Making of the British Intelligence Community* (London: Heinemann, 1985), 455.
6. Stephen Marrin, "Training and Educating U.S. Intelligence Analysts," *International Journal of Intelligence and CounterIntelligence* 22:1 (Spring 2009): 131–46.
7. Bruce W. Bidwell, *History of the Military Intelligence Division, Department of the Army General Staff: 1775–1941* (Frederick, MD: University Publications of America, 1986), 2–8.
8. Charles D. Ameringer, *U.S. Foreign Intelligence: The Secret Side of American History* (Lexington, MA: Lexington Books, 1990), 37–39.
9. Antoine-Henri de Jomini, *The Art of War,* in *Roots of Strategy*, book 2, ed. J. D. Hittle (Harrisburg, PA: Stackpole Books, 1987), 529–38.
10. Andrew, *Secret Service*, 104, 106. A more lurid version of the same incident, not naming Jackson, appears in David Kahn, *The Codebreakers: The Story of Secret Writing* (New York: Macmillan, 1967), 272.

11. Huntington, *The Soldier and the State*, 72.
12. "The Weinberger Doctrine," *Washington Post*, Nov. 30, 1984, A18. See also David T. Twining, "The Weinberger Doctrine and the Use of Force in the Contemporary Era," in *The Recourse to War: An Appraisal of the "Weinberger Doctrine,"* ed. Alan N. Sabrosky and Robert L. Sloane (Carlisle, PA: Strategic Studies Institute, 1989), 11–12; and Walter LaFeber, "The Rise and Fall of Colin Powell and the Powell Doctrine," *Political Science Quarterly* 124:1 (Spring 2009): 71–93.
13. Huntington, *The Soldier and the State*, 78.
14. Ameringer, *U.S. Foreign Intelligence*, 378–79.
15. Smist, *Congress Oversees the United States Intelligence Community*, 119–23.
16. Alfred Cumming, "Statuatory Procedures under Which Congress Is to Be Informed of U.S. Intelligence Activities, Including Covert Actions," Congressional Research Service, Jan. 18, 2006.
17. Mary Thornton, "Secrecy Pledges Challenged Openly: Union Lawsuit Alleges Violation of Constitutional Rights," *Washington Post*, Sept. 2, 1987.

Chapter Two. The Intelligence Process

1. U.S. Department of the Army, Field Manual 30-5, *Combat Intelligence* (Washington: Government Printing Office, 1973), 2–14 to 2–15.
2. Richard J. Samuels, *Special Duty: A History of the Japanese Intelligence Community* (Ithaca, NY: Cornell University Press, 2019), 11.
3. Bruce D. Berkowitz and Allan E. Goodman, *Best Truth: Intelligence in the Information Age* (New Haven, CT: Yale University Press, 2000), x.
4. Mark M. Lowenthal, *Intelligence: From Secrets to Policy*, 4th ed. (Washington: CQ Press/Sage, 2009), 58–60.
5. Ross Bellaby, "What's the Harm? The Ethics of Intelligence Collection," *Intelligence and National Security* 27:1 (Feb. 2012): 109.
6. Christopher Andrew, *Defend the Realm: The Authorized History of MI5* (New York: Alfred A. Knopf, 2009), 402, 451, 589–90, 616–37, 658.
7. See Abraham Ben-Zvi, "American Preconceptions and Policies toward Japan, 1940–1941: A Case Study in Misperception," *International Studies Quarterly* 19:2 (June 1975): 235–44.
8. This example occurred to the author when looking at Cold War imagery to train as an imagery interpreter; only the presence of other engineer equipment at the same location justified identifying the object as a mine-laying plow.
9. Michael Herman, *Intelligence Power in Peace and War* (Cambridge: Cambridge University Press, 1996), 100–102.

10. Berkowitz and Goodman, *Best Truth*, 4–21.
11. In addition to the CIA, DIA, and INR, two other organizations are major players in IC discussions because of their wealth of information: the National Security Agency and the National Geospatial-Intelligence Agency. In my limited and perhaps dated experience, however, these agencies often focused their analysis directly on their specific collection capabilities more than on developing broader-gauge assessments.
12. Lowenthal, *Intelligence: From Secrets to Policy*, 124–27.
13. Steve Chan, "The Intelligence of Stupidity: Understanding Failures in Strategic Warning," *American Political Science Review* 73:1 (March 1974): 177–78.
14. A superb overview of this issue is Thomas Fingar, *Reducing Uncertainty: Intelligence Analysis and National Security* (Stanford, CA: Stanford University Press, 2011), esp. 33–53.
15. Fingar, *Reducing Uncertainty*, 33.
16. An earlier version of this description appeared in Jonathan M. House, *Military Intelligence, 1870–1991: A Research Guide* (Westport, CT: Greenwood Press, 1993), 20–21. In turn, that study used various sources, including Patrick Beesly, *Very Special Intelligence: The Story of the Admiralty's Operational Intelligence Centre 1939–1945* (New York: Ballantine Books, 1981); Anthony Cave Brown, *Bodyguard of Lies* (New York: Harper and Row, 1975); Harold C. Deutsch, "The Influence of ULTRA on World War II," *Parameters: Journal of the U.S. Army War College* 8:4 (Dec. 1978): 2–15; and Roger J. Spiller, "Assessing Ultra," *Military Review* 59:8 (Aug. 1979): 13–23.
17. For indications prior to the 1941 invasion, see David E. Murphy, *What Stalin Knew: The Enigma of Barbarossa* (New Haven, CT: Yale University Press, 2005), 116–20, 63–72; Barton Whaley, *Codeword Barbarossa* (Cambridge, MA: MIT Press, 1973), 30–34, 48; and Jonathan Haslam, *Near and Distant Neighbors: A New History of Soviet Intelligence* (New York: Farrar, Straus, and Giroux, 2015), 97–98.
18. Francis H. Hinsley, E. E. Thomas, C. F. G. Ransom, and R. C. Knight, *British Intelligence in the Second World War: Its Influence on Strategy and Operations*, vol. I (London: Her Majesty's Stationery Office, 1979), 144; Beesly, *Very Special Intelligence*, 110–13.
19. Hinsley et al., *British Intelligence in the Second World War*, vol. II, 582–87, 739–46, 757–63; Hugh Skillen, *Spies of the Airwaves: A History of Y Sections During the Second World War* (Pinner, England: privately printed, 1989), 88–202.

20. Robert Jervis, *How Statesmen Think: The Psychology of International Politics* (Princeton, NJ: Princeton University Press, 2017), 160.
21. Michelle Nichols, "Ex-CIA Chief Says 'Slam Dunk' Iraq Quote Misused," Reuters, April 26, 2007. Tenet later said he did not recall any such statement and believed that someone in the administration gave the story to a reporter to shift blame to him. George Tenet and Bill Harlow, *At the Center of the Storm: My Years at the CIA* (New York: HarperCollins, 2007), 479–85.
22. Office of the Director of National Intelligence, "The Terrorist: Threat to the U.S. Homeland," National Intelligence Estimate, July 17, 2007, 4.
23. Michael J. Adamski, "Enhancing the ODNI Analytic Standards: An Evolving Framework," *American Intelligence Journal* 29:1 (2011): 116.
24. U.S. Code of Federal Regulations (CFR), 18 CFR § 3a.11, Classification of official information.
25. Christopher Andrew, *Secret Service: The Making of the British Intelligence Community* (London: Heinemann, 1985), 330–32. Negligent Soviet security officers sometimes compromised the security of one-time codes by reusing the same code sheet on another occasion.

Chapter Three. The Operator-Analyst Interface

1. Thucydides, *The Landmark Thucydides: A Comprehensive Guide to the Peloponnesian War*, ed. Robert B. Strassler (New York: Free Press, 1996), 4.108[4], 282.
2. Quoted in Kevin M. Woods et al., *The Iraqi Perspectives Report: Saddam's Senior Leadership on Operation Iraqi Freedom from the Official U.S. Joint Forces Command Report* (Annapolis, MD: Naval Institute Press, 2006), 12.
3. Martin Petersen, "What I Learned in 40 Years of Doing Intelligence Analysis for U.S. Foreign Policy Makers," *Studies in Intelligence* 55:1 (March 2011): 13–20.
4. Mark M. Lowenthal, *Intelligence: From Secrets to Policy*, 4th ed. (Washington: CQ Press/Sage, 2009), 186.
5. Matthew H. Wahlert, "The 'Motivated Bias' Dilemma in Warfare and Intelligence," *Defense & Security Analysis* 28:3 (Sep. 2012): 247–59.
6. Keren Yarhi-Milo, *Knowing the Adversary: Leaders, Intelligence, and Assessment of Intentions in International Relations* (Princeton, NJ: Princeton University Press, 2014), 45.
7. Roberta Wohlstetter, *Pearl Harbor: Warning and Decision* (Stanford, CA: Stanford University Press, 1982), 3, 197, quotation 387.

8. David H. Petraeus, "Lessons of History and Lessons of Vietnam," *Parameters: Journal of the U.S. Army War College* 16:3 (Autumn 1986): 43–53.
9. Douglas Porch, *The French Secret Services: From the Dreyfus Affair to the Gulf War* (New York: Farrar, Straus, and Giroux, 1995), 70.
10. See, for example, Ahron Bregman, *Israel's Wars: A History Since 1947*, 2nd ed. (London: Routledge, 2002), 114.
11. Saad el Shazly, *The Crossing of the Suez*, rev. ed. (San Francisco: American Mideast Research, 2003), 18–48.
12. Yarhi-Milo, *Knowing the Adversary*, 47–55.
13. Bryon D. Mushrush, "Improved Intelligence Warning in an Age of Complexity," research monograph, School for Advanced Military Studies (Fort Leavenworth, KS: U.S. Army Command and General Staff College, 2015), 17–18.
14. Richard J. Samuels, *Special Duty: A History of the Japanese Intelligence Community* (Ithaca, NY: Cornell University Press, 2019), 46.
15. Horst Borg, "German Air Intelligence in World War II," *Aerospace Historian* 33:2 (Summer 1986): 121–29; Horst Borg, "German Air Intelligence in the Second World War," *Intelligence and National Security* 5:2 (April 1990): 350–424.
16. Richard D. White Jr., "George Tenet and the Last Great Days of the CIA," *Public Administration Review* 68:3 (June 2008): 423, 425; James Risen, *State of War: The Secret History of the CIA and the Bush Administration* (New York: Free Press, 2006), 17–18.
17. U.S. Commission on the Intelligence Capabilities of the United States Regarding Weapons of Mass Destruction, *Report to the President of the United States, March 31, 2005* (Washington: Government Printing Office, 2005), cover letter, p. 3.
18. Samuels, *Special Duty*, 244.
19. Herbert R. McMaster, *Dereliction of Duty: Lyndon Johnson, Robert McNamara, the Joint Chiefs of Staff, and the Lies that Led to Vietnam* (New York: HarperCollins, 1997), 58.
20. Edward J. Drea, *McNamara, Clifford, and the Burdens of Vietnam: 1965–1969.* Secretaries of Defense Historical Series, vol. VI (Washington: Historical Office, Office of the Secretary of Defense, 2011), 63–64. See also the more ambivalent assessment of May 3, 1965, by the Board of National Estimates, Memorandum 5-3-65. Subject: Consequences of a Pause in Bombings of the DRV, CIA FOIA Reading Room, the Vietnam Collection.
21. United Nations Security Council Resolution 687, 1991.
22. UNSCOM, "Thirteenth Quarterly Report of the Executive Chairman of the United Nations Monitoring, Verification and Inspection Commission

in Accordance with Paragraph 12 of Security Council Resolution 1284 (1999)," UN Security Council document S/2003/580, dated May 30, 2003, 40, https://www.un.org/Depts/unmovic/documents/S-2003-580.pdf, accessed March 26, 2021.

23. See, for example, Charles Duelfer, *Hide and Seek: The Search for Truth in Iraq* (New York: Public Affairs/Perseus Group, 2009), 77–161.
24. Beth Bailey and Richard H. Immerman, eds., *Understanding the U.S. Wars in Iraq and Afghanistan* (New York: New York University Press, 2015), 86.
25. See, for example, David Hannay, "Three Iraq Intelligence Failures Reconsidered," *Survival* 51:6 (Dec. 2009–Jan. 2010): 15–16.
26. Robert Jervis, *Why Intelligence Fails: Lessons from the Iranian Revolution and the Iraq War* (Ithaca, NY: Cornell University Press, 2010), 148.
27. Woods et al., *The Iraqi Perspectives Report*, 92–93, 41–42.
28. According to Khidir Hamza, one of the Iraqi nuclear scientists, part of the Iraqi nuclear weapons program continued to operate under cover in the immediate aftermath of Desert Storm. Hamza, however, defected in 1994, making it difficult for him to document continued nuclear research after that date. Khidir Hamza with Jeff Stein, *Saddam's Bombmaker: The Terrifying Inside Story of the Iraqi Nuclear and Biological Weapons Agenda* (New York: Scribner, 2000), 258–62.
29. UNSCOM, "Thirteenth Quarterly Report of the Executive Chairman," 5.
30. Woods et al., *The Iraqi Perspectives Report*, 95.
31. See, for example, the Defense Department news release by Linda D. Kozaryn, "Patrolling Iraq's Northern Skies," June 1, 1998, http://www.defense.gov/news/newsarticle.aspx?id=43185, accessed June 7, 2014.
32. Independent Inquiry Committee into the United Nations Oil-for-Food Programme, Paul A. Volcker, chair, "Manipulation of the Oil-for-Food Programme by the Iraqi Regime," October 27, 2005, https://web.archive.org/web/20130823070841/http://www.iic-offp.org/documents/IIC%20Final%20Report%2027Oct2005.pdf, accessed March 26, 2021.
33. Samuel Helfont, *Compulsion in Religion: Saddam Hussein, Islam, and the Roots of Insurgencies in Iraq* (New York: Oxford University Press, 2018), 24, 54, 67.
34. White House Press Secretary's Office, "President Delivers State of the Union Address," January 29, 2002, http://georgewbush-whitehouse.archives.gov/news/releases/2002/01/print/20020129–11.html, accessed June 9, 2014.
35. Defense Department news release by Linda D. Kozaryn, "Rumsfeld: Suicide Bombing Is Terrorism," April 3, 2002, http://www.defense.gov/

news/newsarticle.aspx?id=44197, accessed June 9, 2014. Robert Jervis contends that this was the main point of friction between the administration and the IC—that intelligence officials saw no likelihood that Saddam would share WMD with Islamic terrorists. Robert Jervis, *How Statesmen Think: The Psychology of International Politics* (Princeton, NJ: Princeton University Press, 2017), 152–53. While this was a point of disagreement, the basic issue of WMD in Iraqi hands was the more urgent question.

36. Seymour M. Hersh, "The Stovepipe," Annals of National Security, *The New Yorker*, Oct. 27, 2003, 77.
37. Seymour M. Hersh, "Selective Intelligence," Annals of National Security, *The New Yorker*, May 12, 2003, 44–51.
38. The quotation is from "Hussein-Qaeda Link 'Inappropriate,' Report Says," *New York Times*, April 6, 2007, 8. At the behest of Senator Carl Levin, the Department of Defense acting inspector general later confirmed that the actions of Feith and his office were "inappropriate." Department of Defense Office of Inspector General, Report No. 07-INTEL-04, "Review of Pre-Iraqi War Activities of the Office of the Under Secretary of Defense for Policy," February 9, 2007, ii. Redacted version at http://www.fas.org/irp/agency/dod/ig020907-decl.pdf, accessed June 22, 2020. See also Terry H. Anderson, *Bush's Wars* (Oxford: Oxford University Press, 2011), 104–5.
39. Quoted by Admiral Lowell Jacoby in David P. Oakley, *Subordinating Intelligence: The DoD/CIA Post-Cold War Relationship* (Lexington: University Press of Kentucky, 2019), 146.
40. White, "George Tenet and the Last Great Days of the CIA," 423–25.
41. Risen, *State of War*, 71–73.
42. Douglas J. Feith, *War and Decision: Inside the Pentagon at the Dawn of the War on Terrorism* (New York: HarperCollins, 2008), 224–28. The July date is based on Anderson, *Bush's Wars*, 101–2.
43. The author was deputy commander of the Iraq intelligence working group at the time and received this account from the commander immediately after he saw Feith. No proof of the alleged biological weapon system was ever found. Instead, the Commission on the Intelligence Capabilities of the United States concluded that the IC had made "too much of an inferential leap" about this supposed system (U.S. Commission on the Intelligence Capabilities of the United States, *Report to the President*, 560).
44. Anderson, *Bush's Wars*, 181.
45. United Nations Security Council Resolution 1441 (2002), November 8, 2002, 3, http://www.un.org/depts/unmovic/new/documents/resolutions/s-res-1441.pdf, accessed March 26, 2021.

46. UNSCOM, "Thirteenth Quarterly Report of the Executive Chairman," 21–23.
47. U.S. Commission on the Intelligence Capabilities of the United States, *Report to the President*, cover letter, p. 1. Pages 168 and 561 of the actual report criticized analysts for demanding proof that Iraq did *not* have WMD, which was the question posed by the administration.
48. Jervis, *How Statesmen Think*, 154.
49. Jack Davis, "The Challenge of Managing Uncertainty: Paul Wolfowitz on Intelligence-Policy Relations," *Studies in Intelligence* 39:5 (1996): 37.
50. Moni Chorev, "Surprise Attack: The Case of the Yom-Kippur War," research project (Washington: Industrial College of the Armed Forces, National Defense University, 1996), 18.

Chapter Four. The European Precedents

1. Quoted in Christopher Andrew, *Defend the Realm: The Authorized History of MI5* (New York: Alfred A. Knopf, 2009), 844.
2. Robert Pape has argued eloquently that recent terrorist attacks use Islamic or other religious reasons as a means to build social support, whereas the actual objective of such terrorism is to force the withdrawal of foreign forces from a national area. Robert A. Pape, *Dying to Win: The Strategic Logic of Suicide Terrorism* (New York: Random House, 2005), 4, 104.
3. Derek Wilson, *Sir Francis Walsingham: A Courtier in an Age of Terror* (New York: Carroll & Graf, 2007), 57–58.
4. Wilson, *Sir Francis Walsingham*, 93–94, 106, 142–43, 170, 207.
5. John Hughes-Wilson, *The Secret State: A History of Intelligence and Espionage* (New York: Pegasus Books, 2016), 19.
6. Andrew, *Secret Service*, 1.
7. David McCullough, *John Adams* (New York: Simon & Schuster, 2001), 199–201.
8. Andrew, *Secret Service*, 1–6.
9. Steven E. Maffeo, *Most Secret and Confidential: Intelligence in the Age of Nelson* (Annapolis, MD: Naval Institute Press, 2012).
10. Mary McGrigor, *Wellington's Spies* (Barnsley, South Yorkshire: Leo Cooper/Pen and Sword Books, 2005), 156–66.
11. Mark Urban, *The Man Who Broke Napoleon's Codes: The Story of George Scovell* (London: Faber and Faber, 2001), esp. 108–28, 174, 237, 257–66, 280–89.
12. Alan Judd, *The Quest for C: Sir Mansfield Cumming and the Founding of the British Secret Service* (London: HarperCollins, 1999), 35–72.

13. Judd, *The Quest for C*, 94–181.
14. Andrew, *Defend the Realm*, 50–52, 72–76, 84, 102–7, 232–33.
15. Keith Jeffery, *MI6: The History of the Secret Intelligence Service, 1909–1949* (London: Bloomsbury, 2010), 50–55, 75, 79; Judd, *The Quest for C*, 381–97.
16. Donald C. Watt, "British Intelligence and the Coming of the Second World War in Europe," in *Knowing One's Enemies: Intelligence Assessment Before the Two World Wars*, ed. Ernest R. May (Princeton, NJ: Princeton University Press, 1984), 243–45.
17. Jeffery, *MI6*, 138, 176–84.
18. Christopher Andrew and Vasili Mitrokhin, *The Sword and the Shield: The Mitrokhin Archive and the Secret History of the KGB* (New York: Basic Books, 1999), 36–67.
19. Jonathan Haslam, *Near and Distant Neighbors: A New History of Soviet Intelligence* (New York: Farrar, Straus, and Giroux, 2015), 68–81.
20. Jeffery, *MI6*, 194, 245–48.
21. See, for example, Aaron L. Goldman, "Two Views of Germany: Nevile Henderson vs. Vansittart and the Foreign Office, 1937–1939," *British Journal of International Studies* 6:3 (Oct. 1980): 247–77.
22. Norrin M. Ripsman and Jack S. Levy, "Wishful Thinking or Buying Time? The Logic of British Appeasement in the 1930s," *International Security* 33:2 (Fall 2008): 148–81.
23. Watt, "British Intelligence and the Coming of the Second World War," 243–44, 246–47, 254–59.
24. Christopher Andrew, "Churchill and Intelligence," *Intelligence and National Security* 3:3 (1988): 181–93.
25. Michael S. Goodman, *The Official History of the Joint Intelligence Committee*, vol. I, *From the Approach of the Second World War to the Suez Crisis* (London: Routledge, 2014), 4–5, 419–26.
26. Mark Urban, *UK Eyes Alpha: Inside British Intelligence* (London: Faber and Faber, 1996), 286.
27. Richard J. Aldrich, "Counting the Cost of Intelligence: The Treasury, National Service and GCHQ," *English Historical Review* 128:532 (June 2013): 596–98, 607.
28. Douglas Porch, *The French Secret Services: From the Dreyfus Affair to the Gulf War* (New York: Farrar, Straus, and Giroux, 1995), 5–6.
29. Alan Williams, *The Police of Paris, 1718–1789* (Baton Rouge: Louisiana State University Press, 1979), xvii; Philip J. Stead, *The Police of Paris* (London: Staples, 1957), 15, 22–37. See also Honore-Antoine Frégier, *Histoire de l'Administration de la Police de Paris depuis Philippe-Auguste jusqu'aux États Généraux de 1789*, vol. I (Paris: Guillaumin, 1850), 5–14.

30. Jonathan M. House, *Controlling Paris: Armed Forces and Counter-Revolution, 1789–1848* (New York: New York University Press, 2014), 11–28.
31. Stead, *The Police of Paris*, 69.
32. Nils Forssell, *Fouché: The Man Napoleon Feared*, trans. Anna Borwell (New York: Frederick A. Stokes Co., 1928), 96–109.
33. Forssell, *Fouché*, 135–69.
34. Porch, *The French Secret Services*, 10–11.
35. Stead, *The Police of Paris*, 90–91; Clive Emsley, *Policing and its Context, 1750–1870* (New York: Schocken, 1984), 53–57.
36. Maurice Dommanget, *Auguste Blanqui: Des Origines a la Révolution de 1848* (Paris: Mouton, 1969), 177–203; David H. Pinkney, "The Pacification of Paris: The Military Lessons of 1830," in *1830 in France*, ed. John M. Merriman (New York: New Viewpoints, 1975), 186–97.
37. Hsi-Huey Liang, *The Rise of Modern Police and the European State System from Metternich to the Second World War* (Cambridge: Cambridge University Press, 1992), 52.
38. Porch, *The French Secret Services*, 12–15. On the border collection efforts, see also Christopher Andrew, *Secret World: A History of Intelligence* (New Haven, CT: Yale University Press, 2019), 453.
39. Liang, *The Rise of Modern Police and the European State System*, 97–99.
40. Porch, *The French Secret Services*, 37–38, 50–54. 41. Liang, *The Rise of Modern Police and the European State System*, 114–20; Porch, *The French Secret Services*, 25–26.
42. Terrence J. Finnegan, *Shooting the Front: Allied Aerial Reconnaissance and Photographic Interpretation on the Western Front—World War I* (Washington, DC: National Defense Intelligence College, 2006), 34.
43. Finnegan, *Shooting the Front*, 61; James L. Gilbert, *World War I and the Origins of U.S. Military Intelligence* (Lanham, MD: Scarecrow/Rowman & Littlefield, 2012), 66.
44. Porch, *The French Secret Services*, 83–90, 99–100.
45. Porch, *The French Secret Services*, 135–43.
46. Karl-Heinz Frieser, *The Blitzkrieg Legend: The 1940 Campaign in the West* (Annapolis, MD: Naval Institute Press, 2005), 62–63.
47. Stephen A. Schuker, "Seeking a Scapegoat: Intelligence and Grand Strategy in France, 1919–1940," in *Secret Intelligence in the European States System, 1918–1989*, ed. Jonathan Haslam and Karina Urbach (Stanford, CA: Stanford University Press, 2014), chap. 3, 84–86.
48. Roger Faligot and Pascal Krop, *La Piscine: The French Secret Service since 1944*, trans. W. D. Halls (Oxford: Basil Blackwell, 1989), 11–16, 21–25.

49. Faligot and Krop, *La Piscine*, 72–73.
50. Porch, *The French Secret Services*, 278 and passim.
51. Faligot and Krop, *La Piscine*, 77–93, 128–32.
52. Porch, *The French Secret Services*, 408, 419, 421, 447–50; Faligot and Krop, *La Piscine*, 281.
53. Faligot and Krop, *La Piscine*, 288–96.
54. Porch, *The French Secret Services*, 494.
55. This section is based upon Siegfried Beer and Marianne Walle, "Les services du renseignement habsbourgeois ont-ils échoué? La défaite des services du renseignement austro-hongrois dans la première guerre mondiale," *Guerres mondiales et conflits contemporains*, no. 232 (2008): 73–85.
56. Ian D. Armour, "Colonel Redl: Fact and Fantasy," *Intelligence and National Security* 2:1 (1987): 170–83.
57. The otherwise brilliant Michael Howard and Peter Paret translation of *On War* (Princeton, 1976), 117, uses "intelligence," whereas the now-obsolete J. J. Graham translation (London, 1873) uses "information," which was probably more accurate. See Roger Z. George and Robert D. Kline, eds., *Intelligence and the National Security Strategist: Enduring Issues and Challenges* (Washington: National Defense University, 2004), 17.
58. Wilhelm J. C. E. Stieber, *The Chancellor's Spy: The Revelations of the Chief of Bismarck's Secret Service*, trans. Jan van Heurck (New York: Grove Press, 1979), 23–35, 68–71.
59. Stieber, *The Chancellor's Spy*, 93–164.
60. Andrew, *Defend the Realm*, 6, 12, 30–36.
61. Kenneth Campbell, "Major General Friedrich Gempp: German Intelligence Leader," *American Intelligence Journal* 25:1 (Summer 2007): 75–78.
62. Campbell, "Major General Friedrich Gempp," 78–79.
63. Lauran Paine, *German Military Intelligence in World War II: The Abwehr* (New York: Stein & Day, 1984), 11.
64. Mark M. Hull, "The Irish Interlude: German Intelligence in Ireland, 1939–1943," *Journal of Military History* 66:3 (July 2002): 695–96.
65. Andrew, *Secret Service*, 438–39.
66. Jeffery, *MI6*, 520–21.
67. Robert Hutchinson, *German Foreign Intelligence from Hitler's War to the Cold War: Flawed Assumptions and Faulty Analysis* (Lawrence: University Press of Kansas, 2019), 2, 4, 20–36, 90–93, 122–24, 222.
68. David Thomas, "Foreign Armies East and German Military Intelligence in Russia, 1941–45," *Journal of Contemporary History* 22:2 (April 1987): 269, 276, 279–80, 290. For the wartime organization and functioning of

FHO, see U.S. War Department, Military Intelligence Division, *German Military Intelligence, 1939–1945* (Frederick, MD: University Publications of America, 1984), esp. 1–33.

69. Kenneth Campbell, "Walter Schellenberg, SD Chief," *American Intelligence Journal* 25:2 (Winter 2007–8): 91.
70. John R. Deane Jr., *Lessons in Leadership: My Life in the US Army from World War II to Vietnam, ed. Jack C. Mason* (Lexington: University Press of Kentucky, 2012), 43–55.
71. Jérôme Mellon, "The Foreign Intelligence-Gathering of the MfS's *Hauptverwaltung Aufklärung*," October 2001, http://cv.jmellon.com/mfs.pdf, accessed October 23, 2017.
72. Hutchinson, *German Foreign Intelligence from Hitler's War to the Cold War*, 174–84.
73. Ronald Hingley, *The Russian Secret Police: Muscovite, Imperial Russian, and Soviet Political Security Operations* (New York: Simon & Schuster, 1970), 1–2.
74. Hingley, *The Russian Secret Police*, 5–37.
75. Hingley, *The Russian Secret Police*, 63–77.
76. Rita T. Kronenbitter, "Paris Okhrana, 1885–1905," *Studies in Intelligence* 10:3 (Summer 1966): 55–63.
77. Rita T. Kronenbitter, "The Okhrana's Female Agents: Part I: Russian Women," *Studies in Intelligence* 9:2 (Spring 1965): 25–41.
78. Alex Marshall, "Russian Military Intelligence, 1905–1917: The Untold Story behind Tsarist Russia in the First World War," *War in History* 11:4 (Nov. 2004): 395–407.
79. Marshall, "Russian Military Intelligence," 410–22.
80. Andrew and Mitrokhin, *The Sword and the Shield*, 23; Hingley, *The Russian Secret Police*, 183–225.
81. Emil Draitser, *Stalin's Romeo Spy: The Remarkable Rise and Fall of the KGB's Most Daring Operative. The True Life of Dmitri Bystrolyotov* (Evanston, IL: Northwestern University Press, 2010), esp. 62–245.
82. Draitser, *Stalin's Romeo Spy*, 366–69.
83. David E. Murphy, *What Stalin Knew: The Enigma of Barbarossa* (New Haven, CT: Yale University Press, 2005), 7–13, 54–61.
84. Robert Stephan, "SMERSH: Soviet Military Counter-Intelligence during the Second World War," *Journal of Contemporary History* 22:4 (Oct. 1987): 585–613.
85. Hingley, *The Russian Secret Police*, 203, 212–13.
86. Haslam, *Near and Distant Neighbors*, 147–57; Andrew, *Defend the Realm*, 368–69, 378, 381–84, 431–35.

87. Christopher Andrew and Oleg Gordievsky, *KGB: The Inside Story of Its Foreign Operations from Lenin to Gorbachev* (London: Scepter/Hodder and Stoughton, 1990), 486–88.
88. Christopher Andrew and Vasili Mitrokhin, *The Mitrokhin Archive II: The KGB and the World* (London: Penguin, 2006), 21; John Barron, *The KGB Today: The Hidden Hand* (London: Hodder and Stoughton, 1983), 143.
89. Barron, *The KGB Today*, 145.
90. Benjamin B. Fischer, "CANOPY WING: The U.S. War Plan That Gave the East Germans Goose Bumps," *International Journal of Intelligence and CounterIntelligence* 27:3 (May 2014): 434–37.
91. Barron, *The KGB Today*, 13–14, 403–4.
92. Benjamin B. Fischer, "The Soviet-American War Scare of the 1980s," *International Journal of Intelligence and CounterIntelligence* 19:3 (Nov. 2006): 480–518.
93. Martin Ebon, *KGB: Death and Rebirth* (Westport, CT: Praeger, 1994), 3, 36–41.
94. Ebon, *KGB: Death and Rebirth*, 97–99, 106.
95. Bettina Renz, *Russia's Military Revival* (Cambridge: Polity Press, 2018), 105, 114–15.

Chapter Five. The U.S. Intelligence Community, 1882–1961

1. Charles D. Ameringer, *U.S. Foreign Intelligence: The Secret Side of American History* (Lexington, MA: Lexington Books, 1990), 50–61.
2. Wyman H. Packard, *A Century of Naval Intelligence* (Washington: Department of the Navy, 1996), 2–3; Henry P. Beers, "The Development of the Office of the Chief of Naval Operations," *Military Affairs* 10:1 (Spring 1946): 47–48.
3. Bruce W. Bidwell, *History of the Military Intelligence Division, Department of the Army General Staff: 1775–1941* (Frederick, MD: University Publications of America, 1986), 52–54; Elizabeth Bethel, "The Military Information Division: Origin of the Intelligence Division," *Military Affairs* 11:1 (Spring 1947): 17–18.
4. W. Dirk Ratt, "U.S. Intelligence Operations and Covert Action in Mexico, 1900–47," *Journal of Contemporary History* 22:4 (Oct. 1987): 622.
5. Ameringer, *U.S. Foreign Intelligence*, 86; Ratt, "U.S. Intelligence Operations and Covert Action in Mexico," 621, 623.
6. Ward Churchill, "From the Pinkertons to the PATRIOT Act: The Trajectory of Political Policing in the United States, 1870 to the Present," *The New Centennial Review* 4:1 (Spring 2004): 11–44.

7. 5 USC §3108. See also Jeffrey L. Vagle, *Being Watched: Legal Challenges to Government Surveillance* (New York: New York University Press, 2017), 22.
8. Brian A. Jackson, ed., *The Challenge of Domestic Intelligence in a Free Society: A Multidisciplinary Look at the Creation of a U.S. Domestic Counterterrorism Intelligence Agency* (Santa Monica, CA: RAND, 2009), 16.
9. Tim Weiner, *Enemies: A History of the FBI* (New York: Random House, 2012), 7–11.
10. Bidwell, *History of the Military Intelligence Division*, 110–208; David Kahn, *The Reader of Gentlemen's Mail: Herbert O. Yardley and the Birth of American Codebreaking* (New Haven, CT: Yale University Press, 2004), 19–21.
11. Ratt, "U.S. Intelligence Operations and Covert Action in Mexico," 616–17, 627.
12. Agnes Gereben Schaefer, "The History of Domestic Intelligence in the United States," in Jackson, *The Challenge of Domestic Intelligence in a Free Society*, chap. 2, 20.
13. Alex Goodall, *Loyalty and Liberty: American Countersubversion from World War I to the McCarthy Era* (Champaign: University of Illinois Press, 2013), 61–81.
14. Goodall, *Loyalty and Liberty*, 74.
15. Mark Ellis, "J. Edgar Hoover and the 'Red Summer' of 1919," *Journal of American Studies* 28:1 (April 1994), 39–50.
16. David Williams, "The Bureau of Investigation and Its Critics, 1919–1921: The Origins of Federal Political Surveillance," *Journal of American History* 68:3 (Dec. 1981): 568–76.
17. Williams, "The Bureau of Investigation and Its Critics," 56; Schaefer, "The History of Domestic Intelligence in the United States," in Jackson, *The Challenge of Domestic Intelligence in a Free Society*, 22–25.
18. Neal Katyal and Richard Caplan, "The Surprisingly Strong Case for the Legality of the NSA Surveillance Program: The FDR Precedent," *Stanford Law Review* 60:4 (Feb. 2008): 1025–37. Both the Justice Department and the Supreme Court claimed to find exceptions to the 1934 prohibition against wiretaps (1039–40).
19. Athan G. Theoharis, "Dissent and the State: Unleashing the FBI, 1917–1985," *History Teacher* 24:1 (Nov. 1990): 43–48; Weiner, *Enemies: A History of the FBI*, 85–90; Katyal and Caplan, "The Surprisingly Strong Case," 1039, 1058.
20. James Bamford, *The Puzzle Palace: A Report on America's Most Secret Agency* (New York: Penguin Books, 1983), 20–27; Bidwell, *History of the Military Intelligence Division*, 124, 240, 253–54.

21. Bamford, *The Puzzle Palace*, 27–35, quotation 34; Bidwell, *History of the Military Intelligence Division*, 327–34.
22. John Prados, *Combined Fleet Decoded: The Secret History of American Intelligence and the Japanese Navy in World War II* (New York: Random House, 1995), 7–10.
23. Gordon W. Prange, Donald M. Goldstein, and Katherine V. Dillon, *At Dawn We Slept: The Untold Story of Pearl Harbor* (New York: Penguin Books, 1991), 80–86.
24. Christopher Andrew, *Secret World: A History of Intelligence* (New Haven, CT: Yale University Press, 2019), 628.
25. Weiner, *Enemies: A History of the FBI*, 96–106.
26. Richard Harris Smith, *OSS: The Secret History of America's First Central Intelligence Agency* (Berkeley: University of California Press, 1972), 1–2.
27. Thomas F. Troy, *Donovan and the CIA: A History of the Establishment of the Central Intelligence Agency* (Frederick, MD: University Publications of America, 1981), 63, 123, 150, 156, 174–76, 184–87.
28. Smith, *OSS: The Secret History*, 8–17.
29. Rhodri Jeffreys-Jones, *Cloak and Dollar: A History of American Secret Intelligence* (New Haven, CT: Yale University Press, 2002), 133, 153.
30. Harold C. Relyea, *Evolution and Organization of Intelligence Activities in the United States* (Laguna Hills, CA: Aegean Park Press, 1988), 138.
31. Thomas L. Ahern Jr., *The Way We Do Things: Black Entry Operations into North Vietnam, 1961–1964* (Washington: Center for the Study of Intelligence/CIA, 2005), 4.
32. Troy, *Donovan and the CIA*, 214–65.
33. Michael Warner, ed., *The CIA under Harry Truman*, CIA Cold War Records series (Washington: Center for the Study of Intelligence, 1994), xii–xvii.
34. Steven L. Reardon, *History of the Office of the Secretary of Defense*, vol. I, *The Formative Years, 1947–1950* (Washington: Center for the Study of Intelligence, 1984), 23–26.
35. National Security Act of 1947, Section 202.
36. Warner, *CIA under Harry Truman*, xiv–xvii; Relyea, *Evolution and Organization of Intelligence Activities*, 134–35, 241.
37. National Security Act of 1947, Section 102, (a) and (d).
38. Schaefer, "The History of Domestic Intelligence in the United States," in Jackson, *The Challenge of Domestic Intelligence in a Free Society*, 31–34.
39. Trevor Barnes, "The Secret Cold War: The C.I.A. and American Foreign Policy in Europe, 1946–1956, Part I," *Historical Journal* 24:2 (June 1981): 400, 405–6.

40. *The History of SIGINT in the Central Intelligence Agency, 1947–70*, vol. I (Arlington, VA: CIA Historical Staff, 1971), 23–24, 39–44, https://archive.org/details/HistoryOfSIGINTInTheCIA19471970, accessed March 27, 2021.
41. Samuel F. Wells Jr., *Fearing the Worst: How Korea Transformed the Cold War* (New York: Columbia University Press, 2019), 415; Raat, "U.S. Intelligence Operations and Covert Action in Mexico," 633.
42. Richard J. Aldrich, *The Hidden Hand: Britain, America, and Cold War Secret Intelligence* (New York: Overlook Press/Peter Mayer Publishers, 2001), 86–87; David F. Rudgers, "The Origins of Covert Action," *Journal of Contemporary History* 35:2 (April 2000): 251–54.
43. Rudgers, "The Origins of Covert Action," 419–20; Warner, *CIA under Harry Truman*, xvi–xxi; Anne Karalekas, *History of the Central Intelligence Agency* (Laguna Hills, CA: Aegean Park Press, 1977), 11–12, 30–33.
44. Wells, *Fearing the Worst*, 422, 460, 465–66.
45. Douglas Little, "Mission Impossible: The CIA and the Cult of Covert Action in the Middle East," *Diplomatic History* 28:5 (Nov. 2004): 663–701; Douglas Little, "Cold War and Covert Action: The United States and Syria, 1945–1958," *Middle East Journal* 44:1 (Winter 1990): 51–75.
46. Reproduced in William M. Leary, ed., *The Central Intelligence Agency: History and Documents* (Tuscaloosa: University of Alabama Press, 1984), 134–42.
47. Wells, *Fearing the Worst*, 416–18.
48. Wells, *Fearing the Worst*, 446–49; Rudgers, "The Origins of Covert Action," 258–59.
49. Ludwell L. Montague, *General Walter Bedell Smith as Director of Central Intelligence , October 1950–February 1953* (University Park: Pennsylvania State University Press, 1992), 46–58, 218; Wells, *Fearing the Worst*, 458–70. The United States declined to support a third force in China; see Roger B. Jeans Jr., "Ghost Guerrillas: The CIA and 'Tiger General' Li Zongren's Third Force during the Early Cold War," *Journal of Military History* 81:2 (April 2017): 491–512.
50. Thomas L. Burns, *The Origins of the National Security Agency, 1940–1952*, United States Cryptologic History series V, vol. I (Fort Meade, MD: Center for Cryptologic History, National Security Agency, 1990), 31–32, 34–37, 51–59.
51. Bamford, *The Puzzle Palace*, 15–17.
52. *History of SIGINT in the CIA*, vol. I, 87–92; National Security Council Intelligence Directive [NSCID] No. 9: Communications Intelligence, December 29, 1952, Dwight D. Eisenhower Presidential Library

(hereafter "Eisenhower Library"), Special Assistant for National Security Affairs (hereafter "SpAsst for NSA"), box 6.

53. *National Photographic Interpretation Center: Antecedents and Early Years, 1952–1956*, The Directorate of Intelligence Historical series, vol. I (Langley, VA: CIA Historical Staff, 1972), 1–11.
54. Montague, *General Walter Bedell Smith*, 263–65.
55. James W. Fester, "Administrative Literature and the Second Hoover Commission Reports," *American Political Science Review* 51:1 (March 1957): 143.
56. Michael Warner and J. Kenneth McDonald, *US Intelligence Community Reform Studies Since 1947* (Washington: Center for the Study of Intelligence, 2005), 15–17.
57. "Report on Intelligence Activities in the Federal Government," compilation with agency responses (undated, c. 1955), Eisenhower Library, Office of the Staff Secretary, box 13.
58. "Report on Intelligence Activities in the Federal Government," appendix I.
59. "Report by the Commission on Organization of the Executive Branch," in U.S. Department of State, *Foreign Relations of the United States, 1950–1955: The Intelligence Community, 1950–1955* (Washington: Department of State, 2005), #221.
60. Montague, *General Walter Bedell Smith*, 91–93, 264.
61. Montague, *General Walter Bedell Smith*, 264.
62. President to Doolittle, July 26, 1954, in "Report on the Covert Activities of the Central Intelligence Agency," September 30, 1954.
63. "Report on the Covert Activities," conclusions 2.
64. "Report on the Covert Activities," discussion 6.
65. "Report on the Covert Activities," conclusions 8, discussion 3.
66. Memorandum for Record of presidential meeting with Doolittle and his committee, October 19, 1954, Eisenhower Library, Ann Whitman File, Papers as President, box 13.
67. Memorandum for Record of presidential meeting with Doolittle.
68. Memorandum for Record of presidential meeting with Doolittle.
69. See, for example, Edgar M. Bottome, *The Missile Gap: A Study of the Formulation of Military and Political Policy* (Cranbury, NJ: Associated University Presses, 1971.)
70. Richard V. Damms, "James Killian, the Technological Capabilities Panel, and the Emergence of President Eisenhower's 'Scientific-Technological Elite,'" *Diplomatic History* 24:1 (Winter 2000): 61–62.
71. Dwight D. Eisenhower, *Waging Peace, 1956–1961: The White House Years* (Garden City, NY: Doubleday and Company, 1965), 208, 224, 243.

72. Eisenhower, *Waging Peace*, 69–71; Philip Taubman, *Secret Empire: Eisenhower, the CIA, and the Hidden Story of America's Space Espionage* (New York: Simon & Schuster, 2003), 79–105.
73. "Deterrence and Survival in the Nuclear Age," November 7, 1957, Eisenhower Library, Office of the Staff Secretary, box 13.
74. Philip K. Edwards, "The President's Board: 1956–1960," *Studies in Intelligence* 13 (Summer 1969): 113; "Report by the Commission on Organization of the Executive Branch."
75. Edwards, "The President's Board," 113–14.
76. President to James Killian, January 11, 1956, Eisenhower Library, Office of the Staff Secretary, box 5, file PBCFIA (5).
77. Edwards, "The President's Board," 114. See also correspondence in Eisenhower Library, Office of the Staff Secretary, boxes 5 and 6, PBCFIA files. Ambassador Kennedy later resigned, ostensibly because his son was running for president, and was replaced by Colgate Darden, politician and president of the University of Virginia.
78. For example, see Memorandum of Conference with President, February 2, 1960, Eisenhower Library, Office of the Staff Secretary, box 6, intelligence file.
79. See Memorandum for members of NSC, January 17, 1957, Eisenhower Library, SpAsst for NSA, box 7, file PBCFIA (2).
80. Memorandum, Director of Bureau of the Budget to Executive Secretary of NSC, January 25, 1957, and Memorandum, DCI to NSC Executive Secretary, January 25, 1957, both in Eisenhower Library, SpAsst for NSA, box 7, file PBCFIA.
81. See, for example, Brief for Discussion with the President, 5th Report of PBCFIA, Strategic Warning Mechanism, March 7, 1960, Eisenhower Library, SpAsst for NSA, box 4; Brief for Discussion with the President, Fusion of COMINT-ELINT, March 11, 1960, Eisenhower Library, SpAsst for NSA, box 4.
82. Letter to the President, [1st] report of PBCFIA, December 20, 1956, Eisenhower Library, SpAsst for NSA, box 7, file PBCFIA (2).
83. Memorandum of Conference with the President, January 17, 1957, Eisenhower Library, Office of the Staff Secretary, box 6, intelligence file.
84. Memorandum of Conference with the President, October 24, 1957, Eisenhower Library, Office of the Staff Secretary, box 6; 3rd Report of PBCFIA, October 30, 1958, Eisenhower Library, Office of SpAsst for NSA, box 7, 1959 file.
85. Undated memorandum (c. 1960), DCI responses to PBCFIA recommendations, Eisenhower Library, Office of SpAsst for NSA, box 8, 1960(2) file.

86. Memorandum of Conference with the President, February 2, 1960, Eisenhower Library, Office of the Staff Secretary, box 6, intelligence file.
87. U.S. Department of State, *Foreign Relations of the United States, 1950–1955: The Intelligence Community*, #250, NSC 5412/2, Covert Operations (Washington: Department of State, 2005), 746–49; Memorandum, Historical Background of Functioning of the NSC 5412/2 Special Group and Its Predecessors, January 19, 1959, CIA FOIA Library/Reading Room.
88. Letter to the President, [1st] report of PBCFIA, December 20, 1956, Eisenhower Library, SpAsst for NSA, box 7, file PBCFIA (2).
89. Memorandum to all holders of NSC 5412/2 from NSC Executive Secretary, March 26, 1957, Eisenhower Library, SpAsst for NSA, box 3.
90. Memorandum of meeting with the president, January 29, 1959, Eisenhower Library, SpAsst for NSA, box 3.
91. Memorandum, Gray to Christian Herter, Allen Dulles, and John Irwin, 5412/2 Group, January 19, 1959, Eisenhower Library, Office of the Staff Secretary, box 15.
92. 3rd Report of PBCFIA, October 30, 1958, Eisenhower Library, SpAsst for NSA, box 7.
93. Memorandum, DCI to NSC Executive Secretary, Subject: Third Report by PBCFIA, July 28, 1959, Eisenhower Library, SpAsst for NSA, box 7, file 1959(1); unlabeled memorandum, DCI responses to PBCFIA recommendations, c. 1960, SpAsst for NSA, box 8, file 1960(2).
94. David Binder, "Richard M. Bissell, 84, Is Dead; Helped Plan Bay of Pigs Invasion," *New York Times*, February 8, 1994.
95. Quoted in Memorandum, Coyne to Gray, Subject: Recommendation No. 3 of the Third Report of the PBCFIA, February 18, 1959, Eisenhower Library, SpAsst for NSA, box 4, file Meetings with the President 1959 (5).
96. Unnumbered report of PBCFIA, January 5, 1961, Eisenhower Library, Office of the Staff Secretary, box 6.
97. Richard Bissell Jr., *Reflections of a Cold Warrior* (New Haven, CT: Yale University Press, 1996), 99–111.
98. Jonathan M. House, *A Military History of the Cold War, 1944–1962* (Norman: University of Oklahoma Press, 2012), 401–5.
99. Letter to the President, [1st] report of PBCFIA, December 20, 1956, Eisenhower Library, SpAsst for NSA, box 7, file PBCFIA (2).
100. 3rd Report of PBCFIA, October 24, 1957, Eisenhower Library, Office of the Staff Secretary, box 6, file PBCFIA.
101. This paragraph is based on *The History of SIGINT in the CIA*, vol. II, 80–88.

102. Memorandum, Subject: The Baker Report (Scientific Judgement on Foreign Communications Intelligence), February 5, 1958; Memorandum of conference with the President, February 10, 1958, both in Eisenhower Library, Ann Whitman File, Papers as President, box 30.
103. *History of SIGINT in the CIA*, vol. II, 90–91.
104. For example, Chairman, USIB, to NSC Executive Secretary, Subject: Status Report, Elimination of Unnecessary Duplication in Foreign Intelligence Publications, January 5, 1961, Eisenhower Library, SpAsst for NSA, box 8.
105. 5th Report of PBCFIA, October 30, 1958; Memorandum, NSC Executive Secretary to Secretaries of State and Defense, DCI, and DIRNSA, January 19, 1950, both in Eisenhower Library, SpAsst for NSA, box 7.
106. Brief for Discussion with the President, Subject: 7th Report of PBCFIA, Recommendation on ELINT Ferret Missions, December 23, 1960, Eisenhower Library, SpAsst for NSA, box 5, file 1960 Meetings with the President, vol. II (1). The president approved continued missions with precautions.
107. Memorandum, DCI and Secretary of Defense to NSC Executive Secretary, Subject: 5th Report by PBCFIA (Recommendation Regarding Fusion of COMINT/ELINT Activities), July 6, 1960, Eisenhower Library, SpAsst for NSA, box 8, file PBCFIA 1960 (2).
108. Brief for Discussion with the President, Subject: 6th Report of PBCFIA, Recommendation on Direction of COMINT-ELINT, Eisenhower Library, SpAsst for NSA, box 5, file 1960 Meetings with the President, vol. II (7).
109. Vladislav M. Zubok and Constantine Pleshakov, *Inside the Kremlin's Cold War: From Stalin to Khrushchev* (Cambridge, MA: Harvard University Press, 1996), 14.
110. Killian to the President, April 15, 1956, Eisenhower Library, Office of the Staff Secretary, box 6.
111. FBI Director to Secretary of Defense, October 23, 1956, Eisenhower Library, SpAsst for NSA, box 3.
112. Memorandum, Chair of ICIS to NSC Executive Secretary, October 22, 1956, Eisenhower Library, SpAsst for NSA, box 3.
113. Memorandum, Subject: Discussion at the 473rd Meeting of the NSC, Thursday, January 5, 1961, Eisenhower Library, Ann Whitman File, Papers as President, NSC Series, box 13.
114. Memorandum of Conference with the President, December 26, 1958, Eisenhower Library, SpAsst for NSA, box 3, file Meetings with the President, 1958 (3).

115. Memorandum, Discussion at 358th NSC Meeting, March 13, 1958, Eisenhower Library, Ann Whitman File, Papers as President, box 13.
116. *History of SIGINT in the CIA*, vol. II, 2–5.
117. Briefing Note on Hull Board Recommendations, Subject: 5th Report of PBCFIA, January 18, 1960, Eisenhower Library, SpAsst for NSA, box 4.
118. Memorandum for Record, President's meeting with PBCFIA, dated February 8, 1960, Eisenhower Library, Office of the Staff Secretary, box 15.

Chapter Six. The U.S. Intelligence Community since 1961

1. Philip K. Edwards, "The President's Board: 1956–1960," *Studies in Intelligence* 13 (Summer 1969), 128; Executive Order 10938, cited in National Archives, https://www.archives.gov/federal-register/executive-orders/1961-kennedy.html#10938.
2. Lawrence S. Kaplan, Ronald D. Landa, and Edward J. Drea, *History of the Office of the Secretary of Defense*, vol. V, *The McNamara Ascendancy, 1961–1965* (Washington: Office of the Secretary of Defense, 2006), 22–23.
3. Memorandum for Record, Considerations to the Establishment of a Defense Intelligence Agency, April 21, 1961, Central Intelligence Agency (CIA) FOIA Reading Room.
4. Memorandum, Secretary of Defense to President, the Establishment of a Defense Intelligence Agency, July 6, 1961, CIA FOIA Reading Room.
5. Kaplan, Landa, and Drea, *The McNamara Ascendancy*, 23.
6. Jack Zlotnick, *National Security Management: National Intelligence* (Washington: National Defense University, 1964), 5–9.
7. Marilyn B. Young, *The Vietnam Wars, 1945–1990* (New York: HarperCollins, 1991), 42–45; Cecil B. Currey, *Edward Lansdale: The Unquiet American* (Washington: Brassey's, 1998), 156–65; Thomas L. Ahern Jr., *CIA and the House of Ngo: Covert Action in South Vietnam, 1954–63* (Washington: Center for the Study of Intelligence/CIA, 2000), ix, 6, 15.
8. Ahern, *CIA and the House of Ngo*, 41–93.
9. Ahern, *CIA and the House of Ngo*, 89–91, 94; Thomas L. Ahern Jr., *The Way We Do Things: Black Entry Operations into North Vietnam, 1961–1964* (Washington: Center for the Study of Intelligence/CIA, 2005), 7–10.
10. Ahern, *The Way We Do Things*, 15–57.
11. Ahern, *The Way We Do Things*, 25, 31, 33, 43; Richard H. Shultz Jr., *The Secret War against Hanoi: Kennedy's and Johnson's Use of Spies, Saboteurs, and Covert Warriors in North Vietnam* (New York: HarperCollins, 1999), 28–50.

12. On Diem's conduct of the war and his eventual fall, see Edward Miller, *Misalliance: Ngo Dinh Diem, the United States, and the Fate of South Vietnam* (Cambridge, MA: Harvard University Press, 2013); and Philip E. Catton, *Diem's Final Failure: Prelude to America's War in Vietnam* (Lawrence: University Press of Kansas, 2002), esp. 17–45.
13. Schultz, *The Secret War against Hanoi*, 34–35; Randall B. Woods, *Shadow Warrior: William Egan Colby and the CIA* (New York: Basic Books/Perseus, 2013), 184.
14. Ahern, *The CIA and the House of Ngo*, 173–85, 190, 197.
15. Ahern, *The CIA and the House of Ngo*, 192, 196, 205–12; Thomas L. Ahern Jr., *CIA and the Generals: Covert Support to Military Government in South Vietnam* (Washington: Center for the Study of Intelligence/CIA, 1998), 2; Woods, *Shadow Warrior*, 191–96.
16. The most sophisticated study of the measurement issue is Gregory A. Daddis, *No Sure Victory: Measuring U.S. Army Effectiveness and Progress in the Vietnam War* (Oxford: Oxford University Press, 2011), esp. 225–235.
17. Frank Leith Jones, *Blowtorch: Robert Komer, Vietnam, and American Cold War Strategy* (Annapolis, MD: Naval Institute Press, 2013), esp. 135–208.
18. Dale Andradé and James H. Willbanks, "CORDS/Phoenix: Counterinsurgency Lessons from Vietnam for the Future," *Military Review* 86:2 (March–April 2006): 9–23. For a negative evaluation, see Douglas Valentine, *The Phoenix Program* (New York: William Morrow and Company, 1990), 253–66.
19. Jill Lepore, "The Long Blue Line: Inventing the Police," *New Yorker*, July 20, 2020, 68–69.
20. Paul J. Scheips, *The Role of Federal Military Forces in Domestic Disorders, 1945–1992* (Washington: U.S. Army Center of Military History, 2005), 177–203; Barrye L. Price, "Against All Enemies: A Study of Civil Unrest and Federal Intervention within the United States from 1794 to 1968" (PhD diss., Texas A&M University, 1997), 52–75.
21. Scheips, *The Role of Federal Military Forces in Domestic Disorders*, 39, 75, 122–23.
22. Agnes Gereben Shaeffer, "The History of Domestic Intelligence in the United States," in *The Challenge of Domestic Intelligence in a Free Society: A Multidisciplinary Look at the Creation of a U.S. Domestic Counterterrorism Intelligence Agency*, ed. Brian A. Jackson (Santa Monica, CA: RAND, 2009), chap. 2, 35–36; Tim Weiner, *Enemies: A History of the FBI* (New York: Random House, 2012), 271–72.
23. Christopher H. Pyle, *Military Surveillance of Civilian Politics, 1967–1970* (New York: Garland Publishing, 1986); Jeffrey L. Vagle, *Being Watched:*

Legal Challenges to Government Surveillance (New York: New York University Press, 2017), 24–29.

24. Department of the Army, Army Regulation 380-13, *Acquisition and Storage of Information Concerning Non-Affiliated* [with the Army] *Persons and Organizations* (Washington: Government Printing Office, 1974).
25. The most infamous break-ins of the period were done not by the FBI but by Howard Hunt's "plumbers," working for the Committee to Re-Elect the President. In 1971, a year before Watergate, Hunt and two others broke into the Los Angeles offices of Daniel Ellsberg's psychiatrist, seeking information to discredit Ellsberg concerning the so-called Pentagon Papers. Owen Edwards, "The Ellsberg Files," *Smithsonian* 43:6 (2012): 70–71.
26. Schaefer, "The History of Domestic Intelligence in the United States," in Jackson, *The Challenge of Domestic Intelligence in a Free Society*, 33–34, 36, 37.
27. Weiner, *Enemies*, 267–70.
28. Seymour M. Hersh, "Huge C.I.A. Operation Reported in U.S. Against Antiwar Forces, Other Dissidents in Nixon Years," *New York Times*, Dec. 22, 1974, 1.
29. *Report to the President by the Commission on CIA Activities within the United States* [Rockefeller Commission] (Washington: Government Printing Office, 1975), ix–18.
30. Frank J. Smist Jr., *Congress Oversees the United States Intelligence Community, 1947–1989* (Knoxville: University of Tennessee Press, 1990), 10–13, 33, 78, 182–83. See also Gerald K. Haines, "The Pike Committee Investigations and the CIA," *Studies in Intelligence* 42:5 (Winter 1998–99): 81–92.
31. Smist, *Congress Oversees the United States Intelligence Community*, 35–51, 86.
32. Woods, *Shadow Warrior*, 399–462.
33. U.S. National Commission on Terrorist Attacks upon the United States, *The 9/11 Commission Report* (Washington: Government Printing Office, 2004), 75–78.
34. 50 U.S. Code § 1803, 1802.
35. U.S. National Commission on Terrorist Attacks, *The 9/11 Commission Report*, 74.
36. Richard A. Clarke, *Against All Enemies: Inside America's War on Terror* (New York: Free Press, 2004), 13, 24, 91, 215–16.
37. U.S. Executive Order 12306, United States Foreign Intelligence Activities, Jan. 24, 1978.

38. Charles D. Ameringer, *U.S. Foreign Intelligence: The Secret Side of American History* (Lexington, MA: Lexington Books, 1990), 376, 365; David P. Oakley, *Subordinating Intelligence: The DoD/CIA Post–Cold War Relationship* (Lexington: University Press of Kentucky, 2019), 15.
39. Kenneth M. Absher, Michael C. Desch, and Roman Popadiuk, *Privileged and Confidential: The Secret History of the President's Intelligence Advisory Board* (Lexington: University Press of Kentucky, 2012), 225–30.
40. James Stejskal, *Special Forces Berlin: Clandestine Cold War Operations of the US Army's Elite, 1956–1990* (Philadelphia: Casemate Publishers, 2017), 127–35; James H. Kyle and John R. Eidson, *The Guts to Try: The Untold Story of the Iran Hostage Rescue Mission by the On-Scene Desert Commander* (New York: Orion Books/Crown Publishers, 1990), 95, 97.
41. William E. Odom, *Fixing Intelligence: For a More Secure America* (New Haven, CT: Yale University Press, 2003), 144–49.
42. Ameringer, *U.S. Foreign Intelligence*, 373–76.
43. Loch K. Johnson, *Secret Agencies: U.S. Intelligence in a Hostile World* (New Haven, CT: Yale University Press, 1998), 43, 48–49.
44. Beth Bailey and Richard H. Immerman, eds., *Understanding the U.S. Wars in Iraq and Afghanistan* (New York: New York University Press, 2015), 80.
45. Ameringer, *U.S. Foreign Intelligence*, 367–68, 377–79.
46. The assistant secretary of state for inter-American affairs, Thomas Enders, tried and failed to persuade the administration to adopt a more neutral policy on Nicaragua. In the late summer of 1982, the House Intelligence Committee, which Edward Boland chaired, attached classified language to the Intelligence Authorization Act to forbid CIA funds from being spent on the Contras; the same language was then explicitly added to a defense authorization bill in December. James M. Scott, "Interbranch Rivalry and the Reagan Doctrine in Nicaragua," *Political Science Quarterly* 112:2 (Summer 1997): 242–44.
47. National Security Decision Directive 77, Jan. 14, 1983, https://fas.org/irp/offdocs/nsdd/23-1966t.gif, accessed Aug. 6, 2020.
48. Robert Parry and Peter Kornbluh, "Iran-Contra's Untold Story," *Foreign Policy*, no. 72 (Autumn 1988): 9–26. On MiG-21s for Nicaragua, see Oswaldo Bonilla, "Sandinista Leader Defends Right to Acquire Soviet MiGs," UPI Archives, Sept. 17, 1984; Philip Taubman, "U.S. Warns Soviets It Won't Tolerate MiGs in Nicaragua," *New York Times*, Nov. 8, 1984, 1; and CIA, Directorate of Intelligence, "Will Nicaragua Get MiGs?" Nov. 24, 1986, CIA FOIA Reading Room.
49. Scott Glabe, "The Original Privatization of Intelligence: Iran-Contra Revisited," *American Intelligence Journal* 28:1 (2010): 113–20.

50. Iran-Contra has been the subject of much commentary; a good brief summary may be found in Pierre Razoux, *The Iran-Iraq War*, trans. Nicholas Elliott (Cambridge, MA: Harvard University Press, 2015), 379–87.
51. Michael J. Sulick, *American Spies: Espionage against the United States from the Cold War to the Present* (Washington: Georgetown University Press, 2013), 7–8, 93–95, 159–61, 267–69.
52. Jeff McConnell, "Israeli Spies in the U.S.," *MERIP Middle East Report* no. 138 (Jan.–Feb. 1986), 35–37; P. R. Kumaraswamy, "The Politics of Pardon: Israel and Jonathan Pollard," *Arab Studies Quarterly* 18:3 (Summer 1996): 17–22.
53. Robert Service, *The End of the Cold War, 1985–1991* (New York: Public Affairs/Perseus, 2015), 281–82.
54. Thomas A. Keany and Eliot Cohen, *Gulf War Airpower Survey, Summary Report* (Washington: Department of the Air Force, 1993), 121, 130.
55. Johnson, *Secret Agencies*, 49–51; Richard D. White Jr., "George Tenet and the Last Great Days of the CIA," *Public Administration Review* 68:3 (June 2008): 422–23.
56. William J. Clinton, "National Priorities for Intelligence: Remarks to the Intelligence Community," *American Intelligence Journal* 16:1 (Spring/Summer 1995): 15–17.
57. Oakley, *Subordinating Intelligence*, 1, 16–21.
58. James Risen, *State of War: The Secret History of the CIA and the Bush Administration* (New York: Free Press, 2006), 8.
59. Gordon Corera, *Shopping for Bombs: Nuclear Proliferation, Global Insecurity, and the Rise and Fall of the A Q Khan Network* (New York: Oxford University Press, 2006), 5–13, 44–46, 89–109.
60. Robert Zarate, "The Nonuse and Abuse of Nuclear Proliferation in the Cases of North Korea and Iran," in *Moving Beyond Pretense: Nuclear Power and Nonproliferation*, ed. Henry Sokolski (Carlisle, PA: Strategic Studies Institute and U.S. Army War College Press, 2014), chap. 14, 378–84.
61. Zarete, "The Nonuse and Abuse of Nuclear Proliferation," in Sokolski, *Moving Beyond Pretense*, 385–86.
62. Brian L. Davis, *Qaddafi, Terrorism, and the Origins of the U.S. Attack on Libya* (New York: Praeger, 1990), 78–108.
63. Daniel P. Bolger, *Americans at War, 1975–1986, An Era of Violent Peace* (Novato, CA: Presidio Press, 1988), 403–4.
64. James C. McKinley Jr., "Two U.S. Embassies in East Africa Bombed," *New York Times*, Aug. 8, 1998, 1.
65. Clarke, *Against All Enemies*, 209.

66. Tenet and Harlow, *At the Center of the Storm*, 151–55; on the al Qaeda effort in the later 1990s, see Clarke, *Against All Enemies*, 133–204.
67. Bailey and Immerman, *Understanding the U.S. Wars in Iraq and Afghanistan*, 88–89.
68. Samuel Helfont, *Compulsion in Religion: Saddam Hussein, Islam, and the Roots of Insurgencies in Iraq* (New York: Oxford University Press, 2018), 213–23.
69. Bailey and Immerman, *Understanding the U.S. Wars in Iraq and Afghanistan*, 78, 92.
70. Douglas A. Pryer, "The Fight for the High Ground: The U.S. Army and Interrogation during Operation Iraqi Freedom I, May 2003–April 2004," (MMAS / Fort Leavenworth, KS, thesis, U.S. Army Command and General Staff College, 2009), 5–6, 19–20, 22, 29, 41.
71. *Report of the Senate Select Committee on Intelligence Committee Study of the Central Intelligence Agency's Detention and Interrogation Program* [Feinstein Report], U.S. Senate, 113th Cong., 2nd Sess., Senate Report 113–288 (Washington: Government Printing Office, 2014), vi–xx.
72. Risen, *State of War*, 23–25.
73. Michael Hayden, Frontline interview, Aug. 19, 2010, https://www.pbs.org/wgbh/pages/frontline/are-we-safer/interviews/michael-hayden.html, accessed March 27, 2021.
74. Schaefer, "The History of Domestic Intelligence in the United States," in Jackson, *The Challenge of Domestic Intelligence in a Free Society*, 43.
75. Neal Katyal and Richard Caplan, "The Surprisingly Stronger Case for the Legality of the NSA Surveillance Program: The FDR Precedent," *Stanford Law Review* 60:4 (Feb. 2008): 1030–34.
76. Peter Bergen et al., "Do NSA's Bulk Surveillance Programs Stop Terrorists?" New America Foundation (Jan. 2014), 1–2.
77. U.S. 107th Congress, Public Law 107-296, Nov. 25, 2002, Titles II, V, VIII, and IX.
78. Hayden, Frontline interview.
79. Richard A. Posner, *The Reorganized U.S. Intelligence System After One Year* (Washington: American Enterprise Institute, 2006), 4–5.
80. Risen, *State of War*, 68–73.
81. Tenet and Harlow, *At the Center of the Storm*, 66–71.

Chapter Seven. The Paradox of Warning

1. Michael I. Handel, "The Yom Kippur War and the Inevitability of Surprise," *International Studies Quarterly* 21:3 (Sept. 1977): 479.

2. Steve Chan, "The Intelligence of Stupidity: Understanding Failures in Strategic Warning," *American Political Science Review* 73:1 (March 1974): 174.
3. Thomas Fingar, DDNI for Analysis, Speech to Commonwealth Club, San Francisco, Feb. 14, 2008.
4. John A. Gentry and Joseph S. Gordon, *Strategic Warning Intelligence: History, Challenges, and Prospects* (Washington: Georgetown University Press, 2019), 19–20.
5. Chan, "The Intelligence of Stupidity," 172.
6. Handel, "The Yom Kippur War and the Inevitability of Surprise," 483, 493; Avi Shlaim, "Failures in National Intelligence Estimates: The Case of the Yom Kippur War," *World Politics* 28:3 (April 1976): 358–59.
7. John A. Gentry, "Intelligence Failure Reframed," *Political Science Quarterly* 123:2 (Summer 2008): 249.
8. See, for example, Scott R. Feil, *Preventing Genocide: How the Early Use of Force Might Have Succeeded in Rwanda* (New York: Carnegie Corporation, 1998).
9. Michael Breen, "Icons & Influencers: (16) Chun Doo-hwan: the Last Dictator," *Korea Times*, November 23, 2011, http://www.koreatimes.co.kr/www/nation/2012/02/363_99434.html, accessed March 27, 2021.
10. Michael Breen, "Assassination of President Park Chung-hee in 1979," *Korea Times*, May 17, 2016.
11. "A Bomb Wreaks Havoc in Rangoon," *Time*, Oct. 17, 1983, 36; CIA, "Rangoon Bombing Incident: The Case against the North Koreans," Oct. 19, 1983, CIA FOIA Reading Room, https://www.cia.gov/library/readingroom/docs/DOC_0000408056.pdf, accessed Aug. 25, 2020.
12. Abraham Ben-Zvi, "The Study of Surprise Attacks," *British Journal of International Studies* 5:2 (July 1979): 129–41.
13. David M. Glantz and Jonathan M. House, *When Titans Clashed: How the Red Army Stopped Hitler*, rev. and exp. ed. (Lawrence: University Press of Kansas, 2015), 50–51.
14. For an account of this evolution, see Gentry and Gordon, *Strategic Warning Intelligence*, 67–73.
15. Memorandum of conference with the President, October 24, 1957, Eisenhower Library, Office of the Staff Secretary, box 6.
16. Unlabeled memorandum, c. 1960, DCI responses to PBCFIA recommendations, Eisenhower Library, SpAsst for NSA, box 8, 1960 file.
17. William Tidwell, "Notes on the CRITIC System," *Studies in Intelligence* 14:2 (Spring 1960): 19–23.
18. Memorandum, DCI and Deputy Secretary of Defense to NSC Executive Secretary, December 15, 1959, Eisenhower Library, SpAsst for NSA, box 8.

19. Gabriel Gorodetsky, *Grand Delusion: Stalin and the German Invasion of Russia* (New Haven, CT: Yale University Press, 1999), 4–15; Geoffrey Roberts, "The Soviet Decision for a Pact with Nazi Germany," *Soviet Studies* 44:1 (1992): 57–72.
20. Barton Whaley, *Codeword Barbarossa* (Cambridge, MA: MIT Press, 1973), 24–129.
21. David E. Murphy, *What Stalin Knew: The Enigma of Barbarossa* (New Haven, CT: Yale University Press, 2005), 63–72, 116–20.
22. Jonathan Haslam, *Near and Distant Neighbors: A New History of Soviet Intelligence* (New York: Farrar, Straus, and Giroux, 2015), 97–98.
23. Whaley, *Codeword Barbarossa*, 192–194.
24. Murphy, *What Stalin Knew*, 7–13, 54–61.
25. Murphy, *What Stalin Knew*, 173–74; Whaley, *Codeword Barbarossa*, 172–75, 248.
26. Glantz and House, *When Titans Clashed*, 50.
27. L. Dvoinykh and N. Tarkhova, "What Military Intelligence Reported: Historians Have a Chance to Analyze Soviet Intelligence Dispatches on the Eve of the War," *Russian Studies in History* 36:3 (Winter 1997–1998): 81.
28. Glantz and House, *When Titans Clashed*, 50–51.
29. Roberta Wohlstetter, *Pearl Harbor: Warning and Decision* (Stanford, CA: Stanford University Press, 1982), 139.
30. Roberta Wohlstetter, "Cuba and Pearl Harbor: Hindsight and Foresight," *Foreign Affairs* 43:4 (July 1965): 693; David Kahn, "The Intelligence Failure of Pearl Harbor," *Foreign Affairs* 70:5 (Winter 1991): 145.
31. James R. Stobie, "More to the Story: A Reappraisal of U.S. Intelligence Prior to the Pacific War" (MMAS thesis, U.S. Army Command and General Staff College, Fort Leavenworth, KS, 2007), 27–28.
32. Wohlstetter, *Pearl Harbor*, 8–16.
33. Gordon W. Prange, Donald M. Goldstein, and Katherine V. Dillon, *At Dawn We Slept: The Untold Story of Pearl Harbor* (New York: Penguin Books, 1991), 80–86.
34. Wohlstetter, *Pearl Harbor*, 187, 389–90.
35. Stobie, "More to the Story," 11.
36. Wohlstetter, *Pearl Harbor*, 230–31, 273–75.
37. John T. Kuehn, "The War in the Pacific, 1941–1945," in *The Cambridge History of the Second World War*, vol. I, *Fighting the War*, ed. John Ferris and Evan Mawdsley (Cambridge: Cambridge University Press, 2015), 423.
38. Jonathan M. House, *A Military History of the Cold War, 1944–1962* (Norman: University of Oklahoma Press, 2012), 50–51, 166–68.

39. Allan R. Millett, *The War for Korea, 1945–1950: A House Burning* (Lawrence: University Press of Kansas, 2005), 142–50, 198–212.
40. Millett, *The War for Korea*, 241–43, 250–51.
41. See, for example, Sergei N. Goncharov, John W. Lewis, and Xue Litai, *Uncertain Partners: Stalin, Mao, and the Korean War* (Stanford, CA: Stanford University Press, 1993), 130–40; Geoffrey Roberts, *Stalin's Wars: From World War to Cold War, 1939–1953* (New Haven, CT: Yale University Press, 2006), 366–69.
42. Alexander L. George and Richard Smoke, *Deterrence in American Foreign Policy: Theory and Practice* (New York: Columbia University Press, 1974), 145–66.
43. Ben-Zvi, "The Study of Surprise Attacks," 144.
44. George and Smoke, *Deterrence in American Foreign Policy*, 186.
45. George and Smoke, *Deterrence in American Foreign Policy*, 216–18.
46. Jian Chen, *China's Road to the Korean War: The Making of the Sino-American Confrontation* (New York: Columbia University Press, 1994), 186–88, 196–202, 208–9.
47. Goncharov, Lewis, and Xue, *Uncertain Partners*, 159–63; Jian Chen, *Mao's China and the Cold War* (Chapel Hill: University of North Carolina Press, 2001), 87–90.
48. Goncharov, Lewis, and Xue, *Uncertain Partners*, 187–95; Chen, *Mao's China and the Cold War*, 89–90.
49. This paragraph is based upon the following: Clay Blair, *The Forgotten War: America in Korea, 1950–1953* (New York: Times Books/Random House, 1987), 370–90; Roy E. Appleman, *South to the Naktong, North to the Yalu (June–November 1950)* (Washington: Office of the Chief of Military History, 1961), 673–75; Xiaobing Li, Allan R. Millett, and Bin Yu, trans. and eds., *Mao's Generals Remember Korea* (Lawrence: University Press of Kansas, 2001), 14.
50. Abraham Ben-Zvi, "Hindsight and Foresight: A Conceptual Framework for the Analysis of Surprise Attacks," *World Politics* 28:3 (April 1976): 390.
51. Steven J. Zaloga, *Target America: The Soviet Union and the Strategic Arms Race, 1945–1964* (Novato, CA: Presidio Press, 1993), 193–97.
52. Norman Polmar and John D. Gresham, *DEFCON-2: Standing on the Brink of Nuclear War During the Cuban Missile Crisis* (Hoboken, NJ: John Wiley and Sons, Inc., 2006), 6, 28–31.
53. George and Smoke, *Deterrence in American Foreign Policy*, 468–69.
54. Klaus Knorr, "Failure in National Intelligence Estimates: The Case of the Cuban Missiles," *World Politics* 16:3 (April 1964): 456–57.

55. Joseph F. Bouchard, "Use of Naval Force in Crises: A Theory of Stratified Crisis Interaction" (PhD diss., Stanford University, 1988), 516–17, 527–30. The data described by Bouchard are not mentioned specifically in the CIA's after-action report, although the Department of Defense unquestionably began its preparations at the start of October rather than mid-October. See James Q. Rever, "Memorandum for Deputy Director of Central Intelligence, Subject: Historical Analysis of U-2 Overflights of Cuba, 24 October 1962," document CIA-RDP92B01090R002600080068-8, available through CIA FOIA Reading Room, accessed Sept. 2, 2020.
56. See House, *A Military History of the Cold War*, 421–40.
57. Lien-Hang T. Nguyen, *Hanoi's War: An International History of the War for Peace in Vietnam* (Chapel Hill, NC: University of North Carolina Press, 2012), 98–101.
58. John Prados, "The Warning That Left Something to Chance: Intelligence at Tet," *Journal of American-East Asian Relations* 2:2 (Summer 1993): 172–79.
59. Prados, "The Warning That Left Something to Chance," 177–78.
60. William M. Hammond, *Public Affairs: The Military and the Media, 1962–1968* (Washington: U.S. Army Center of Military History, 1988), 332–38; William M. Hammond, "The Tet Offensive and the News Media: Some Thoughts on the Effects of News Reporting," *Army History* 70 (Winter 2009): 8–11.
61. Dominic D. P. Johnson and Dominic Tierney, *Failing to Win: Perceptions of Victory and Defeat in International Politics* (Cambridge, MA: Harvard University Press, 2006), 184–87.
62. Quotation from the 1974 interim report of the Agranat Commission of Inquiry, contained in Bernard Reich, ed., *Arab-Israeli Conflict and Conciliation: A Documentary History* (Westport, CT: Praeger, 1995), 121.
63. Handel, "The Yom Kippur War," 489.
64. Dani Asher, *The Egyptian Strategy for the Yom Kippur War*, trans. Moshe Tlamim (Jefferson, NC: McFarland and Co., 2003), 9–10, 61.
65. Dina Rezk, *The Arab World and Western Intelligence: Analysing the Middle East, 1956–1981* (Edinburgh: Edinburgh University Press, 2017), 252–54, 257.
66. Shlaim, "Failures in National Intelligence Estimates," 366.
67. Shlaim, "Failures in National Intelligence Estimates," 268–270; Handel, "The Yom Kippur War," 473–76, 485, 498–99.
68. Handel, "The Yom Kippur War," 482.
69. Richard K. Betts, *Surprise Attack: Lessons for Defense Planning* (Washington: Brookings Institution, 1982), 78.

70. Handel, "The Yom Kippur War," 500–501.
71. Mohamed Heikal, *The Road to Ramadan* (New York: Quadrangle Books, 1975), 204–5.
72. Saad el Shazly, *The Crossing of the Suez*, rev. ed. (San Francisco: American Mideast Research, 2003), 71–75.
73. Rezk, *The Arab World and Western Intelligence*, 265.
74. Agranat Commission report in Reich, *Arab-Israeli Conflict and Conciliation*, 123.
75. Shlaim, "Failures in National Intelligence Estimates," 349.
76. Handel, "The Yom Kippur War," 468.

Chapter Eight. Conclusions

1. Ryan Gingeras, "How the Deep State Came to America: A History," *War on the Rocks*, Feb. 4, 2019, https://warontherocks.com/2019/02/how-the-deep-state-came-to-america-a-history/, accessed March 27, 2021.
2. Neal Katyal and Richard Caplan, "The Surprisingly Stronger Case for the Legality of the NSA Surveillance Program: The FDR Precedent," *Stanford Law Review* 60:4 (Feb. 2008): 1039.

Bibliography

Documents and Unpublished Sources

Dwight D. Eisenhower Presidential Library

Ann Whitman Files, NSC Series
Ike Skelton Combined Arms Research Library
National Security Council Series, Administrative Subseries
Office of the Staff Secretary Subject Series, Alphabetical Subseries
Special Assistant Series, Special Assistant for National Security Affairs
U.S. Army Center of Military History
U.S. Army Military History Institute

Digital Collections

Central Intelligence Agency FOIA Library/Reading Room
Intelligence Resource Program, Federation of American Scientists
National Security Archives, George Washington University

Published Works

Absher, Kenneth M., Michael C. Desch, and Roman Popadiuk. *Privileged and Confidential: The Secret History of the President's Intelligence Advisory Board.* Lexington: University Press of Kentucky, 2012.

Adamski, Michael J. "Enhancing the ODNI Analytic Standards: An Evolving Framework." *American Intelligence Journal* 29:1 (2011): 116–19.

Ahern, Thomas L. Jr. *CIA and the Generals: Covert Support to Military Government in South Vietnam.* Washington: Center for the Study of Intelligence/CIA, 1998.

———. *CIA and the House of Ngo: Covert Action in South Vietnam, 1954–63.* Washington: Center for the Study of Intelligence/CIA, 2000.

———. *The Way We Do Things: Black Entry Operations into North Vietnam, 1961–1964.* Washington: Center for the Study of Intelligence/CIA, 2005.

Aldrich, Richard J. "Counting the Cost of Intelligence: The Treasury, National Service and GCHQ." *English Historical Review* 128:532 (June 2013): 596–627.

———. *The Hidden Hand: Britain, America, and Cold War Secret Intelligence.* New York: Overlook Press/Peter Mayer Publishers, 2001.

Ambrose, Stephen E., and Richard H. Immermann. *Ike's Spies: Eisenhower and the Espionage Establishment.* Garden City, NY: Doubleday & Co., 1981.

Ameringer, Charles D. *U.S. Foreign Intelligence: The Secret Side of American History.* Lexington, MA: Lexington Books, 1990.

Anderson, Terry H. *Bush's Wars.* Oxford: Oxford University Press, 2011.

Andradé, Dale, and James H. Willbanks, "CORDS/Phoenix: Counterinsurgency Lessons from Vietnam for the Future." *Military Review* 86:2 (March–April 2006): 9–23.

Andrew, Christopher. "American Presidents and Their Intelligence Communities." *Intelligence and National Security* 10:4 (Jan. 2008): 95–112.

———. "Churchill and Intelligence." *Intelligence and National Security* 3:3 (1988): 181–93.

———. *Defend the Realm: The Authorized History of MI5.* New York: Alfred A. Knopf, 2009.

———. *Secret Service: The Making of the British Intelligence Community.* London: Heinemann, 1985.

———. *Secret World: A History of Intelligence.* New Haven, CT: Yale University Press, 2019.

Andrew, Christopher, and Julie Elkner. "Stalin and Foreign Intelligence." *Totalitarian Movements and Political Religions* 4:1 (2003): 69–94.

Andrew, Christopher, and Oleg Gordievsky. *KGB: The Inside Story of Its Foreign Operations from Lenin to Gorbachev.* London: Scepter/Hodder and Stoughton, 1990.

Andrew, Christopher, and Vasili Mitrokhin. *The Mitrokhin Archive II: The KGB and the World* London: Penguin, 2006.

———. *The Sword and the Shield: The Mitrokhin Archive and the Secret History of the KGB.* New York: Basic Books, 1999.

Appleman, Roy E. *South to the Naktong, North to the Yalu (June–November 1950).* Washington: Office of the Chief of Military History, 1961.

Armour, Ian D. "Colonel Redl: Fact and Fantasy." *Intelligence and National Security* 2:1 (1987): 170–83.

Asher, Dani. *The Egyptian Strategy for the Yom Kippur War.* Trans. by Moshe Tlamim Jefferson, NC: McFarland & Co., 2003.

Bailey, Beth, and Richard H. Immerman, eds. *Understanding the U.S. Wars in Iraq and Afghanistan.* New York: New York University Press, 2015.

Bamford, James. *The Puzzle Palace: A Report on America's Most Secret Agency.* New York: Penguin Books, 1983.

Barnes, Trevor. "The Secret Cold War: The C.I.A. and American Foreign Policy in Europe, 1946–1956, Part I." *Historical Journal* 24:2 (June 1981): 399–415.

Barrass, Gordon. "Able Archer 83: What Were the Soviets Thinking?" *Survival* 56:8 (Dec. 2016–Jan. 2017): 7–30.

Barron, John. *The KGB Today: The Hidden Hand.* London: Hodder and Stoughton, 1983.

Barry, James A., Jack Davis, David D. Gries, and Joseph Sullivan. "Bridging the Intelligence-Policy Divide." *Studies in Intelligence* 37:3 (1994): no page numbers.

Beer, Siegfried and Marianne Walle. "Les services du renseignement habsbourgeois ont-ils échoué? La défaite des services du renseignement austro-hongrois dans la première guerre mondiale." *Guerres mondiales et conflits contemporains*, no. 232 (2008): 73–85.

Beers, Henry P. "The Development of the Office of the Chief of Naval Operations." *Military Affairs* 10:1 (Spring 1946): 40–68.

Beesly, Patrick. *Very Special Intelligence: The Story of the Admiralty's Operational Intelligence Centre 1939–1945.* New York: Ballantine Books, 1981.

Bellaby, Ross. "What's the Harm? The Ethics of Intelligence Collection." *Intelligence and National Security* 27:1 (Feb. 2012): 93–117.

Ben-Zvi, Abraham. "American Preconceptions and Policies toward Japan, 1940–1941: A Case Study in Misperception." *International Studies Quarterly* 19:2 (June 1975): 228–48.

———. "Hindsight and Foresight: A Conceptual Framework for the Analysis of Surprise Attacks." *World Politics* 28:3 (April 1976), 381–95.

———. "The Study of Surprise Attacks." *British Journal of International Studies* 5:2 (July 1979): 129–49.

Bergen, Peter, David Sterman, Emily Schneider, and Bailey Cahall. "Do NSA's Bulk Surveillance Programs Stop Terrorists?" New America Foundation, Jan. 2014.

Berkowitz, Bruce D., and Allan E. Goodman. *Best Truth: Intelligence in the Information Age.* New Haven, CT: Yale University Press, 2000.

Bethel, Elizabeth. "The Military Information Division: Origin of the Intelligence Division." *Military Affairs* 11:1 (Spring 1947): 17–24.

Betts, Richard K. "Analysis, War, and Decision: Why Intelligence Failures Are Inevitable." *World Politics* 31:1 (October 1978): 61–89.

———. "Policy-Makers and Intelligence Analysts: Love, Hate, or Indifference?" *Intelligence and National Security* 3:1 (Jan. 1988): 181–89.

———. *Surprise Attack: Lessons for Defense Planning.* Washington: Brookings Institution, 1982.

Bidwell, Bruce W. *History of the Military Intelligence Division, Department of the Army General Staff: 1775–1941.* Frederick, MD: University Publications of America, 1986.

Bissell, Richard M. Jr., with Jonathan E. Lewis and Frances T. Pudlo. *Reflections of a Cold Warrior: From Yalta to the Bay of Pigs.* New Haven, CT: Yale University Press, 1996.

Blair, Clay. *The Forgotten War: America in Korea, 1950–1953.* New York: Times Books/Random House, 1987.

Bolger, Daniel P. *Americans at War, 1975–1986, An Era of Violent Peace.* Novato, CA: Presidio Press, 1988.

Borg, Horst. "German Air Intelligence in the Second World War." *Intelligence and National Security* 5:2 (April 1990): 350–424.

———. "German Air Intelligence in World War II." *Aerospace Historian* 33:2 (Summer 1986): 121–29.

Bottome, Edgar M. *The Missile Gap: A Study of the Formulation of Military and Political Policy.* Cranbury, NJ: Associated University Presses, 1971.

Bouchard, Joseph F. "Use of Naval Force in Crises: A Theory of Stratified Crisis Interaction." PhD dissertation, Stanford University, 1988.

Bregman, Ahron. *Israel's Wars: A History Since 1947.* 2nd ed. London: Routledge, 2002.

Brown, Anthony Cave. *Bodyguard of Lies.* New York: Harper and Row, 1975.

Burns, Thomas L. *The Origins of the National Security Agency, 1940–1952.* United States Cryptologic History Series V, Vol. I. Fort Meade, MD: Center for Cryptologic History, National Security Agency, 1990.

Campbell, Kenneth. "Major General Friedrich Gempp: German Intelligence Leader." *American Intelligence Journal* 25:1 (Summer 2007): 75–81.

———. "Walter Schellenberg, SD Chief." *American Intelligence Journal* 25:2 (Winter 2007–8): 88–94.

Catton, Philip E. *Diem's Final Failure: Prelude to America's War in Vietnam.* Lawrence: University Press of Kansas, 2002.

Chan, Steve. "The Intelligence of Stupidity: Understanding Failures in Strategic Warning." *American Political Science Review* 73:1 (March 1974): 171–80.

Chen, Jian. *China's Road to the Korean War: The Making of the Sino-American Confrontation.* New York: Columbia University Press, 1994.

———. *Mao's China and the Cold War.* Chapel Hill, NC: University of North Carolina Press, 2001.

Chorev, Moni. "Surprise Attack: The Case of the Yom-Kippur War." Research Project. Washington: Industrial College of the Armed Forces, National Defense University, 1996.

Churchill, Ward. "From the Pinkertons to the PATRIOT Act: The Trajectory of Political Policing in the United States, 1870 to the Present." *The New Centennial Review* 4:1 (Spring 2004): 1–72.

Clarke, Richard A. *Against All Enemies: Inside America's War on Terror.* New York: Free Press, 2004.

Clinton, William J. "National Priorities for Intelligence: Remarks to the Intelligence Community." *American Intelligence Journal* 16:1 (Spring/Summer 1995): 15–17.

Commission on the Intelligence Capabilities of the United States Regarding Weapons of Mass Destruction. *Report to the President of the United States, March 31, 2005* [Silberman-Robb Report]. Washington: Government Printing Office, 2005.

Corera, Gordon. *Shopping for Bombs: Nuclear Proliferation, Global Insecurity, and the Rise and Fall of the A Q Khan Network.* New York: Oxford University Press, 2006.

Crist, David. *The Twilight War: The Secret History of America's Thirty-Year Conflict with Iran.* New York: Penguin, 2012.

Cumming, Alfred. "Statutory Procedures under Which Congress Is to Be Informed of U.S. Intelligence Activities, Including Covert Actions." Congressional Research Service, Jan. 18, 2006.

Currey, Cecil B. *Edward Lansdale: The Unquiet American.* Washington: Brassey's, 1998.

Daddis, Gregory A. *No Sure Victory: Measuring U.S. Army Effectiveness and Progress in the Vietnam War.* Oxford: Oxford University Press, 2011.

Damms, Richard V. "James Killian, the Technological Capabilities Panel, and the Emergence of President Eisenhower's 'Scientific-Technological Elite.'" *Diplomatic History* 24:1 (Winter 2000): 57–78.

Davis, Brian L. *Qaddafi, Terrorism, and the Origins of the U.S. Attack on Libya.* New York: Praeger, 1990.

Davis, Jack. "The Challenge of Managing Uncertainty: Paul Wolfowitz on Intelligence-Policy Relations." *Studies in Intelligence* 39:5 (1996): 35–42.

———. "Intelligence Analysts and Policymakers: Benefits and Dangers of Tensions in the Relationship." *Intelligence and National Security* 21:6 (Dec. 2006): 999–1021.

Deane, John R. Jr. *Lessons in Leadership: My Life in the US Army from World War II to Vietnam.* Lexington: University Press of Kentucky, 2012.

Deutsch, Harold C. "The Influence of ULTRA on World War II." *Parameters: Journal of the U.S. Army War College* 8:4 (Dec. 1978): 2–15.

Dommanget, Maurice. *Auguste Blanqui: Des Origines a la Révolution de 1848.* Paris: Mouton, 1969.

Draitser, Emil. *Stalin's Romeo Spy: The Remarkable Rise and Fall of the KGB's Most Daring Operative. The True Life of Dmitri Bystrolyotov.* Evanston, IL: Northwestern University Press, 2010.

Drea, Edward J. *McNamara, Clifford, and the Burdens of Vietnam 1965–1969.* Secretaries of Defense Historical Series, Vol. VI. Washington: Historical Office, Office of the Secretary of Defense, 2011.

Duelfer, Charles. *Hide and Seek: The Search for Truth in Iraq.* New York: Public Affairs/Perseus Group, 2009.

Dvoinykh, L., and N. Tarkhova, "What Military Intelligence Reported: Historians Have a Chance to Analyze Soviet Intelligence Dispatches on the Eve of the War." *Russian Studies in History* 36:3 (Winter 1997–1998); originally published in *Nauka i zhizn'* 3 (1995).

Dziak, John J. *Chekisty: A History of the KGB.* Lexington, MA: Lexington Books, 1988.

Ebon, Martin. *KGB: Death and Rebirth.* Westport, CT: Praeger, 1994.

Edwards, Owen. "The Ellsberg Files." *Smithsonian* 43:6 (2012): 70–71.

Edwards, Philip K. "The President's Board 1956–1960." *Studies in Intelligence* 13 (Summer 1969): 113–28.

Eisenhower, Dwight D. *Waging Peace, 1956–1961: The White House Years.* Garden City, NY: Doubleday and Company, 1965.

Ellis, Mark. "J. Edgar Hoover and the 'Red Summer' of 1919." *Journal of American Studies* 28:1 (April 1994): 39–59.

Emsley, Clive. *Policing and its Context, 1750–1870.* New York: Schocken, 1984.

Faligot, Roger, and Pascal Krop. *La Piscine: The French Secret Service since 1944.* Translated by W. D. Halls. Oxford: Basil Blackwell, 1989; original Paris: Editions du Seuil, 1985.

Feil, Scott R. *Preventing Genocide: How the Early Use of Force Might Have Succeeded in Rwanda.* New York: Carnegie Corporation, 1998.

Feith, Douglas J. *War and Decision: Inside the Pentagon at the Dawn of the War on Terrorism.* New York: HarperCollins, 2008.

Fester, James W. "Administrative Literature and the Second Hoover Commission Reports." *American Political Science Review* 51:1 (March 1957): 135–57.

Fingar, Thomas. *Reducing Uncertainty: Intelligence Analysis and National Security.* Stanford, CA: Stanford University Press, 2011.

Finnegan, Terrence J. *Shooting the Front: Allied Aerial Reconnaissance and Photographic Interpretation on the Western Front—World War I.* Washington: National Defense Intelligence College, 2006.

Fischer, Benjamin B. "Canopy Wing: The U.S. War Plan That Gave the East Germans Goose Bumps." *International Journal of Intelligence and CounterIntelligence* 27:3 (May 2014): 431–64.

———. "The Soviet-American War Scare of the 1980s." *International Journal of Intelligence and CounterIntelligence* 19:3 (Nov. 2006): 480–518.

Ford, Christopher, and David Rosenberg. *The Admirals' Advantage: U.S. Navy Operational Intelligence in World War II and the Cold War.* Annapolis, MD: Naval Institute Press, 2005.

Forssell, Nils. *Fouché: The Man Napoleon Feared.* Translated by Anna Borwell. New York: Frederick A. Stokes Co., 1928.

Frégier, Honore-Antoine. *Histoire de l'Administration de la Police de Paris depuis Philippe-Auguste jusqu'aux états Généraux de 1789*, Vol. I Paris: Guillaumin, 1850.

Frieser, Karl-Heinz. *The Blitzkrieg Legend: The 1940 Campaign in the West.* Annapolis, MD: Naval Institute Press, 2005.

Garthoff, Raymond L. "Foreign Intelligence and the Historiography of the Cold War." *Journal of Cold War Studies* 6:2 (Spring 2004): 21–56.

Gentry, John A. "Intelligence Failure Reframed." *Political Science Quarterly* 123:2 (Summer 2008): 247–70.

Gentry, John A., and Joseph S. Gordon. *Strategic Warning Intelligence: History, Challenges, and Prospects.* Washington: Georgetown University Press, 2019.

George, Alexander L., and Richard Smoke. *Deterrence in American Foreign Policy: Theory and Practice.* New York: Columbia University Press, 1974.

George, Roger Z., and Robert D. Kline, eds. *Intelligence and the National Security Strategist: Enduring Issues and Challenges.* Washington: National Defense University, 2004.

Gilbert, James L. *World War I and the Origins of U.S. Military Intelligence.* Lanham, MD: Scarecrow/Rowman & Littlefield, 2012.

Gingeras, Ryan. "How the Deep State Came to America: A History." *War on the Rocks*, Feb. 4, 2019. https://warontherocks.com/2019/02/how-the-deep-state-came-to-america-a-history/. Accessed March 27, 2021.

Glabe, Scott. "The Original Privatization of Intelligence: Iran-Contra Revisited." *American Intelligence Journal* 28:1 (2010): 113–20.

Glantz, David M., and Jonathan M. House. *When Titans Clashed: How the Red Army Stopped Hitler.* Rev. and expanded ed. Lawrence: University Press of Kansas, 2015.

Goldman, Aaron L. "Two Views of Germany: Nevile Henderson vs. Vansittart and the Foreign Office, 1937–1939" *British Journal of International Studies* 6:3 (Oct. 1980): 247–77.

Goncharov, Sergei N., John W. Lewis, and Xue Litai. *Uncertain Partners: Stalin, Mao, and the Korean War.* Stanford, CA: Stanford University Press, 1993.

Goodall, Alex. *Loyalty and Liberty: American Countersubversion from World War I to the McCarthy Era.* Champaign: University of Illinois Press, 2013.

Goodman, Michael S. *The Official History of the Joint Intelligence Committee.* Vol. I, *From the Approach of the Second World War to the Suez Crisis.* London: Routledge, 2014.

Gorodetsky, Gabriel. *Grand Delusion: Stalin and the German Invasion of Russia.* New Haven, CT: Yale University Press, 1999.

Haines, Gerald K. "The Pike Committee Investigations and the CIA." *Studies in Intelligence* 42:5 (Winter 1998–99): 81–92.

Hammond, William M. *Public Affairs: The Military and the Media, 1962–1968.* CMH Pub 91-13. Washington: U.S. Army Center of Military History, 1988.

———. "The Tet Offensive and the News Media: Some Thoughts on the Effects of News Reporting." *Army History* 70 (Winter 2009): 7–15.

Hamza, Khidir, with Jeff Stein. *Saddam's Bombmaker: The Terrifying Inside Story of the Iraqi Nuclear and Biological Weapons Agenda.* New York: Scribner, 2000.

Handel, Michael I. "Intelligence and the Problem of Strategic Surprise." *Journal of Strategic Studies* 7:3 (September 1984): 229–81.

———. "The Yom Kippur War and the Inevitability of Surprise." *International Studies Quarterly* 21:3 (September 1977): 461–502.

Hannay, David. "Three Iraq Intelligence Failures Reconsidered." *Survival* 51:6 (Dec. 2009–Jan. 2010): 13–20.

Haslam, Jonathan. *Near and Distant Neighbors: A New History of Soviet Intelligence.* New York: Farrar, Straus, and Giroux, 2015.

Haslam, Jonathan, and Karina Urbach, eds. *Secret Intelligence in the European State System, 1918–1989.* Stanford, CA: Stanford University Press, 2014.

Heikal, Mohamed. *The Road to Ramadan.* New York: Quadrangle Books, 1975.

Heinrichs, Waldo. *Threshold of War: Franklin D. Roosevelt and American Entry into World War II.* Oxford: Oxford University Press, 1988.

Helfont, Samuel. *Compulsion in Religion: Saddam Hussein, Islam, and the Roots of Insurgencies in Iraq.* New York: Oxford University Press, 2018.

Herman, Michael. *Intelligence Power in Peace and War.* Cambridge: Cambridge University Press, 1996.

Hersh, Seymour M. "Huge C.I.A. Operation Reported in U.S. Against Antiwar Forces, Other Dissidents in Nixon Years." *New York Times*, Dec. 22, 1974, 1.

———. "Selective Intelligence." Annals of National Security. *The New Yorker*, May 12, 2003, 44–51.

———. "The Stovepipe." Annals of National Security. *The New Yorker*, Oct. 27, 2003, 77.

Hingley, Ronald. *The Russian Secret Police: Muscovite, Imperial Russian, and Soviet Political Security Operations.* New York: Simon & Schuster, 1970.

Hinsley, Francis H., E. E. Thomas, C. F. G. Ransom, and R. C. Knight. *British Intelligence in the Second World War: Its Influence on Strategy and Operations.* 5 Vols. London: Her Majesty's Stationery Office, 1979–1990.

The History of SIGINT in the Central Intelligence Agency, 1947–70. 2 Vols. Arlington, VA: CIA Historical Staff, 1971. (Top Secret; declassified July 18, 2013.) https://archive.org/details/HistoryOfSIGINTInThe CIA19471970. Accessed March 27, 2021.

Hittle, J. D., ed. *Roots of Strategy*, Book 2. Harrisburg, PA: Stackpole Books, 1987.

House, Jonathan M. *Controlling Paris: Armed Forces and Counter-Revolution, 1789–1848.* New York: New York University Press, 2014.

———. *A Military History of the Cold War, 1944–1962.* Norman: University of Oklahoma Press, 2012.

———. *A Military History of the Cold War, 1962–1991.* Norman: University of Oklahoma Press, 2020.

———. *Military Intelligence, 1870–1991: A Research Guide.* Westport, CT: Greenwood Press, 1993.

Hughes-Wilson, John. *The Secret State: A History of Intelligence and Espionage.* New York: Pegasus Books, 2016.

Hull, Mark M. "The Irish Interlude: German Intelligence in Ireland, 1939–1943." *Journal of Military History* 66:3 (July 2002): 695–717.

Huntington, Samuel P. *The Soldier and the State: The Theory and Politics of Civil-Military Relations.* Paperback ed. New York: Vintage/Random House, 1957.

Hutchinson, Robert. *German Foreign Intelligence from Hitler's War to the Cold War: Flawed Assumptions and Faulty Analysis.* Lawrence: University Press of Kansas, 2019.

Jackson, Brian A., ed. *The Challenge of Domestic Intelligence in a Free Society: A Multidisciplinary Look at the Creation of a U.S. Domestic Counterterrorism Intelligence Agency.* Santa Monica, CA: RAND, 2009.

Jeans, Roger B. Jr. "Ghost Guerrillas: The CIA and 'Tiger General' Li Zongren's Third Force during the Early Cold War." *Journal of Military History* 81:2 (April 2017): 491–512.

Jeffery, Keith. *MI6: The History of the Secret Intelligence Service, 1909–1949.* London: Bloomsbury, 2010.

Jeffreys-Jones, Rhodri. *Cloak and Dollar: A History of American Secret Intelligence.* New Haven, CT: Yale University Press, 2002.

Jervis, Robert. *How Statesmen Think: The Psychology of International Politics.* Princeton, NJ: Princeton University Press, 2017.

———. *Why Intelligence Fails: Lessons from the Iranian Revolution and the Iraq War.* Ithaca, NY: Cornell University Press, 2010.

Johnson, Dominic D. P., and Dominic Tierney. *Failing to Win: Perceptions of Victory and Defeat in International Politics.* Cambridge, MA: Harvard University Press, 2006.

Johnson, Loch K. *Secret Agencies: U.S. Intelligence in a Hostile World.* New Haven, CT: Yale University Press, 1998.

Johnson, Tom. "What Every Cryptologist Should Know about Pearl Harbor." *Cryptologic Quarterly* 6:2 (Summer 1987): 55–67.

de Jomini, Antoine-Henri. *The Art of War.* In *Roots of Strategy,* book 2, edited by J. D. Hittle, 529–38. Harrisburg, PA: Stackpole Books, 1987.

Jones, Frank Leith. *Blowtorch: Robert Komer, Vietnam, and American Cold War Strategy.* Annapolis, MD: Naval Institute Press, 2013.

Judd, Alan. *The Quest for C: Sir Mansfield Cumming and the Founding of the British Secret Service.* London: HarperCollins, 1999.

Kahn, David. *The Codebreakers: The Story of Secret Writing.* New York: Macmillan, 1967.

———. "The Intelligence Failure of Pearl Harbor." *Foreign Affairs* 70:5 (Winter 1991): 138–52.

———. *The Reader of Gentlemen's Mail: Herbert O. Yardley and the Birth of American Codebreaking.* New Haven, CT: Yale University Press, 2004.

Kaplan, Lawrence S., Ronald D. Landa, and Edward J. Drea. *History of the Office of the Secretary of Defense. Vol. V, The McNamara Ascendancy, 1961–1965.* Washington: Office of the Secretary of Defense, 2006.

Karalekas, Anne. *History of the Central Intelligence Agency.* Laguna Hills, CA: Aegean Park Press, 1977. Originally a 1976 report to the Senate Select Committee to Study Governmental Operations with Respect to Intelligence Activities, or Church Committee.

Katyal, Neal, and Richard Caplan. "The Surprisingly Stronger Case for the Legality of the NSA Surveillance Program: The FDR Precedent." *Stanford Law Review* 60:4 (Feb. 2008): 1023–77.

Keany, Thomas A., and Eliot Cohen. *Gulf War Airpower Survey, Summary Report*. Washington: Department of the Air Force, 1993.

Killian, James R. Jr. *The Education of a College President*. Cambridge, MA: MIT Press, 1985.

———. *Sputnik, Scientists, and Eisenhower: A Memoir of the First Special Assistant to the President for Science and Technology*. Cambridge, MA: MIT Press, 1977; paperback 1982.

Kinzer, Stephen. *The Brothers: John Foster Dulles, Allen Dulles, and their Secret World War*. New York: St. Martin's Griffin, 2014.

Knorr, Klaus. "Failure in National Intelligence Estimates: The Case of the Cuban Missiles." *World Politics* 16:3 (April 1964): 455–67.

Kronenbitter, Rita T. "The Okhrana's Female Agents: Part I: Russian Women." *Studies in Intelligence* 9:2 (Spring 1965): 25–41.

———. "Paris Okhrana, 1885–1905." *Studies in Intelligence* 10:3 (Summer 1966): 55–66.

Kuehn, John T. "The War in the Pacific, 1941–1945." *The Cambridge History of the Second World War*, , edited by John Ferris and Evan Mawdsley Vol. I, *Fighting the War* 389–419. Cambridge: Cambridge University Press, 2015.

Kumaraswamy, P. R. "The Politics of Pardon: Israel and Jonathan Pollard." *Arab Studies Quarterly* 18:3 (Summer 1996): 17–35.

Kyle, James H., and John R. Eidson. *The Guts to Try: The Untold Story of the Iran Hostage Rescue Mission by the On-Scene Desert Commander*. New York: Orion Books/Crown Publishers, 1990.

LaFeber, Walter. "The Rise and Fall of Colin Powell and the Powell Doctrine." *Political Science Quarterly* 124:1 (Spring 2009): 71–93.

Leary, William M., ed. *The Central Intelligence Agency: History and Documents*. Tuscaloosa: University of Alabama Press, 1984.

Lepore, Jill. "The Long Blue Line: Inventing the Police." *New Yorker*, July 20, 2020, 64–69.

Liang, Hsi-Huey. *The Rise of Modern Police and the European State System from Metternich to the Second World War*. Cambridge: Cambridge University Press, 1992.

Little, Douglas. "Cold War and Covert Action: The United States and Syria, 1945–1958." *Middle East Journal* 44:1 (Winter 1990): 51–75.

———. "Mission Impossible: The CIA and the Cult of Covert Action in the Middle East." *Diplomatic History* 28:5 (Nov. 2004): 663–701.

Lowenthal, Mark M. *Intelligence: From Secrets to Policy*, 4th ed. Washington: CQ Press/Sage, 2009.

Maffeo, Steven E. *Most Secret and Confidential: Intelligence in the Age of Nelson*. Annapolis, MD: Naval Institute Press, 2012.

Marrin, Stephen. "Training and Educating U.S. Intelligence Analysts." *International Journal of Intelligence and CounterIntelligence* 22:1 (Spring 2009): 131–46.

Marshall, Alex. "Russian Military Intelligence, 1905–1917: The Untold Story behind Tsarist Russia in the First World War." *War in History* 11:4 (Nov. 2004): 393–423.

May, Ernest R., ed. *Knowing One's Enemies: Intelligence Assessment Before the Two World Wars.* Princeton, NJ: Princeton University Press, 1984.

McConnell, Jeff. "Israeli Spies in the U.S." *MERIP Middle East Report,* no. 138 (Jan.–Feb. 1986): 35–37, 45.

McCullough, David. *John Adams.* New York: Simon & Schuster, 2001.

McGrigor, Mary. *Wellington's Spies.* Barnsley, South Yorkshire: Leo Cooper/ Pen and Sword Books, 2005.

McMaster, Herbert R. *Dereliction of Duty: Lyndon Johnson, Robert McNamara, the Joint Chiefs of Staff, and the Lies that Led to Vietnam.* New York: HarperCollins, 1997.

Mellon, Jérôme. "The Foreign Intelligence-Gathering of the MfS's *Hauptverwaltung Aufklärung.*" By the author, October 16, 2001. http://cv.jmellon.com/mfs.pdf. Accessed October 23, 2017.

Merriman, John, ed. *1830 in France.* New York: Franklin Watts, 1975.

Miller, Edward. *Misalliance: Ngo Dinh Diem, the United States, and the Fate of South Vietnam.* Cambridge, MA: Harvard University Press, 2013.

Millett, Allan R. *The War for Korea, 1945–1950: A House Burning.* Lawrence: University Press of Kansas, 2005.

———. *The War for Korea, 1950–1951: They Came from the North.* Lawrence: University Press of Kansas, 2010.

Montague, Ludwell L. *General Walter Bedell Smith as Director of Central Intelligence.* University Park: Pennsylvania State University Press, 1992.

Murphy, David E. *What Stalin Knew: The Enigma of Barbarossa.* New Haven, CT: Yale University Press, 2005.

Mushrush, Bryon D. "Improved Intelligence Warning in an Age of Complexity." Research monograph, School for Advanced Military Studies. Fort Leavenworth, KS: U.S. Army Command and General Staff College, 2015.

National Photographic Interpretation Center. Vol. I: *Antecedents and Early Years, 1952–1956.* The Directorate of Intelligence Historical Series. Langley, VA: CIA Historical Staff, December 1972.

Nguyen, Lien-Hang T. *Hanoi's War: An International History of the War for Peace in Vietnam.* Chapel Hill: University of North Carolina Press, 2012.

Oakley, David P. *Subordinating Intelligence: The DoD/CIA Post–Cold War Relationship*. Lexington: University Press of Kentucky, 2019.

Odom, William E. *Fixing Intelligence: For a More Secure America*. New Haven, CT: Yale University Press, 2003.

Packard, Wyman H. *A Century of Naval Intelligence*. Washington: Department of the Navy, 1996.

Paine, Lauran. *German Military Intelligence in World War II: The Abwehr*. New York: Stein & Day, 1984.

Pape, Robert A. *Dying to Win: The Strategic Logic of Suicide Terrorism*. New York: Random House, 2005.

Parker, Frederick D. "A New View of Pearl Harbor: The U.S. Navy and Communications Intelligence." *Cryptologic Quarterly* 5:3 (Fall 1986): 59–74.

Parry, Robert, and Peter Kornbluh. "Iran-Contra's Untold Story." *Foreign Policy*, no. 72 (Autumn 1988): 3–30.

Petersen, Martin. "What I Learned in 40 Years of Doing Intelligence Analysis for U.S. Foreign Policy Makers." *Studies in Intelligence* 55:1 (March 2011): 13–20.

Petraeus, David H. "Lessons of History and Lessons of Vietnam." *Parameters: Journal of the U.S. Army War College* 16:3 (Autumn 1986): 43–53.

Pillar, Paul R. "Intelligence, Policy, and the War in Iraq." *Foreign Affairs* 85:2 (March–April 2006): 15–27.

Pinkney, David H. "The Pacification of Paris: The Military Lessons of 1830." In *1830 in France*, edited by John M. Merriman, 186–97. New York: New Viewpoints, 1975.

Polmar, Norman, and John D. Gresham. *DEFCON-2: Standing on the Brink of Nuclear War During the Cuban Missile Crisis*. Hoboken, NJ: John Wiley and Sons, Inc., 2006.

Porch, Douglas. *The French Secret Services: From the Dreyfus Affair to the Gulf War*. New York: Farrar, Straus, and Giroux, 1995.

Posner, Richard A. "The Reorganized U.S. Intelligence System After One Year." Washington: American Enterprise Institute, 2006.

Prados, John. *Combined Fleet Decoded: The Secret History of American Intelligence and the Japanese Navy in World War II*. New York: Random House, 1995.

———. "The Warning That Left Something to Chance: Intelligence at Tet." *Journal of American-East Asian Relations* 2:2 (Summer 1993): 161–84.

Prange, Gordon W., Donald M. Goldstein, and Katherine V. Dillon. *At Dawn We Slept: The Untold Story of Pearl Harbor*. New York: Penguin Books, 1991.

Price, Barrye L. "Against All Enemies: A Study of Civil Unrest and Federal Intervention within the United States from 1794 to 1968." PhD dissertation, Texas A&M University, 1997.

Pryer, Douglas A. "The Fight for the High Ground: The U.S. Army and Interrogation During Operation Iraqi Freedom I, May 2003–April 2004." Master of Military Art and Science thesis, U.S. Army Command and General Staff College, Fort Leavenworth, KS, 2009.

Pyle, Christopher H. *Military Surveillance of Civilian Politics, 1967–1970.* New York: Garland Publishing, 1986.

Ratt, W. Dirk. "U.S. Intelligence Operations and Covert Action in Mexico, 1900–47." *Journal of Contemporary History* 22:4 (Oct. 1987): 615–38.

Razoux, Pierre. *The Iran-Iraq War.* Translated by Nicholas Elliott. Cambridge, MA: Harvard University Press, 2015.

Reardon, Steven L. *History of the Office of the Secretary of Defense* Vol. I, *The Form-ative Years, 1947–1950.* Washington: Office of the Secretary of Defense, 1984.

Reich, Bernard, ed. *Arab-Israeli Conflict and Conciliation: A Documentary History.* Westport, CT: Praeger, 1995.

Relyea, C. Harold. *Evolution and Organization of Intelligence Activities in the United States.* Laguna Hills, CA: Aegean Park Press, 1988. Reprint of a 1976 report to the Senate Select Committee to Study Governmental Operations with Respect to Intelligence Activities, or Church Committee.

Renz, Bettina. *Russia's Military Revival.* Cambridge, UK: Polity Press, 2018.

Report to the President by the Commission on CIA Activities Within the United States [Rockefeller Commission]. Washington: Government Printing Office, 1975.

Report of the Senate Select Committee on Intelligence Committee Study of the Central Intelligence Agency's Detention and Interrogation Program [Feinstein Report]. U.S. Senate, 113th Cong., 2nd Sess., Senate Report 113-288. Washington: Government Printing Office, 2014.

Rezk, Dina. *The Arab World and Western Intelligence: Analysing the Middle East, 1956–1981.* Edinburgh: Edinburgh University Press, 2017.

Ripsman, Norrin M., and Jack S. Levy. "Wishful Thinking or Buying Time? The Logic of British Appeasement in the 1930s." *International Security* 33:2 (Fall 2008): 148–81.

Risen, James. *State of War: The Secret History of the CIA and the Bush Administration.* New York: Free Press, 2006.

Roberts, Geoffrey. "The Soviet Decision for a Pact with Nazi Germany." *Soviet Studies* 44:1 (1992): 57–78.

———. *Stalin's Wars: From World War to Cold War, 1939–1953.* New Haven, CT: Yale University Press, 2006.

Rudgers, David F. "The Origins of Covert Action." *Journal of Contemporary History* 35:2 (April 2000): 249–62.

Sabrosky, Alan N., and Robert L. Sloane, eds. *The Recourse to War: An Appraisal of the "Weinberger Doctrine."* Carlisle, PA: Strategic Studies Institute, 1989.

Samuels, Richard J. *Special Duty: A History of the Japanese Intelligence Community.* Ithaca, NY: Cornell University Press, 2019.

Schaefer, Agnes Gereben. "The History of Domestic Intelligence in the United States." In *The Challenge of Domestic Intelligence in a Free Society: A Multidisciplinary Look at the Creation of a U.S. Domestic Counterterrorism Intelligence Agency*, edited by Brian A. Jackson, 13–48. Santa Monica, CA: RAND, 2009.

Scheips, Paul J. *The Role of Federal Military Forces in Domestic Disorders, 1945–1992.* Washington: U.S. Army Center of Military History, 2005.

Schuker, Stephen. "Seeking a Scapegoat: Intelligence and Grand Strategy in France, 1919–1940." In *Secret Intelligence in the European State System, 1918–1989*, edited by Jonathan Haslam and Karina Urbach, 81–127. Stanford, CA: Stanford University Press, 2014.

Scott, James M. "Interbranch Rivalry and the Reagan Doctrine in Nicaragua." *Political Science Quarterly* 112:2 (Summer 1997): 237–60.

Scott, Len. "Intelligence and the Risk of Nuclear War: Able Archer-83 Revisited." *Intelligence and National Security* 26:2 (Dec. 2011): 759–77.

Service, Robert. *The End of the Cold War, 1985–1991.* New York: Public Affairs/Perseus, 2015.

Shlaim, Avi. "Failures in National Intelligence Estimates: The Case of the Yom Kippur War." *World Politics* 28:3 (April 1976): 348–80.

el Shazly, Saad. *The Crossing of the Suez*. Rev. ed. San Francisco: American Mideast Research, 2003.

Shultz, Richard H. Jr. *The Secret War against Hanoi: Kennedy's and Johnson's Use of Spies, Saboteurs, and Covert Warriors in North Vietnam*. New York: HarperCollins, 1999.

Skillen, Hugh. *Spies of the Airwaves: A History of Y Sections During the Second World War.* Pinner, England: privately printed, 1989.

Smist, Frank J. Jr. *Congress Oversees the United States Intelligence Community, 1947–1989.* Knoxville: University of Tennessee Press, 1990.

Smith, Richard Harris. *OSS: The Secret History of America's First Central Intelligence Agency.* Berkeley: University of California Press, 1972.

Sokolski, Henry, ed. *Moving Beyond Pretense: Nuclear Power and*

Nonproliferation. Carlisle, PA: Strategic Studies Institute and U.S. Army War College Press, 2014.

Spiller, Roger C. "Assessing Ultra." *Military Review* 59:8 (Aug. 1979): 13–23.

Stead, Philip J. *The Police of Paris*. London: Staples, 1957.

Stejskal, James. *Special Forces Berlin: Clandestine Cold War Operations of the US Army's Elite, 1956–1990*. Philadelphia: Casemate Publishers, 2017.

Stephan, Robert. "SMERSH: Soviet Military Counter-Intelligence during the Second World War." *Journal of Contemporary History* 22:4 (Oct. 1987): 585–613.

Stieber, Wilhelm J. C. E. *The Chancellor's Spy: The Revelations of the Chief of Bismarck's Secret Service*. Translated by Jan van Heurck. New York: Grove Press, 1979; original Stuttgart: Seewald Verlag.

Stobie, James R. "More to the Story: A Reappraisal of U.S. Intelligence Prior to the Pacific War." MMAS thesis, U.S. Army Command and General Staff College, Fort Leavenworth, KS, 2007.

Sulick, Michael J. *American Spies: Espionage against the United States from the Cold War to the Present*. Washington: Georgetown University Press, 2013.

Taubman, Philip. *Secret Empire: Eisenhower, the CIA, and the Hidden Story of America's Space Espionage*. New York: Simon & Schuster, 2003.

Tenet, George, and Bill Harlow. *At the Center of the Storm: My Years at the CIA*. New York: HarperCollins, 2007.

Theoharis, Athan G. "Dissent and the State: Unleashing the FBI, 1917–1985." *History Teacher* 24:1 (Nov. 1990): 41–52.

Thomas, David. "Foreign Armies East and German Military Intelligence in Russia, 1941–45." *Journal of Contemporary History* 22:2 (April 1987), 261–301.

Thucydides. *The Landmark Thucydides: A Comprehensive Guide to the Peloponnesian War*. Edited by Robert B. Strassler. New York: Free Press, 1996.

Tidwell, William. "Notes on the CRITIC System." *Studies in Intelligence* 14:2 (Spring 1960): 19–23.

Troy, Thomas F. *Donovan and the CIA: A History of the Establishment of the Central Intelligence Agency*. Frederick, MD: University Publications of America, 1981.

Twining, David T. "The Weinberger Doctrine and the Use of Force in the Contemporary Era." In *The Recourse to War: An Appraisal of the "Weinberger Doctrine,"* edited by Alan N. Sabrosky and Robert L. Sloane, 9–38. Carlisle, PA: Strategic Studies Institute, 1989.

U.S. Department of the Army. Field Manual 30-5, *Combat Intelligence*. Washington: Government Printing Office, 1973.

U.S. Department of State. *Foreign Relations of the United States, 1945–1950: Emergence of the Intelligence Establishment.* Washington: Department of State, 1996.

———. *Foreign Relations of the United States, 1950–1955: The Intelligence Community, 1950–1955.* Washington: Department of State, 2005.

U.S. Executive Order 12306, United States Foreign Intelligence Activities, Jan. 24, 1978. Superseded Dec. 4, 1981.

U.S. National Commission on Terrorist Attacks upon the United States. *The 9/11 Commission Report.* Washington: Government Printing Office, 2004.

U.S. Office of the Director of National Intelligence. "The Terrorist: Threat to the U.S. Homeland." National Intelligence Estimate, July 17, 2007.

U.S. War Department, Military Intelligence Division. *German Military Intelligence, 1939–1945.* Frederick, MD: University Publications of America, 1984.

Urban, Mark. *The Man Who Broke Napoleon's Codes: The Story of George Scovell.* London: Faber and Faber, 2001.

———. *UK Eyes Alpha: Inside British Intelligence.* London: Faber and Faber, 1996.

Vagle, Jeffrey L. *Being Watched: Legal Challenges to Government Surveillance.* New York: New York University Press, 2017.

Valentine, Douglas. *The Phoenix Program.* New York: William Morrow and Company, 1990.

Wahlert, Matthew H. "The 'Motivated Bias' Dilemma in Warfare and Intelligence." *Defense & Security Analysis* 28:3 (Sept. 2012): 247–59.

Walsh, Lawrence E. *Final Report of the Independent Counsel for Iran/Contra Matters.* Vol. I, *Investigations and Prosecutions.* U.S. Court of Appeals for the District of Columbia Circuit, Division for the Purpose of Appointing Independent Counsel, Division No. 86-6. Washington, 1993.

Warner, Michael, ed. *The CIA under Harry Truman.* CIA Cold War Records series. Washington: Center for the Study of Intelligence, 1994.

Warner, Michael, and J. Kenneth McDonald. *US Intelligence Community Reform Studies Since 1947.* Washington: Center for the Study of Intelligence, 2005.

Watt, Donald C. "British Intelligence and the Coming of the Second World War in Europe." In *Knowing One's Enemies: Intelligence Assessment Before the Two World Wars,* edited by Ernest R. May, 243–45. Princeton, NJ: Princeton University Press, 1984.

Weiner, Tim. *Enemies: A History of the FBI.* New York: Random House, 2012.

Wells, Samuel F. Jr. *Fearing the Worst: How Korea Transformed the Cold War.* New York: Columbia University Press, 2019.

Whaley, Barton. *Codeword Barbarossa.* Cambridge, MA: MIT Press, 1973.

White, Richard D. Jr. "George Tenet and the Last Great Days of the CIA." *Public Administration Review* 68:3 (June 2008): 420–27.

Williams, Alan. *The Police of Paris, 1718–1789.* Baton Rouge: Louisiana State University Press, 1979.

Williams, David. "The Bureau of Investigation and Its Critics, 1919–1921: The Origins of Federal Political Surveillance." *Journal of American History* 68:3 (Dec. 1981): 560–79.

Wilson, Derek. *Sir Francis Walsingham: A Courtier in an Age of Terror.* New York: Carroll & Graf, 2007.

Wilson, Ray, and Ian Adams. *Special Branch: A History, 1882–2006.* London: Biteback Publishing, 2015.

Wohlstetter, Roberta M. "Cuba and Pearl Harbor: Hindsight and Foresight." *Foreign Affairs*, 43:4 (July 1965): 691–707.

———. *Pearl Harbor: Warning and Decision.* Stanford, CA: Stanford University Press, 1982.

Wood, Joe. "Persuading the President: Jimmy Carter and American Troops in Korea." *Studies in Intelligence* 40:4 (1996): 97–113.

Woods, Kevin M., Michael R. Pease, Mark E. Stout, Williamson Murray, and James G. Lacey. *The Iraqi Perspectives Report: Saddam's Senior Leadership on Operation Iraqi Freedom from the Official U.S. Joint Forces Command Report.* Annapolis, MD: Naval Institute Press, 2006.

Woods, Randall B. *Shadow Warrior: William Egan Colby and the CIA.* New York: Basic Books/Perseus, 2013.

Xiaobing Li, Allan R. Millett, and Bin Yu, trans. and eds. *Mao's Generals Remember Korea.* Lawrence: University Press of Kansas, 2001.

Yarhi-Milo, Keren. *Knowing the Adversary: Leaders, Intelligence, and Assessment of Intentions in International Relations.* Princeton, NJ: Princeton University Press, 2014.

Young, Marilyn B. *The Vietnam Wars, 1945–1990.* New York: HarperCollins, 1991.

Zaloga, Steven J. *Target America: The Soviet Union and the Strategic Arms Race, 1945–1964.* Novato, CA: Presidio Press, 1993.

Zlotnick, Jack. *National Security Management: National Intelligence.* Washington: National Defense University, 1964.

Zubok, Vladislav M., and Constantine Pleshakov. *Inside the Kremlin's Cold War: From Stalin to Khrushchev* Cambridge, MA: Harvard University Press, 1996.

Index

About the Author

Jonathan M. House is a retired Army intelligence officer and military historian. He received his doctorate and his commission at the University of Michigan. He served as an intelligence analyst on the Joint Staff during both the 1991 and 2003 conflicts and is the author or co-author of numerous military histories, most notably *When Titans Clashed: How the Red Army Stopped Hitler* and *A Military History of the Cold War* (2 vols.).

The Naval Institute Press is the book-publishing arm of the U.S. Naval Institute, a private, nonprofit, membership society for sea service professionals and others who share an interest in naval and maritime affairs. Established in 1873 at the U.S. Naval Academy in Annapolis, Maryland, where its offices remain today, the Naval Institute has members worldwide.

Members of the Naval Institute support the education programs of the society and receive the influential monthly magazine *Proceedings* or the colorful bimonthly magazine *Naval History* and discounts on fine nautical prints and on ship and aircraft photos. They also have access to the transcripts of the Institute's Oral History Program and get discounted admission to any of the Institute-sponsored seminars offered around the country.

The Naval Institute's book-publishing program, begun in 1898 with basic guides to naval practices, has broadened its scope to include books of more general interest. Now the Naval Institute Press publishes about seventy titles each year, ranging from how-to books on boating and navigation to battle histories, biographies, ship and aircraft guides, and novels. Institute members receive significant discounts on the Press' more than eight hundred books in print.

Full-time students are eligible for special half-price membership rates. Life memberships are also available.

For a free catalog describing Naval Institute Press books currently available, and for further information about joining the U.S. Naval Institute, please write to:

Member Services
U.S. Naval Institute
291 Wood Road
Annapolis, MD 21402-5034
Telephone: (800) 233-8764
Fax: (410) 571-1703
Web address: www.usni.org